CONQUERING DEPRESSION

How to Recognize It,
How to Treat It,
How to Control It

by
Wina Sturgeon

(original title: DEPRESSION)

CORNERSTONE LIBRARY
Published by Simon & Schuster
NEW YORK

Reprinted 1981

Copyright © 1979, 1981 by Wina Sturgeon
All rights reserved
including the right of reproduction
in whole or in part in any form
Published by Cornerstone Library, Inc.
A Simon & Schuster Division of
Gulf & Western Corporation
Simon & Schuster Building
1230 Avenue of the Americas
New York, New York 10020

CORNERSTONE LIBRARY and colophon are
trademarks of Simon & Schuster, registered in
the U.S. Patent and Trademark Office.

Manufactured in the United States of America

10 9 8 7 6 5 4 3 2 1

Library of Congress Cataloging in Publication Data

Sturgeon, Wina, 1942—
    Conquering Depression, how to recognize it, how to treat it,
how to control it.

    1. Depression, Mental.   I. Title.
RC537.S86   1981   616.85'27   80-29419

ISBN 0-346-12514-6

Author's Note

You may have bought this book because you know someone who seems depressed or who has been diagnosed as having a clinical case of depression. Or, you may be wondering if you yourself have the illness; if you are, you'll find all the information you need to judge your symptoms and decide if they come from the biochemical illness known as depression.

This book is for you if: (1) You *know* that you have talent and ability but you have never been able to show any of it. (2) You feel that you're carrying a huge guilty secret about how unlovable and unworthy you really are and that if anyone ever found out, they would turn from you in disgust. (3) Nothing turns out right for you or quite the way you wanted it. (4) You feel there is some secret that, could you only learn it, would make everything right again.

It's true that there *are* some people who are complete incompetents, whose every disappointment is of their own making. But through the years I have discovered that this kind of person is rare, rare enough to be considered unusual.

Depression is an incapacitating illness, a crippling disease. It cripples in precisely those areas which cause emotional unhappiness, in social relationships and in work. It will get in your way no matter how much talent or creativity or ability you have. In this book you will learn how to recognize this illness in yourself and in others. But more, you will learn how to protect yourself against it, so that while you may pass through the normal low periods which are part of all our lives, you will never be the victim of one of mankind's oldest maladies.

Contents

Introduction

Important advances in medicine are usually made in a reverse manner: the treatment is discovered before the disease is identified. Let me give an illustration—At the beginning of the last century doctors in England wrote about "Miasmal Fever." The miasma (or mist) which often occurred at night, especially in swampy areas, was believed to be the cause of fevers which were accompanied by diarrhea and sometimes were fatal. Hence, sensible people kept their windows tightly closed at night. Probably your own grandparents followed this advice—or at least knew some older person who did.

Eventually it was found that "Jesuit's Bark" from the cinchona tree (which the Jesuits had brought back from America) was good for treating some patients with miasmal fever but had no effect on others. No wonder! The cinchona contained quinine which is good for malaria. Only when the treatment became available was the connection really made that these were patients who did not have daily fevers but ones that occurred every three or four days. Later it was discovered that the mosquito carried the malaria parasite. Thus, keeping the windows closed so that mosquitoes didn't get in and bite you was good preventive medicine at that time.

When people began purifying water (and with the discovery of the microscope), it was found that if the typhoid bacillus seeped into drinking water it could cause typhoid fever. Another disease reduced still further the patients with "Miasmal Fever."

Finally, a third disease, typhus fever, which is carried by rat lice who would then bite people (the lice, not the rats) was identified. Naturally there were lots of rodents in swampy areas. With this discovery, miasmal fever disappeared since it turned out to be three different diseases.

The reason for this long introduction about miasmal fever is because today we are not very certain about how to classify emotional and mental disorders. Only this year (1979), the official classification system of the American Psychiatric Association did away with the category "Neuroses." Not all psychiatrists agree that this was a good idea and many still believe it is a useful way to describe certain kinds of behavior. The real trouble is the same as with miasmal fever—we don't know what causes emotional, behavioral and mental disorders. We have some interesting theories—but so did those who believed it was the miasma (mist) which brought on the fever.

In the past, people with psychiatric disorders were believed to be "possessed" by demons and devils. At times they were "prayed over" and at other times they were flogged with chains to "drive out the devils." More recently psychoanalysis (starting with Freud) and electroshock therapy (since 1938) have been used. Each of these treatments had some degree of success but there were also many patients who did not respond, or only partially responded, or who got better for only a short time. Only 25 years ago we started using "tranquilizers" which caught on very rapidly. A few years later we introduced antidepressant drugs but for some reason they were not so rapidly accepted and even today, more than 20 years after they were first used, there are people who have not heard about them.

Wina Sturgeon's book makes clear how dramatic the antidepressant drug effects can be. She does it in a fashion and with a personal knowledge that makes the story much more real than any medical text. She also touches on novel aspects such as the problem of living with a depressed person.

There will be psychiatrists and pharmacologists and other experts who will disagree with some of the statements she has made. I don't agree with all of them myself. But then, we experts don't always agree with each other either. The book is not meant to be used for teaching conventional pharmacology or psychology or psychiatry so that such differences are not the point. Wina Sturgeon's book can be used in psychiatry courses of medical schools to teach the other side—the patient's side—of what it is really like to experience depression and how it feels to have that most cursed weight lifted.

Nathan S. Kline, M.D.

Biographical Note

Dr. Kline was a pioneer in the use of both tranquilizers and antidepressant drugs (for which he received Lasker Awards in 1957 and again in 1964). For the past 25 years he has been doing research at what is now the Rockland Research Institute, part of the New York State Office of Mental Health. In addition to being Director of the Rockland Research Institute, he is Clinical Professor of Psychiatry at Columbia University, a member of the Expert Committee on Mental Health of the World Health Organization, an Honorary Fellow of the Royal College of Psychiatrists (of England) and has been awarded decorations and honors from a number of foreign governments. Most importantly, in his private practice in mid-Manhattan he has treated more than 5,000 patients with depression so that he speaks from direct clinical experience.

Preface

The first "breakthrough" in depression was recognition that it existed. That came in the fourth century, B.C. Hippocrates made the first clinical description of a disease called melancholia . . . that's what they called it then.

The next "breakthrough" happened some two thousand years later, in 1956, by accident. A type of medication used to treat tuberculosis was found to have euphoric side effects. Doctors thought it could be used to treat depression, which was *then* thought of as a mental disorder.

The mood elevator was isolated and a strange thing was discovered. The drug didn't really lift the spirits. It just changed the production of certain chemicals produced by the central nervous system. Doctors wanted to find out how that cured depression, and their research led to the discovery that depression is not just a mood. It's an organic, biologically caused disease.

The discovery of that fact makes me grateful I was born only the decade before it happened. Without that breakthrough, I would probably now be dead.

I found out about depression the hard way: by breaking down from the strain of trying to cope with it. But I was lucky. The doctor who treated me specialized in clinical depressions. He recognized what was wrong and was able to help me cure myself. That's one of the most striking aspects about this illness: the doctor can maintain your sanity, can ease you through the worst symptoms, but only the patient can cure himself.

Finding out there was a name for my condition was the biggest help of all. I'd been living with it for most of my life without understanding what was wrong. And something certainly was wrong. My I.Q. tested at 147, yet there were times when I couldn't use my head for even the simplest of things. My behavior was erratic; I seemed to have no control over it. I was horribly lonely; I couldn't make or keep friends. And it was bewildering. I never knew what it was that caused me to lose job after job, to be labeled incompetent and to see proof of my incompetence when I knew it wasn't true.

It was so bad that I remember once holding a job for three months—a record for me. The day I got fired was still a cause for elation. I had actually held a job for three months! (I held 21 different jobs my first 18 months away from home.)

It seems strange now. Inside, I knew what I was capable of if given the chance—yet I ruined every chance I got. Even the knowledge of my capabilities was only subliminal. Consciously, I pretty much agreed with what I believed to be the world's opinion of me. I was abnormal, "different," inferior, guilty of every sin and doomed to failure.

The breakdown—or should I say breakthrough?—came in 1966, when I was 25. Two years before, I had run to England, just as I'd run away from home to go to New York and from there to California. In London I'd gotten a job as a staff reporter on a weekly feature newspaper, the simplest kind of writing. Yet it was getting harder and harder to write. It was during the beginning of the hippy movement, and I thought maybe that was the problem. Perhaps I wasn't meant for the "straight" life. I was meant to be a hippy. I moved in with a 20-year-old rock musician who had never lived away from his parents before.

The arrangement was disastrous on many levels. I had guilt

conflicts about living with a man without being married. I didn't like the fact that my salary was supporting us while he just seemed to be having fun. We each lived in different worlds and had no common ground of communication. Yet I needed this young man for my self-esteem. The emphasis was on youth, and I felt I was old . . . old. And I needed acceptance, even if it was from a bunch of people I was unable at the time to respect. At least the guitar player would allow me to ignore the approaching end of my girlhood, while showing the world that someone could care enough to live with me.

I started taking birth control pills. They caused a lump in my breast and a missed period. I told the boy I was living with and he panicked. On top of that, my mother suddenly sent a telegram saying she was coming to England in four days and wanted to stay with me. She would know I was living with someone. I would have to tell her I thought I was pregnant. I was positive the lump in my breast was cancerous. To top it off, the relationship between the guitar player and myself had now degenerated to the snapping stage.

The stress was too much. The day after the telegram came, I felt twitchy and unable to concentrate. I was afraid to drive home from work and had to force myself to start the car. Traffic was heavy that evening. It would move a few feet, then stop. I felt a sense of menace every time the car in front flashed its brake lights. I lit a cigarette, then realized the smoke had fingers which were going to strangle me. The car started growing smaller, the roof and sides closing in, and I knew I was going to be crushed.

You have to understand that I still had a faint connection to reality. I realized that none of this was actually happening, so I must be going crazy. But that realization only added to my terror.

I pulled the car over to the curb and began looking for a telephone booth. The urge to scream was almost impossible to resist, yet I knew if I gave in to that urge, I would never, never stop screaming. I found a phone booth and dialed the operator, crying that I needed help. Then I began babbling and sobbing. She didn't call the funny farm, and bless her for it. She evidently knew a doctor, because the next thing I knew, someone was trying to soothe me over the phone. It was a psychiatrist.

He asked if I could drive to his office, which was only a few blocks away. No . . . impossible. He told me which bus to take. I tried, but the bus was really a hungry monster, and after half a block of riding I jumped off it.

I'd copied down the doctor's address and telephone number, and somehow managed to call him. He sent his wife to get me. By this time, a sort of numbness had set in. I don't remember much of what happened next, but I found out later that the doctor had talked with me for two hours, diagnosed my state as a severe anxiety attack, and told me I had a classic case of endogenous depression.

He suggested hospitalization. Oh, God . . . that was unthinkable! So he sent me to a specialist in depression therapy named Dr. Hopkins who gave me a prescription for a powerful tranquilizing drug.

The anti-depressant took two weeks to begin working. Most of them do take some time to start, since they aren't really mood-lifters but stabilizers of certain chemicals produced by the body. The pills controlled the anxiety and depression, but there was still a lot of hard work to be done before the cure.

The next six months became a constant struggle for possession of my mind, a mind that had been possessed by a chemical imbalance for most of its years. The doctor helped me gain the needed insights. Long hours were spent on things which I had never been able to see before . . . and the bewilderment began to end. Not only had I been unable to understand *why* I did the things I did, but I didn't even know *what* it was I did that caused me so much trouble.

It helped to find out that many of my actions had been out of my control, the result of an imbalance in my central nervous system. It helped even more to find out that my confused mental state was due mainly to that imbalance, and it could be corrected.

I had to relearn everything, including the way my mind worked. That meant I had to get to know myself. I had to learn a new perception, a new way of making judgments. It was like being reborn. For the first time, I was beginning to find out that I wasn't abnormal and different, and that the instinctive feeling of hidden potential was accurate. And best of all, I was now able to touch that hidden potential. I could begin using my abilities to get satisfactory results.

Semiweekly therapy sessions became weekly, and four doses a day of one of the most powerful anti-depressants became three, then changed to a less powerful drug. I was progressing!

Yet during the entire recovery time, I lived like a zombie. Most depression attacks leave the patient with a dull, leaden feeling which even pills won't help. There's no desire to do anything, and the urge for sleep is constant.

My relationship with the rock musician had broken up a few days after the depression breakdown. I would go to work (my employers were aware of what was happening, and even though I could produce practically nothing, they kept me until I was able to function normally again), then would come home, eat dinner, and go to sleep. The round of work, dinner, sleep, breakfast, and work was an unvarying routine.

"Recovery" came six months and three days after the onset of the depression attack. The disease often lifts that suddenly, and when it does, the patient is always aware of its happening. I was trying to read a book when it happened. (Reading is nearly impossible in severe depression because the mind is often unable to retain information long enough to make sense of it.) I had tried to read this book before. It was a psychiatric examination of neurotic states, and part of the book was about depression—the only explanation of the illness I had ever seen in print. Making sense of the words became almost an obsession. I would read and reread one sentence, I would repeat it out loud, and still the information would slip out of my mind.

On this particular night, I was underlining each word with a highlighter as I read. There was a sort of . . . *flash* inside my head, like a silent pop. I put the book down for a moment. The feeling is hard to describe. It was like a shift in equilibrium, or if you prefer, like a sinus clearing suddenly after a head cold.

I picked up the book again, read a few sentences . . . and stopped. There was no difficulty in retention. I leafed back through the pages I had so carefully underlined before, and couldn't even relate to the trouble I had been having understanding them. My mind was working on several levels at once. I was thinking I should allow myself enough time to stop and get a new pair of pantyhose before work the next morning; there was an idea for a feature story beginning to dawn (something that hadn't happened in the last six months); I remembered that I hadn't written to an aquaintance in America for a long time. In short, I was thinking normally, the way most people do.

As soon as I realized that, I knew it was going to be all right. The feeling was an instinctive certainty, and I called Dr. Hopkins to tell him so.

He was cautious. He said the depression may have lifted—it wasn't uncommon for it to happen that way—but there was still work to be done and a lot to be learned if I were to really be able to cope with this disease.

The passing of the depression does not mean a cure. The illness is unpredictable, like cancer. You can recover from one episode, but it can recur again. The difference is that with proper care, the depressive can learn to cope if it does come back, and the recurrence will be less severe and over sooner.

It was two years before I was finally able to say that I was "cured." By cured, I mean able to maintain my equilibrium, able to recognize approaching depressive cycles, able to handle them without drugs and without descent into a vegetative state. The depressive cycles differ from the episodes of severe depression in that they rarely cause symptoms bad enough to require hospitalization, but they still make life miserable. There's no sure proof that anti-depressants help get the central nervous system into a *pattern* of producing the right balance of chemicals, yet it's a fact that after a course of these drugs, many people never have another bout of severe depression.

Of course no one can maintain a constant positive mood. I've had to put up with several minor episodes of depression in the eleven years since that day of near madness. And each time I have been able to look upon it as something outside myself, rather like a bad cold which can be minimized as far as symptoms go but which needs special care to be over with quickly. My subconscious, and the workings of my body, are no longer mysteries to me.

My life has changed so radically that I can't feel very much kinship with that unhappy person who struggled to understand what was wrong before the depression hit with a wallop. I can maintain a loving relationship with other human beings now. I can love and care for my child in a satisfying way. Behavioral psychologists are discovering that a large percentage of the increasing cases of child battering involves parents who show many of the symptoms of depression—and a large number have even been diagnosed as being ill with depressive syndromes. Depression . . . the disease that wraps people in Saran Wrap and keeps them from feeling any emotion except anxiety and fear.

I'm now able to use that creative potential that seemed untouchable before. I can hold a job as long as I wish. I worked as a newswriter for a radio station two and a half years before deciding to go into on-air work. Now I'm one of their reporters. Last year I made my first television film documentary. It won an Emmy. There are civic awards on my wall, half a hundred ribbons from the Los Angeles County Fair for handwork and baking, and a house full of laughter and friends. But most of all, I'm happy. Both with the person I now am and with the life I live.

That happiness has given me a responsibility, and that's why I've written this book.

One of the things I learned about depression is that it affects a majority of the American population in varying degrees, and the number of severe cases needing hospitalization is increasing. That's too much ability going to waste. It's too much needless misery, too many wasted lives. And it's unnecessary.

The public is at last becoming aware of depression, and a lot of people are coming to the same realization I have: if this gray film can be lifted, talent and ability now going to waste can be utilized. The world has never needed ability and good minds as it does now. We can't afford to let even one life be wasted through a disease which prevents the full human potential from being realized.

This book is the result of ten years of research into one of the most widespread and most insidious diseases that has ever afflicted our species. It will tell you what depression is and how it's treated. It will give you constructive methods which can be used to keep depression attacks away—and sadly, this is an area in which current research by the medical profession is lacking. It will detail how, and where, to find help if you have severe depression, and it will explain the various kinds of help available. It will also tell you how to protect yourself from the effects of someone else's depression.

Our society has a problem. It manifests itself in drug abuse, high crime rates, social alienation. We look for solutions in religious revivals, meditation, swapping clubs, places like Esalen, personality cults, or special therapy groups. None of these has proved to be the full answer.

Curing all the depression cases in our society won't completely erase the problems that keep life from being joyful and fun to live, but at least it will allow us to deal more constructively with these problems, using all our human potential to do so. There's no reason for anyone to live in mental misery just because he or she doesn't know about depression or what to do about it—either their own depression or a loved one's.

This book is part of my obligation to other people who are going through the same thing I did. Anyone who has ever had depression and been cured from it, feels that same obligation. And with the state of our world right now, it's urgent to do everything possible to eliminate depression from our species.

This book is written toward that end . . . because that "end" is the human race's new beginning.

Wina Sturgeon

Dedication

There are so many people to whom this book should be dedicated that I just don't have enough room to thank them all. Dr. Nathan Kline's help is acknowledged throughout the book, but less notice has been given Dr. George Simpson, who deserves more than just "thank you." Then there are the people who so influenced my life that they made it possible for me to see with more than eyes.

Nancy Barner Marfyak, whose words waited so long to be heard—and it *is* only with the heart that one can see rightly.

J.C., who was the first to make contact.

And Ted, who gave me a son.

I am grateful.

1.

Depression, the Hidden Disease

You've probably seen the illness hit without knowing what it was. A loved one, a relative or friend—your spouse, parent, child—turns into a stranger almost overnight. You can't tell when it started. You don't know how to help.

Let's take a hypothetical case to show how it might be to live with someone as they came down with depression. Let's call him Joe. There would be no real symptoms at the beginning, nothing you could put your finger on. You might notice that Joe doesn't smile as much, that he doesn't seem to enjoy things the way he always did. You might wonder why he's so irritable lately, but you probably dismiss it as one of those personality stages everyone goes through every so often. Then Joe begins waking up early in the morning, around four or five, and can't get back to sleep. You may think that's a bit strange, but everyone goes through periods of insomnia at one time or another. But then you begin to realize that it's happening every night.

You start seeing other things, things that alarm you. Joe becomes withdrawn. He's no longer interested in his friends or family. Hobbies and projects are neglected. He can no longer seem to make decisions; even something as trivial as ordering from a menu gives him trouble.

Maybe at this point you try talking about it. That's when it becomes frightening. In response to your questions, Joe tells you he's no good, he's not worth caring about. He starts hinting how much better off everyone would be if he just weren't around any more. And now you are frightened, because you have no idea what's happening. And you don't know what to do about it.

What is happening with symptoms like these is depression. And knowing what to do about it can save two lives: the depression victim's, and yours.

Two facts: (1) some medical specialists estimate that as much as 80 percent of the U.S. population suffers from varying degrees of depression at any given time; (2) your chances of developing depression if you live or spend a lot of time with someone who has it are 80 percent.

That means that even if you *are* one of the lucky ones who never experiences depression, you're probably still going to have to deal with it. You might have to deal with it in a friend, a relative, or someone who affects your life in other ways: your boss, a fellow worker, a neighbor. But—if you learn *how* to deal with it, you *can* protect yourself.

Before going any further, let me state the most important piece of information in this book: *You* **MUST** *protect yourself*. Although that will not be your only concern, it must be your *first* concern. No matter how cold it seems, your own self-protection must take priority over your feelings for the depressive and over your efforts to help. Otherwise, you run a pretty thorough chance of being dragged into a cycle of depression yourself. Then, instead of being able to help at a time when your help is desperately needed, you too will be immobilized with the illness. There will be two of you sinking into a state of being which may take years to recover from.

Making your own well-being a priority will be a hard lesson to learn. The techniques of protecting yourself against depression are easy. The hard part is the realization that doing so takes precedence over the needs of the other person—in fact, over everything else.

The first part of protecting yourself is knowing what depression is and what it does to its victims. Let's start with some things depression is *not*: It's not anything the victim has any control over, so it's no use telling him or her to "cheer up." It's not directly related to an obvious cause, though there *is* a form of depression which does stem from an obvious cause. It's not a mental illness, but a *physical disease*.

That last statement is not just another attempt to remove a stigma by euphemisim in the way that drug addiction or other social aberrations are sometimes called diseases. The fact is that depression is a malfunction of the central nervous system.

The central nervous system is that part of the body which along with the endocrine glands, produces most of the chemicals we need to live—the chemicals that make us sleep and feel hungry, that regulate our sex drives and appetites. Most important, they allow our brain to function, they let us think and reason. The word *chemical* for some reason has an association primarily with the laboratory. Chemicals that are produced by the body are called *hormones*. This word too has a misleading connotation. Hormones have become connected primarily with the sexual functions. This is strange, when you consider that sex hormones are vastly outnumbered by all the others produced by the body.

While doctors know how depression shows itself, they know very little about its cause. An analogy to this is our understanding of electricity. We've long known almost everything about *how* electricity works, but after all these years we've just discovered *why* it works the way it does.

In depression, the cause (whatever it is eventually discovered to be) creates an imbalance in the chemicals of the central nervous system. The hormones used in brain function are the ones most specifically affected. For some reason, either too much or too little of the necessary hormones is produced. The most obvious symptoms of this imbalance are in the area of thought and behavior, so little attention is paid to the physical symptoms of depression. And it's true that these physical symptoms are minor—constipation, gastric distress, chest and head pains. But however minor, the depressed person physically feels like hell.

This is not to say that there are no emotional factors in depression. Yet because we know so little about the illness, it's a chicken-and-egg situation. Most depressed people do have or did have some emotional problems. But is it the problems that have triggered a depression, or are the problems the *result* of chronic depression?

To understand why this illness creates the mental and emotional symptoms it does, you must know how the chemical process of the brain works. The chemicals used in brain function are called *biogenic amines* rather than hormones. They are compounds made of amino acids. These biogenic amines are the basic building blocks of many proteins. In fact, each of these chemicals in itself is a protein and is used to feed or build other portions of the body.

The brain can be compared to a computer. It is composed mainly of a "memory bank," millions of brain cells which each carry a tiny fraction of data. This fraction is meaningless in itself; it's like a small part of a code which, when combined with hundreds or thousands of other pertinent data fractions, make up a complete sequence. For a more visual example, look closely at a newspaper picture. It is made up of countless dots in various shades of black or gray. One dot alone conveys no information at all. But the proper sequence of dots, each with its proper shading and in a correct place, make up a picture which conveys meaning to anyone who sees it. Each brain cell with its minute part of information can be compared to one dot in a newspaper picture. It takes a large number of cells or dots to make a complete unit of thought or action or to make a newspaper picture.

Brain cells transmit their data in the form of a minute burst of electricity. These electrical bursts are the method by which the brain processes information. The operation is so complicated that it's a wonder it works at all. The brain must sift through conscious and unconscious thoughts, disregard the unimportant, use what is relevant to decide what further thought or action should take place, and still concentrate on what is happening at the present time.

For an idea of how complicated it is, examine an everyday sequence. Suppose you're sitting in a room and you smell smoke from a just-lit cigarette. The smell acts as a stimulus to a whole series of thoughts with possible actions. Your nose perceives the smell, your brain identifies it as smoke. Smoke is a programmed danger signal, so you become more alert. Your brain passes on the signal for an increase in adrenalin. This is the hormone which creates the fear/flight response necessary for potential action. But at the same time that the brain has ordered protective measures, it is riffling through the memory system. Instantly the memory is produced: this is *familiar* smoke, not a fire warning. It is cigarette smoke. Your eyes now take over, looking around until you spot the person who has just lit the cigarette. Your brain registers this, the flow of adrenalin is halted, your sensory system relaxes, and the whole thought sequence disappears from your mind. The entire process is so automatic that it may not have even interrupted your conversation.

The thoughts and perceptions involved in that sequence may have required the data from hundreds and thousands of brain cells, each firing its burst of electricity. These electrical charges travel to the *cerebral cortex*, the part of the brain which gathers information and translates it. The cerebral cortex takes all the cell firings, separates them into groups each related to one thought or action, and integrates them. Then it translates the mass into a usable thought or action.

Now the laws of physics apply regardless of the environment, and electricity in the brain acts pretty much like electricity anywhere else. It needs a conduit to get where it's supposed to go. When you want to guide an electrical charge, you use a wire to carry it. Electricity from the brain cells is directed to its destination by a "wire" made of a balanced chain of chemicals, the biogenic amines.

When a brain cell is stimulated to fire by some external stimuli or by the thought processes, the charge travels to the cerebral cortex along this chemical chain. The composition of this conduit is so delicate that scientists have no accurate way of measuring the chemical amounts involved. But if that balance is upset even in the slightest, it will change the results of the electrical impulses by the time they get to the cerebral cortex. When this occurs, the complete unit of thought or action may be distorted. Parts of the message may get to the cerebral cortex late or not at all.

The cerebral cortex has no power of judgment or discrimination. It works with the information it receives. This part of the brain, which is wrapped around the outside of the gray part of the brain, does not think for itself. It can't perceive whether the countless cell transmissions it is working with make up a distorted sequence. The cerebral cortex does its job and presents the finished product without checking for accuracy. The individual who is presented with that thought or action by his brain has no way of judging and monitoring that accuracy either. So if the cerebral cortex puts together a mixed-up signal, the organism acts on it without question. That's why the symptoms of depression—lack of self-esteem, indecisiveness, anxiety, and confusion—can't be cured by verbal therapy alone. These feelings come as a direct result of the distortion of the thought process. Verbal therapy is actually asking the patient not to believe what his reason and perception tell him; this technique might work if the therapist could also give something else to replace those misperceptions. And that is impossible. Verbal therapy is a valuable help in depression, but it won't do the job of curing serious depressions without medication.

Although some schools of medical science believe they have been able to identify the biogenic amines which most often malfunction, there is no way to analyze exactly what is going on in the brain and come up with an instant diagnosis. However, the symptoms of depression are as typical as those of measles. A doctor trained in the field of depression (and, for that matter, a layman with a knowledge of the illness) can make an accurate diagnosis of a typical case of endogenous depression within ten minutes of verbal examination. Diagnosing the biogenic amines responsible for the condition, which is essential for proper medication, is done by recognizing the extremely subtle differences in symptoms.

For example, although almost every case of depression will include certain basic symptoms, one case may be marked by extreme anxiety as its predominant feature. Anxiety as a major symptom in depression is usually caused by an alteration in the body's production of *monoamine oxidase*. (That is a simplified explanation, of course.) Monoamine oxidase is an enzyme which destroys biogenic amines and stops the signal that causes a brain cell to fire. Once the cell has been triggered (either through the sensory organs or from a mental stimuli) it then receives a sufficient dose of monoamine oxidase to erase the triggering message.

As you can imagine, this is one of the most important chemicals used in the brain. But frequently, the central nervous system produces too much of it. In fact, this is the most common form of depression. Simplifying again, when there's an overproduction of this biogenic amine, it gets to some of the stimulated brain cells *before* they have a chance to fire. The result is that part of the "message" reaching the cerebral cortex is missing. Since the cerebral cortex works with what it has, the missing parts produce a distorted unit of thought or action.

When a doctor believes that an overproduction of monoamine oxidase is at fault in a case of depression, an MAOI drug will be prescribed. This is a *monoamine oxidase inhibitor*. It regulates the central nervous system into producing less of this substance.

There are many other drugs which work on specific biogenic amines or a combination of them. This general class of drugs is known as anti-depressants, but the name is misleading. They don't lift the blue mood, but work directly on the central nervous system.

It is the small, almost unnoticeable differences in symptoms in cases of depression which make one class of anti-depressant preferable over another. We mentioned the anxiety associated with too much monoamine oxidase. In another case there may be only a small amount of anxiety but a high proportion of confusion. One case may have an exaggerated factor of paranoia or else a general slowing of action and intelligence which shows retardation. There may be a slight difference in sleeping and waking patterns. Endogenous depression is marked by early morning insomnia, but one patient may wake at four, another at six. Each of these subtle differences may relate to one or more chemical imbalances and will be treated by a particular category of anti-depressant. Obviously, these drugs are not interchangeable. Some don't work well together, and certain combinations can be fatal (more about that later).

However much these drugs help depression, they are not a panacea. There are two main things to keep in mind when starting to use them, whether you are waiting for their effects on someone else or whether you yourself are taking them. The diagnosis in depression must be honed very finely, and unfortunately there are many doctors who are unable to readily prescribe the proper type of medication. They may try one anti-depressant and then switch to another when results aren't forthcoming. This is quite a time-consuming process, because these drugs take several weeks to begin working. When first taken, they will have several undesirable effects which, while minor, can be disconcerting. When those effects wear off, usually in about two weeks, it then takes more time for the drug to begin regulating the balance of the central nervous system.

It's amazing to think that a substance in an amount so tiny it can barely be measured will have such an effect on a human being. The differences in the severity of the illness are also amazing. It can range from a condition so mild and chronic that it does little more than remove the extra energy needed for *full* expression of an individual's talent and ability. It can go to extremes, leaving the victim little more than a vegetable, unable to cope with the most basic life-sustaining activities such as eating or moving around.

You may wonder how a depressive can slip into the condition without realizing that a drastic personality change has taken place—for although a depressive is aware of the emotional pain caused by the illness, he or she is usually unaware that something is *wrong* until the condition has reached the peak of the symptoms.

If you've never experienced an episode of endogenous depression, it's hard to explain how anyone can slip into such a state without knowing what is happening. In fact, one side benefit of recovery is that the victim comes away with a much greater understanding of how his or her mind works and a greater self-awareness and self-knowledge.

We humans trust our senses so completely that we rarely analyze our perceptions to learn why we have perceived the way we did. This may be because extreme objectivity is necessary to question perceptions or because it requires a great deal of effort. As an example, a woman may be paranoid about walking into a dimly lit parking lot, perhaps because of the generalized, unspecific thought of attack, or because a specific incident has been impressed upon her mind. She is probably aware of the stimuli responsible for her paranoia and rationally knows that it *is* in fact a situation requiring an increased amount of alertness. But the quickened steps, the slight increase in heartbeat and respiration, the rush of adrenalin—they may be due more to a subjective perception based on paranoia than to the reality of the situation. Yet her reaction is not out of control, and since repetition has made it an automatic response, she doesn't examine the perception responsible for the response. She is aware of feelings of fear and discomfort when walking in the parking lot, but normally she will not ask herself: "Are these feelings necessary or have I created their necessity? Is it within my control to disregard this paranoia and would doing so endanger my survival or have no effect on it?"

For a more specific example of how we can slip into a state of being without questioning it, take the case of Loren Singh. At the age of 19 he came to England from India. At the time, England was going through a stage of great dislike for Indians and Loren found himself the victim of discrimination in both job and housing opportunities. After some years of this, he migrated to America, where people from India are rarer and there is practically no prejudice against them. Loren continued to feel discriminated against. He sought the most menial of jobs, lived in the worst part of town because he felt no one would permit him to climb any higher. His perceptions had been ingrained into him: white people didn't like Indian people. He never questioned that idea until he became involved with a group of Americans who convinced him that he *could* look for a better job and apartment. Loren had slipped into accepting, without question, a position he was no longer forced to occupy.

Another common example of unquestioned perceptions is the case of the employee who has a good idea but is afraid to show it to the boss because he or she feels the boss won't like it. Few people with that perception will ask themselves, "*Why* do I feel the boss won't like my idea?" We seldom trace the thought processes involved in a perception, whether it's an inferiority complex or a fear of spiders. That's why an episode of depression will usually be far advanced before the victim will realize something is happening.

In a typical, nonchronic case (*chronic* means lasting for a long time without ever becoming *acute*, or serious), there is an increase in irritability, sometimes to a radical degree. But usually the first thing the depressive notices—and by that I mean *notices* as apart from passively feeling—is a feeling of sadness. *Nothing seems good, nothing seems worth feeling good about.* It's very similar to a case of the blues. The feeling is followed by a feeling of hopelessness. *It's not even worth trying, nothing is going to get any better.* At first this hopelessness comes and goes, but eventually it becomes constant. In the typical pattern of symptom development, the person may become aware of and even preoccupied by the bowel movements, since depression often causes constipation. Although the individual has been aware that fatigue has been increasing, fatigue usually doesn't become a serious problem until about the midpoint of the onset of the illness. The onset of depression, from first vague feelings to full-fledged illness, usually takes about four weeks. When the full onset of fatigue hits, the person becomes listless and no longer has the energy for anything but the most essential tasks. Getting up, dressing, and going to work or beginning the day's chores is hard, but usually possible. Mustering the energy to get dressed to go out for the evening, or to invite friends over for an evening's entertainment, is just too much work. Usually, the first thing to go are social activities. Then hobbies and projects start being neglected. Reading becomes less and less of a pleasure and more and more of a hard job. Only a small part of this reading difficulty is due to a lack of the energy needed to read. Reading actually *does* become difficult because of the illness's symptoms of confusion and inability to concentrate. Depression affects memory *and* concentration, since both those qualities depend so much on each other.

When I had my depression, that symptom was a real wrench. I love to read, but the lack of concentration made it impossible to retain the beginning of a sentence until I'd reached the end of it. I would spend minutes on one line, repeating each word out loud through clenched teeth, underlining each one with a highlighter—and just as I'd finally made sense of it, I'd forget everything that preceded it and have to go back a few pages and start over again. You can imagine how frustrating that is, and why a severely depressed person may begin crying while merely looking at a piece of correspondence or a business form.

About the crying: some depressives will cry dozens of times a day. These tearful episodes can occur with the slightest provocation. A button may come off a garment, or a pet animal may not come when called. A friend may cut a phone conversation short because someone is at the door, but the depressive will take it as a rebuff and cry. Or there may be no provocation at all. Tears may start flowing without the person's being aware of them. Many times the crying isn't within the depressive's conscious control.

The most self-destructive effect of depression is the total loss of self-esteem. It seems unbelievable that self-esteem is controlled in any way by a combination of chemicals, yet when the central nervous system doesn't produce the right amount of biogenic amines, loss of self-esteem is typically one of the most serious symptoms. The depressed person shows this lack in a number of predictable ways. There's a feeling that *no one likes me, not really, they're only tolerating me*, or there's a feeling that everyone is laughing secretly. Self-consciousness grows until it's a source of deep pain. There's also a tendency toward confessions of great guilt. You may hear the depressed person confess that he or she is responsible for the sorry state of the world or for the fact that the neighborhood has an increased crime rate or a friend is going broke. It does no good to point out that none of these things can possibly be true or that it's a strange sort of ego trip to think one is that important. The depressive actually perceives these great guilts as true and no one can laugh him or her out of it. This particular manifestation is an important one. It often provides the first obvious clue when the person is thinking about suicide. He or she will say something to the effect that the world (or the family or the friend listening to the confession) *will be better off without me*. Or, *I'm not good enough to live*. These are subtle hints and mean that some sort of action is necessary, which will be discussed in greater length further on.

From the moment the illness begins, there is a decrease in appetites—for food, sex, and social contact—for life itself. These appetites decrease further every day. By the time of full onset, the person has lost almost all interest in fulfilling any kind of appetite. More than that, he or she is often actively repelled by the very thought of them. This is the factor that is most destructive to marriages and friendships. You may prepare a gourmet meal for a depressed person you know hasn't eaten all day. He or she will refuse to eat it except under duress, and then make expressions of dislike after a few mouthfuls. Or if you're dealing with a spouse or lover, you may begin a sexy seduction, only to be pushed away and ignored. Even someone who fully understands that the behavior is all due to the depression finds it hard not to take such actions personally.

Personal hygiene will often be somewhat neglected, even in mild episodes, but in a more severe case the neglect can reach the repugnant stage. The depressive will not have the energy or concentration and decision-making ability to shower or shave or even change clothing. In many cases, the depressive will sleep in day clothing and continue to wear it the next day. Unless there's someone around to do some prodding, the same clothing can be worn for days or weeks in a serious case.

A major symptom for diagnosing depression is the early morning insomnia. Depression causes intense drowsiness in the late afternoon or early evening. Then, at around three, four, or five o'clock in the morning there is an awakening with feelings of apprehension. Sometimes the feeling is vague and unfocused. But it can also take the form of *something terrible is about to happen*, or a belief that a tragedy is going to befall a specific person. There may be an exaggeration of a minor daytime worry: *I'm never going to get my income tax return done, they're going to come and arrest me! . . . The boss gave me a funny look yesterday, I know he's thinking of firing me! . . . My spouse hung up the phone suddenly when I came into the room, I know it's an affair, tomorrow I'll be asked for a divorce.*

The feeling can range from a slight case of butterflies in the stomach to a deep and pervasive feeling of dread. In some cases a fitful return to sleep may be possible but it will usually be further broken by restlessness and frequent awakenings. In most cases, the person will just lie in bed, tossing and turning without really sleeping until it's time to get out of bed. But whether there's a return to sleep or not, there's no feeling of refreshment from whatever amount of sleep was obtained. There's a dull, leaden feeling, sometimes even a metallic taste in the mouth, and a cloud of gloom that can't be lifted. The feelings of depression are worst in the early morning. While they rarely lift altogether once full onset of symptoms appear, they are lighter in midafternoon.

Sometimes the person will feel a midafternoon surge of drowsiness too intense to resist. (I would often lay my head on my arms and doze for a few minutes. When my co-workers began commenting on it, I would go to the ladies room and doze while sitting on the toilet.) This drowsiness is almost trance-like. It's also common to feel better after giving into it and snoozing for a minute or two. However, the sleepy feelings aren't confined to midafternoon. They may occur in midmorning, around ten or eleven o'clock, and they frequently reoccur near six or seven in the evening.

Dream patterns change, too. In some cases, there are no dreams at all. (There actually are, but the depressive doesn't remember them.) Or dreams may turn very vivid. Someone who has always dreamed in black and white may begin dreaming in color. The dreams may be spot images without story content or strange blurs of color without meaning. There's another thing which happens frequently, and so far no research seems to have been done on it. If people with moderate to severe depression are taking anti-depressives and then smoke marijuana, it puts them to sleep very quickly and gives them excessively vivid and realistic dreams. Sometimes these marijuana-influenced dreams are so real that the person continues to believe they have happened even when he or she awakens. In one such case, a depressed woman was so convinced that her daughter had died that she told one of her telephoning friends of the "death" with complete acceptance and calm. Even a telephone call from her daughter did nothing to dispel the belief. When her daughter rushed over to the house to see what was wrong, the woman's first response was confusion. She couldn't understand how her daughter was alive. While the connection between marijuana and this type of dreaming is not a subject of any major study, it's interesting to note that in many Far Eastern cultures marijuana or hashish has been used as a cure for depression throughout history. Even in experimental cases in England and parts of Europe, the active principal of marijuana, THC, is sometimes prescribed instead of anti-depressants.

The physical effects of depression are not a reliable means of making a diagnosis because they're so vague. In fact, the physical symptoms are usually ignored because there's so much emotional pain. But descriptions of how these physical symptoms feel are remarkably similar from case to case. "There's a band across my chest and it's so tight that I can't draw a full breath." "Something is constricting my chest, it's hard to breathe." "I've got a funny feeling in my stomach, not a pain, but like a big lump is in there somewhere." "My food doesn't go anywhere, it seems like it just stays sitting in my stomach." "My head feels like it's stuffed with cotton and my thoughts can't get through," though many complaints are far more vague.

Complaints of headache are common, and so are descriptions of a feeling of wearing a too-tight hat. Many depressives feel unexplained pressures in the head, ears, or neck area. Sometimes there is difficulty in swallowing and very often there is dryness of the mouth. There will be periods of sweating and hot flashes, sometimes with tingling of the hands and feet. Old injuries may ache.

In some cases, rather than loss of appetites, there may be an overindulgence in sexual activity, or a heavy weight gain from overeating. But those symptoms are far less common than a serious loss of normal appetites. In fact, the greater the seriousness of the depression, the more the appetite loss.

Like every other disease with a set of symptoms and a prognosis (*prognosis* refers to the doctor's being able to tell how serious it is and how the patient can be expected to do), depression also has an average duration. Depending on the degree of the illness, there are several possible average durations. A mild case typically lasts three to six months. A moderate case, in which *all* symptoms are present in varying degrees, will last about six to nine months. More serious cases of depression, in which the depressive may require hospitalization and/or may be unable to care for him or herself without help, usually needs a minimum of nine months for recovery, though it may take much longer. Of course, these time spans are most typical in cases that are being treated chemically with anti-depressants. Chronic untreated cases can last a lifetime.

Using the Right Terms

I must interject a word here about terminology. Specialists in the field of depression, like specialists everywhere else, like to update their findings by renaming everything every so often. That's why a janitor becomes a *sanitation engineer* or an interior decorator becomes an *environmental design specialist*. It's also why a word like *good*, for example, goes through such periodic changes as *groovy* or *ginchy* or *wild* or *far out*. And so on.

The earlier terms used for the classes of depression were more explanatory than current terms. They were named after the qualities that best expressed the causes of and differences between the various types. Those terms were easy to understand, even by lay people with little medical training. Perhaps that's why doctors began using other terms, ones which *do* need a bit of medical background to understand, and which hardly explain the illness in an understandable way. I'm going to stick to the old terms throughout this book. Language is meant to communicate, and the old terms communicate easily. True, the newer names may be more accurate in describing brain function, but for them you need an awful lot of medical knowledge which isn't essential to understanding what depression is. And understanding depression, protecting yourself against it, or helping someone else through the depressive episode is really the only essential information needed.

The type of depression we've been talking about so far is *endogenous* depression, which is the most common form of this illness. There are some medical specialists who believe that all depressions are a form of manic-depressive illness. *Manic depression* is a condition in which the person passes through cycles of hyperactivity and extreme euphoria and then descends to a deep depression. These cycles can happen over a period of hours, months, or even years. Some doctors believe endogenous depression to be a condition in which the "up" cycle never happens. They now call endogenous depression *unipolar*, or single-cycle depression. The manic form is called a *bipolar*, or double-cycle depression. Bipolar depressions, or manic-depressive syndromes, are much less common, accounting for only about 5 percent of all depressions.

Since the terms "unipolar" and "bipolar" contain a basic inaccuracy in language (why should an illness which consists of at least a good portion spent in a wildly active, manic phase be categorized as a *depression*?), they don't convey much information. But because these new words are being used by many doctors, it's a good idea to familiarize yourself with them so you know what the doctor is talking about.

Endogenous is one of four main categories of depression. The other three may overlap into or become the endogenous form. Endogenous, by the way, is a good description of the difference between this type and the other forms of depression. It means "stemming from within." This form has no obvious cause and is not based on any obvious event.

The category of depression which *is* caused by an obvious event is *reactive* depression. Its name is self-explanatory. Reactive depression is at first a healthy response to some personal loss— the death of a loved one, losing a job, a serious financial setback. It's normal, and in fact desirable, to feel depressed when undergoing a serious personal upset. Allowing oneself to fully experience feelings of grief, rather than suppressing them, can prevent a future neurosis. But when the reaction to a negative experience goes on for a longer time than the experience is worth, it becomes a form of chronic depression. Now that sounds too clinical for subjective judgment. You may be thinking, "Who's to gauge whether the mourning of a loss has a warranted time period?" And it's true that some griefs will last a lifetime—the death of a loved one or a financial upset from which full recovery is never made. But if a man, ten years after his wife's death, is still refusing to go out with friends and still cries every evening, his grief is abnormal. So is the reaction of a person who, months after being fired, is still unable to look for work because of the depression of being fired.

Unlike endogenous depression, reactive depression doesn't hit over a period of weeks. There's no gradual descent into the depths of illness. It comes on almost instantly, as a response. In some cases, reactive depression isn't even caused by a negative event. There's an intimate connection between stress and depression. Any kind of change, good or bad, is stressful. You may have worked and planned for years to move into your dream home, only to feel slightly depressed for weeks after you move in. Achievement of a goal is a stress. But these positive stresses rarely result in an actual case of reactive depression. And while the reactive category may often, if prolonged and left untreated, turn into endogenous depression (if it doesn't just go away by itself), it differs from the endogenous form in a number of ways.

The same feelings of constant sadness are there, of course,

but the major emotional symptoms rarely occur. Concentration is undisturbed and there are no episodes of confusion. Memory is unaffected in reactive depression, though there is a great memory loss in endogenous depressions. There may be periods of anxiety as there are in endogenous illnesses, but with reactive depression this usually happens when the loss was something that affected financial or emotional support. There are few physical symptoms and none of the chest or stomach pains. Reactive depression causes bedtime insomnia. It's hard to fall asleep, but once sleep comes it lasts until morning. On awakening, the person with reactive depression usually feels refreshed; he or she does not feel the leaden mood which comes with the endogenous form.

Suicide is always a risk in any form of depression, but here again there is a difference in these two forms: in the reactive kind the most dangerous time is at the beginning of the depression, whereas the danger in the endogenous form increases as the illness persists. And the appetites are also affected differently; they become passive in reactive depression but still exist. The person may make no move toward food or sex, but if a meal is prepared, he or she will eat. Sexual desire is usually still there, though greatly decreased.

If you're dealing with another person's reactive depression, your main problem will be gauging the point at which the reaction is not the normal, appropriate response, but a genuine chronic condition. It's at that point that professional help is necessary. As in all cases of depression, the sooner some kind of therapy is begun the less serious the episode will be and the quicker there will be a recovery. Since the judgment must be made on an individual basis, because it depends on the personality of the person involved, you'll have to use a rule of thumb, which, to be honest, is pretty vague. A quiet, normally calm person should begin showing moments of cheerfulness and some return to normal social activities within a month, though there will still be a damper on normal personality traits. In other words, don't expect someone to stop *all* mourning in a month. More dramatic personalities will naturally show a more dramatic response to depressing events. Give them a few more weeks to start coming out of their grief.

A third category of depression, far more common than formerly realized, is *toxic* depression, sometimes called *secondary* depression. It comes from an external source, which is toxic to the individual such as drugs, alcohol, or viral infections. Yes, a virus can cause a full-scale depression! Mononucleosis is notorious for this. That disease comes on with mild cold symptoms and takes months for recovery. It leaves the body in such a weakened condition that just climbing a stairway may be so tiring that there is a need to stop and rest halfway up. Infectious hepatitis is another culprit. After a person has recovered and is no longer in danger, toxic depression may come on like a cloud. You may remember that the Beatles' manager, Brian Epstein, committed suicide. At the time, he was recovering from hepatitis. People who saw him before his death remarked on how depressed he seemed. He felt the Beatles weren't happy with him, and he was convinced that he was a failure. He showed all the typical losses in self-esteem and confidence that accompany depression. Even a case of the flu may bring on a mild depression. Knowing this fact might be helpful to *you* if you've just gotten over some virus and suddenly feel the whole world is too much of a burden to face and you don't have the strength or desire to function in your normal manner.

There are also a number of drugs which cause toxic depression. Most specifically, these are the barbiturates and sedatives. These drugs are almost always central nervous system depressants: they work by *depressing* the functions of the central nervous system. This is why an overdose of these drugs can cause death. They depress the central nervous system until it stops working, and since breathing is one of the things controlled by this part of the body, you can see why we can't survive if the central nervous system is depressed too far.

Alcohol is also a central nervous system depressant which will occasionally cause a toxic reaction. This may be due in part to the fact that alcohol uses up a lot of the body's supply of the B vitamins. The B factors are essential to proper nerve and brain cell functioning. Many of the B factors metabolized by the body are made into parts of the proteins used to make the biogenic amines. Many people, knowing that alcohol destroys the stores of this vitamin in the body, have turned that knowledge to their own ends for hangover prevention. By taking a triple dose of the B vitamins, they can overindulge in drink and still feel fine in the morning. But if you intend to test this out, remember that it may eliminate a hangover but it won't keep you from getting drunk!

The easiest kind of toxic depression to cure is the one which comes from an outside substance. Some drugs other than barbiturates and sedatives create a high depressive risk. Cortisone is one, though more commonly depression will come from drugs used to lower high blood pressure. Reserpine is one high blood pressure regulator which is so well known for causing a secondary depression that doctors often warn their patients about it. Our national tendency to want a miracle drug for everything sometimes leads to a real tragedy where depression is concerned. Someone with a case of endogenous depression may have occasional anxiety attacks. Without realizing the basic cause, this person may begin taking a tranquilizer. But since most tranquilizers are central nervous system depressants, the condition then changes from a mild or moderate case to a serious depression, with serious consequences.

This is what happened to me. My case occurred in England, where there's a national health system. The doctor I went to was in her seventies and had been trained long before depression was even identified as an illness. It would never have crossed her mind to look for the symptoms of depression, and besides, she was too busy. She had too many people to see to take time with any one of them. It would have been better if she had prescribed nothing at all. As it was, she gave me librium. Within two weeks, I was a total zombie. My episode might have been much less severe if I hadn't taken a tranquilizer at the beginning of the illness.

Many glandular diseases cause depression as well. Diabetes, hypoglycemia, and especially thyroid illness are often responsible for depression. In the latter case, the thyroid gland underproduces or overproduces *thyroxine*, which regulates energy and metabolic rates and is part of every cell in the body. (The metabolic rate is the speed at which your body takes food, produces proteins, and builds cells, the speed with which your organs and glands function, and in general, the rate of efficiency with which your entire organism works.) You could say that the thyroid is the gas pedal of the body, and when it doesn't produce in the proper amount everything slows down. Underactive thyroid illness (*hypothyroidism*) is very much on the increase. It pays to have your thyroid tested if you show any of the symptoms of low thyroxine production. These symptoms are detailed in the chapter on endocrine imbalances, Chapter Six.

When you are trying to help someone with depression, you should arrange for him or her to take a full metabolic test. There are two reasons for this. One, you want to eliminate the possibility that the illness may be caused by an endocrine gland, since that will require different medication. Two, most depressives will resist getting any kind of therapy for their condition (you can almost say *all* will resist, because resistance against getting help is so common that it can almost be called a symptom), but it's usually easier to persuade a depressive to take a physical test. You'll find full explanations of how to look for signs of hypothyroidism and other glandular malfunctions responsible for depression in Chapter Six.

The fourth type of depression is the one which gives this illness a bad name. This is *psychotic* depression, and it's the only form which is a true psychological disorder. It can be brought on by overexhaustion or brain disease. A brain tumor can cause it. In psychotic depression, there are psychotic behaviors and periods in which the victim isn't in touch with the real world. Often this type of depression may be the first sign of an oncoming nervous breakdown.

A word about nervous breakdowns: I have always disliked this term because it's so meaningless. A true "breakdown" accompanied by strange symptoms such as hearing voices or having periods of wild screaming may be the mind's way of escaping from an unbearable situation for awhile and taking a rest. Sometimes a breakdown is actually a *breakthrough*. The part of the mind that deals in logic is tearing down the old, unworkable structure and rebuilding it with wisdom and sense which has been gained during years of living. Usually this wisdom and sense haven't been integrated into the thought processes because the current way of thinking won't allow it. The words "nervous breakdown" can mean anything from a mind's getting itself in shape to a full-scale dive into insanity—it covers too much territory to communicate any accurate meaning.

Psychotic depression is also sometimes the low end of a

manic-depressive cycle. In this form of the illness, sadness may not be consistent. There will be extreme mood swings. The psychotic depressive may be too blue to do anything buy cry one moment, then become wildly euphoric five minutes later. Frequently there are hallucinations. The emotional symptoms vary with each individual, so there's no set pattern as there is in other types of depression. The person feels best in the morning and gets a leaden feeling as afternoon draws on. Obesity is one side effect of this form of depression, since compulsive overeating is common. Self-esteem fluctuates; one day the person feels worthless, the next there is such overconfidence that he or she takes genuinely foolish risks.

Fortunately, this condition is very rare. There are varying statistics for any fact about depression, but my research seems to grant the most credibility to four out of every one hundred cases of depression being the neurotic form.

Even reactive and toxic depressions are quite rare when measured against the statistical cases of endogenous depression. But these separations for various categories of depression may be meaningless when you realize that without treatment, any type of depression may pass into the endogenous form. While endogenous types are usually easy to diagnose because of the obvious and typical symptoms, it can also take another form which is harder to diagnose. This is *masked* depression. The name comes from the fact that the underlying condition is hidden behind a mask so well constructed that the victim is actually unaware of feeling depressed. Even the most expert doctors have a hard time uncovering masked depression. You may have read Edwin Arlington Robinson's poem about Richard Corey, the man who was the envy of everyone because he had everything going for him and managed his life with correctness and grace. "Whenever Richard Corey went downtown . . . we people on the pavement looked at him. He was a gentleman from sole to crown, clean favored and imperially slim . . . So on we worked and waited for the light, and went without the meat and cursed the bread. And Richard Corey, one calm summer night—went home and put a bullet through his head."

This is a perfect description of the victim of masked depression. And unfortunately, it's a frequent outcome. In masked depression, the person will function in a normal way, taking care of responsibilities and doing what is expected. But the facial expression is a giveaway. The face of any depressive is less mobile, and this is especially true of those with masked depression. It shows very little emotion. The person is aloof and withdrawn. He or she will communicate, but never confide. When you talk to someone who has this illness, you may get the impression that you are only touching their surface and making no deep impression. Masked depression *does* force its victims to live on a superficial plane. They remain aware only of those emotions, feelings, thoughts, and ideas which they can experience without coming into contact with their illness. Everything else is buried and hidden, so that underneath the usually calm exterior is a maelstrom of seething destructiveness and negativity. As the depression expands into their psyche, these people close off more and more of their self to escape the depression. Their level of life becomes more and more superficial.

One of the most extreme cases of masked depression I've ever seen was in a woman named Marta. Marta was the daughter of a brilliant scientist who, with his family, had escaped from Europe during World War II. She was only a few months old when the family relocated in America. Her older sister was beautiful and accomplished, and Marta grew up feeling unloved and unwanted. Of course this may have had a bearing on her depression, but there are many people who also grow up feeling unloved and unwanted and who never experience this illness. One thing Marta's upbringing did do was to teach her to hide her responses. As a child, when she would see her older sister being admired and complimented, she would ask in various ways for the same kind of positive reinforcement. It was done with a "me too, me too" approach. Her parents responded by laughing and accusing her of jealousy. Marta's natural reaction was resentment, which of course was frowned upon. Soon she learned to hide her feelings, for fear of ridicule. When she was barely a teenager, her father died and the family was left with very little money. Marta felt intimidated by her mother, a glamorous, cultured woman whose apartment became a kind of salon for the intellectuals of the city.

When I met Marta, she was in her early twenties. She wanted

to spend the summer in California, and I invited her to stay in my home. She left for the West coast, telling her mother that she was coming here to look after my son, then two years old. I had no idea that she was using this imagined function to give herself a sense of importance. When I met Marta, I had not guessed that she needed anything to bolster her sense of self.

Marta had, upon our first meeting, impressed me with her ability. She had just written a book on interior decorating, and showed me a mock-up for an ad which was to appear in a publishers' magazine about the book. It was the first time in her life she had completed such a major project and she really knew her subject. Or so I thought.

Within a few days after her arrival, I realized there was something seriously wrong with Marta. She acted as though she were hiding a deep secret which she was terrified someone might guess. One night I made a dinner centerpiece of some wicks floating in a bowl of oil. After the meal, when we blew the flames out, I asked her to carry the bowl over to the sink to be emptied and washed. As Marta lifted it, I called out, "Careful with that." She gave me a frightened glance, then immediately *tipped* the bowl over onto the floor. She stood immobilized, making no move to clean up the mess. When the rest of the guests started grabbing towels to wipe up the oil, Marta still made no move to help with the cleaning. Someone told her to lend a hand, since she had spilled it. Marta, with no sign of the discomfort and embarrassment she was certainly feeling, said, "I've got a headache; I can't help," and calmly strolled into the living room.

The visit went downhill after that point. Marta had reluctantly helped out with some of the household chores before that, but now she evaded (rather than refused) to contribute any help at all. She began talking about her health constantly, dropping the facade of social graces which had first impressed me. This facade was easy for Marta to maintain with superficial relationships. But when she spent any length of time with someone, the cover dropped and she showed the self that was manifesting her depressive illness. Her main, and practically only, topic of conversation was the various things which were wrong with her health. She carried an entire compendium of over-the-counter medications with her—there were over twenty of these pill bottles, counting the prescription and nonprescription drugs. She used them all. Marta had migraines, a common affliction among those with masked depression.

After the first week of her visit, I had begun observing Marta, trying to put a finger on this sense of "wrongness" I felt. The lack of mobility in her face was the most obvious. Although she would laugh occasionally, it seemed as though there was no real emotion behind it, once I became acquainted with the way Marta expressed good feelings. Then I realized that the facial expressions of interest, involvement, good feelings, or laughter Marta *did* show were copies—just copies. If others were smiling, she would smile. When others looked serious or interested, so did Marta. It was as if she were playing a constant guessing game, living in a dark world where some game was being played and she didn't know the rules. She would guess, looking to others for guidance and keeping the secret of her ignorance by trying to blend in, by giving the appropriate response without knowing what it should be. Yet she seemed totally unaware of other people as entities. Her personality seemed isolated, as though she were an alien in a human body, trying to prevent everyone from guessing that she wasn't real. This was more than conjecture on my part. In some deep talks we had, she told me this was exactly how she felt. She described herself as feeling "wrapped in Saran Wrap, trying to get through but never making it past the plastic."

Marta had told her mother that there was a necessity for her visit (taking care of my son) in order to impress her. The conversations which did not dwell on her health were composed mainly of little bluffs, statements about what she was doing, had done, or was going to do—all designed to convince the listener (and herself) that there was some substance there, some reality.

When I told Marta about depression, she grew frightened. Rather than feel reassured by the fact that there was a name for her condition, she felt that her desperately kept secret was now revealed. She suddenly decided to go back home, and no one could talk her out of leaving. After spending a lot of time on the phone to New York, she said that she had a reason to leave: she and an old friend were going to open an interior decorating shop.

The opening never happened. Marta's inability to interact with other people soon ended the relationship with her partner, as it ended all her relationships. As it turned out, her book had not even been a truly original work, but a barely disguised rewriting of other authors' works on interior decorating. She actually knew very little about it herself, though her writing showed promise.

Marta moved shortly after, and though I wrote to her, there was never an answer. She was afraid, because I had "guessed" her secret. For her to understand that someone could guess what was wrong and therefore the condition had a name and could be treated would mean admitting there *was* something wrong. This was the thing Marta focused most of her energies on masking. She fled, and soon after that she fled from her mother and sister. Although she showed occasional flashes of brilliance—and even with her illness, her basic intelligence was very high—Marta would never have a chance to use these qualities for the completion of any goal. She drifted away from acquaintances and her family, and no one knew where she was for more than five years. Today she is still running from herself, growing more and more into a robot with each passing year, losing even the little contact she once had with humanity.

I've gone into Marta's case in some depth, because it is so typical of the waste resulting from this illness. Marta came to my home to escape from her old self. She hoped that just by her wishing her past away, it would disappear. She had no way of knowing that she carried her past with her, hidden under blankets of self-protection. Before the dropped oil incident, she believed she had succeeded in hiding her real self from my friends and me and that we accepted her as the new person she wanted to be. But to Marta, the first negative incident meant that she was revealed—now we all knew her secret and would have only contempt for her. So she gave up trying, as she did in relationship after relationship, and withdrew into psychic isolation.

Marta carried the typical signs of masked depression—migraines, hypochondria, the turning to medications in the hopes that one would provide the miracle of making her feel "real," and a masklike face. She also carried the most destructive factor—the total lack of conscious awareness that she actually did have a problem. In all other forms of depression, the victim can *feel* the pain, *knows* that something is wrong. In masked depression, the very ability to function in a seemingly normal way is the biggest disadvantage. Only those very close to the person suspect anything is wrong, and most of these kinds of depressives evade any close relationship. Occasionally the masked depressive will complain to a doctor about the symptoms, and the symptoms will be taken for the actual disease. Masked depressives will be treated for their frequent migraines, told to seek therapy for their hypochondria, dismissed as clumsy because they often evidence lack of coordination and bad muscular control. Or they will be considered lazy because they don't finish projects. What is strangest of all is that this type of depression usually affects people who are extremely intelligent, talented, and creative. Yet the illness stifles those advantages and the abilities all go to waste.

I've described the major types of depression and how the symptoms differ in subtle ways. On the following pages is a chart which allows you to compare these symptoms for a more efficient diagnosis. Remember, this allows only the broadest diagnosis and will give only the *indication* that depression in one of its four main forms exists. Use the chart as if it were a piece of litmus paper; it tells you that something is there, but only in the broadest sense tells you *what*. If the symptom chart shows there is a case of depression present, then begin looking for the right kind of medical help. But keep an open mind—don't feel you know exactly what is wrong just because you have checked off a number of major symptoms. The chart will give you some idea of the existence and degree of this condition, but *by no means* should the chart make you overconfident about the accuracy of your diagnosis. This chart does not replace the opinion of a physician.

DEPRESSION SYMPTOM CHART

Type	Endogenous	Reactive	Toxic	Psychotic
Cause	A chemical imbalance in the central nervous system. Usually unconnected with an obvious external cause.	The death or loss of a loved one, severe personal setback, or the like.	Drugs or other substances which cause a bad reaction in the person, viral illnesses, other outside substances.	Mental disorder or brain disease, overexhaustion, "nervous breakdown."
Mental Symptoms	Inability to concentrate, anxiety, memory loss, periods of confusion, constant sad feelings	Sadness, some periods of anxiety.	Varies from case to case. Hallucinations may be present. Most symptoms similar to those of endogenous form. Listlessness. "dopey" feelings, mood swings.	Varies from case to case. Frequent hallucinations. Occasional manic intensity.
Physical Symptoms	Stomach pains, diarrhea or constipation, headache, feelings of pressure in neck, head, and chest, dryness of mouth.	Usually none.	Few, unless as a side effect of the toxic substance.	A lot of vague complaints which are usually only hypochondria.
Mood	Leaden with periods of anxiety or confusion, apathy, frequent paranoia. Worse in morning, may feel better in early afternoon. Sadness is constant.	Constant sadness.	Swings from hyperactive, to lethargic, slowed down.	Apathetic to intense. Most optimistic in morning, depressed in evening. Behavior unpredictable.

27

DEPRESSION SYMPTOM CHART (Continued)

Type	Endogenous	Reactive	Toxic	Psychotic
Sleep Patterns	Intense sleepiness in early evening, waking between three and dawn, unable to go back to sleep or else falls back to sleep restless and fitful.	Difficulty falling asleep, but then sleeps normally.	Depending on toxic substance, may sleep all the time or suffer from insomnia.	Restless through night, deep sleep in morning.
Waking	No feeling of rest, tired and jittery. May wake with feeling of impending doom, anxiety, or terror.	Feels rested and peaceful.	If substance affects brain or nervous system toxically, may be extremely depressed. Otherwise, may awake feeling better.	Wakes feeling leaden but optimistic.
Eating	Doesn't want food, won't eat, frequent weight loss.	Doesn't want food but will eat if coaxed.	Doesn't make move to get food but will eat if it is ready and waiting.	Varies from case to case. Compulsive overeating common.
Sex	No interest.	Desires are decreased but interest is there.	May be obsessed by sex, or apathetic.	Interest changes from day to day.
Decision Making Ability	None. Unable to make even trivial decisions.	Usually unaffected.	If hyper symptoms, aggressively decisive. If lethargic, too apathetic to make decisions.	Indecisive on large matters, positive decisions on unimportant things.

Self Esteem	None. Feels guilty, worthless, inferior, poor. Feels despised by everyone.	Unaffected. Feeling loss of external factor, not loss of self.	Varies from case to case.	Fluctuates from total lack to overconfidence.
Suicide	Common. Should be expected and watched for. Usually successful if attempted. Will most likely occur when illness is long term or chronic.	Rare, but should be watched for, especially on anniversary of loss.	Extremely rare	Frequent attempts, usually bids for attention. Arranges circumstances to be found in time for rescue.
Energy	None, finds it hard to move.	Usually unaffected.	Varies from case to case.	Swings from intense listlessness to wild burst of action.

2.

Depression Can Be Fatal

Children and Depression

During a recent medical convention there was a special workshop on suicide among patients. One doctor who specializes in the treatment of depression told his colleagues, "I think it would be safe to say that suicide is nothing more or less than a terminal case of depression."

He wasn't being dramatic. Every doctor who treats this illness can tell you of at least one patient lost through suicide. Los Angeles coroner Thomas Nogouchi says that of the suicide victims his office sees, he would estimate that more than *ninety-five percent* were suffering from depression. And his estimates agree with those of other coroners and medical scientists. *Less than five percent of those who die by suicide do not have depression*. It's an even more frightening statistic when you consider that the single largest cause of death among 15- to 25-year-olds is suicide. Depression has very little to do with age, though some age periods are more depression-prone than others. Since endogenous depression is a biochemical disorder, it can strike without any trauma from unhappy life events. This is another reason why depression often escapes an accurate diagnosis until the condition has progressed to an alarming degree. Cases of this disease are even found in very young children, sometimes too young to talk. We rarely think of something like depression in connection with children, yet child psychiatrists are reporting an increasing number of clinical cases. There are definite signs by which a parent can recognize depression in a child. Children who are healthy are energetic, and all healthy children go through periods of rough play, running, shouting, and screaming. The depressed child is listless. He or she shows no signs of enthusiasm about anything. Favorite toys go neglected. The child may avoid playing with friends and withdraw into a quiet shell. Even when part of a group, this child will stand off to the side, not participating in any activity. Homework becomes a chore, far more so than it is to children who merely want to be outside playing. The depressed youngster will sit for hours over a few simple math problems. He or she may start misbehaving and going through periods of rage and aggression.

A parent, living with a child every day, may not see this change because it doesn't happen overnight. A teacher may notice it, but you can't always be sure that the teacher will contact you immediately. Teachers have so many extra details to attend to that they rarely have time to initiate a meeting with a parent unless something is radically and obviously wrong. So if you notice signs such as slipping grades, a lack of interest in outside activities, or a lowering of energy, and especially any periods of sudden violent behavior, it's a good idea to talk to the child's teacher and see if someone else has noticed the change. *That*, of course, is provided that the child isn't able to discuss the problem or doesn't bring up the subject first. You'll find that in cases of depression, children will be vague: *I don't know what's wrong, I just feel sad lately*. Or, *I'm okay, just leave me alone*.

In older children and teenagers the illness may create a sudden leaning toward reckless behavior. One child may start running around with a gang, another may begin driving carelessly. One of the most dangerous things that can happen in this instance is a plunge into the world of drugs. Since a relatively mild drug like marijuana doesn't provide an escape from the pain of depression—in fact, it often makes it worse—stronger and more dangerous drugs are usually used. Cocaine is so expensive that few parents have to worry about a child's having a secret cocaine habit. But it's a different story with heroin and pills. A depressed person, child or adult, may take heroin and feel better for a while. By the time the person is addicted to the drug, it has stopped its euphoric effects and no longer provides even the semblance of an escape from depression's pain. That's because heroin, barbiturates, and tranquilizers are all central nervous system depressants. Too much will stop the respiratory system and cause death. The amphetamines will continue to give artificial energy for some time longer, though the tolerance level drops and more of these dangerous pills have to be taken for the same effect. With the "speed" drugs, the user may stop eating and sleeping. Brain damage may result—*will* result if they are used heavily over an extended time—and eventual death is possible.

The problem is that many young depressives are looking for death. Reckless behavior which incorporates life-taking chances and/or overdoses of life-taking drugs can be indulged in without facing the actual desire—suicide. Few young people, even when depressed, will come right out and admit to themselves that they wish they were dead. That's why a suicide attempt by a teenager usually comes as a shock to everyone. Even if there are veiled hints, people don't tend to take them seriously because, after all, this is a child talking and children don't commit suicide, do they?

Some of the signs of depression can be masked if the child is a heavy television watcher. Sitting in front of the television set for hours may be a normal pattern. The depressed child, though, sits as if in a daze. He or she doesn't retain what passes by on the tube. If you see television watching increase, or notice that it becomes much more important to a child, then start asking questions. *What did you just see? How was it? What came on before this program? How did it end?*

Don't ask these questions as if you were head of the Inquisition. Get involved with the subject. Converse about the shows. You don't want to create a sense of wariness in the child, nor do you want to arouse suspicion about what you may be up to. So talk normally, but be alert to how much the child has retained of what has been watched on television. If you see that none of the programs made *any* impression (and don't expect a full review—children are often vague about something they're describing for you; we're talking here about a day of television watching when the child can't tell you about the programs watched or remembers only one or two program names, and when the story lines are *all* vague or unremembered), then it's time to suspect there may be a depressive episode occurring and to begin watching for other signs of withdrawal. Remember, though, that these symptoms may indicate some other disorder. They are common when there's any kind of upset, mental or physical. Never jump to judgment just because your child has spent a few days in a depressed mood. It's only when the alterations in behavior go on for several weeks that you should even begin to start observing seriously.

Just as the older child avoids confronting the thought of suicide but may begin acting in death-tempting ways, the younger (preschool) child acts out destructive impulses in an almost subconscious way. Dr. Edward Ritvo, of UCLA in Los Angeles, treats many depressed children. He says: "We've only recently come to recognize that children can suffer severe feelings of loss . . . of self-esteem and anger, which is what we mean when we say adults are depressed. Children won't say, 'I feel depressed, lost my appetite, I want to commit suicide.' But little children with those kinds of feelings might do something like kick the neighbor and get mommy to punish them. Or they might throw away something they value."

Dr. Ritvo says parents can spot symptoms of depression in very young children by being aware enough of their child's behavior so that they know when there's a behavior change. He cites unusual behavior such as a dry child suddenly starting to wet the bed, or the sudden onset of nightmares which indicate that something is wrong. There are other signs, such as a child who formerly got along well with others now fighting with friends. Watch for a slide in schoolwork. Dr. Ritvo says a prime sign is a child who formerly did well in school and got along well with others suddenly having behavior problems and not learning.

Depression in children, then, occurs at any age; but later in life there are predictable times when the illness is likely to strike. Certain ages in both men and women are vulnerable times for depression to come on. In women, the most common age for a first depressive episode is in the mid-to-late twenties, often around 25 or 27. This is a time of massive changes in the female body, almost as massive as in puberty and menopause. Externally, this time can be physically observed as the fading of that first "blush" of girlhood. Color begins to ebb from cheeks and lips, the skin begins to lose its moisture, tiny wrinkles start creasing smooth faces. Body weight begins to settle, and figures which were once lithe and supple now need diet and exercise to keep trim and in shape.

Inside, the hormonal composition is changing. It's at this age that women start climbing toward their sexual prime, which won't be reached for another few years. The metabolism starts slowing down. The normal food intake, which maintained a desired weight for years, now contains too many calories for the slower metabolism to use. Pounds start to accumulate.

There are a lot of mental changes going on at this time, too, many of them cultural. With the emphasis on youth and youthful appearance, many women begin feeling that they're over the hill now that they have passed 25. They notice the minute wrinkles (which can't be seen at a distance of more than two inches away) and realize, in many cases for the first time, that their youthful good looks won't last forever. This is probably the heaviest psychic blow a woman can face. Our culture relies so much on appearances that a woman is taught from childhood that her beauty is a measure of her worth. Even now, when a more enlightened age has permitted women to value themselves by their accomplishments as *people*, physical beauty (with its counterpoint of youthfulness) is still an ingrained cultural standard. The realization of aging signals to a woman the end of desirability, the lessening of femaleness. It doesn't matter that this isn't true. It doesn't matter that the mind adjusts to the loss of girlhood so that its passing is almost invisible. The mid-twenties is usually the first time a woman realizes that she is mortal, and that age will take away something which society places a high value upon. It can be an extremely traumatic emotional period. When the emotions are coupled with the metabolic changes happening inside the body, many women slide into depression.

With men, the first episode of depression often happens in the mid-to-late thirties. That period is, for men, the equivalent of women's mid-twenties change. Their metabolism starts to slow down. At this time of life many men develop "beer bellies" which remain with them the rest of their life unless they exercise. Hair begins to thin. A lot of men are surprised when they look in the mirror and see for the first time that their hairline isn't where it was. Most men notice a change in stamina. Where once they could play a game of golf, mow the lawn, and still have enough energy for a few laps around the pool; now muscles begin to ache during strenuous activity. Jowls begin to form on the face. Emotionally, men at this age have to face the fact that for the most part, they *are* now what they are going to be when they grow up. Most men up to this time still have dreams of rising to certain heights or becoming successful in another career. But in the mid-to-late thirties, men realize they are adults—and usually they are too tied down with responsibilities to start all over again and be something, or someone, else.

Again, as with women, the combination of emotional realizations, physical changes, and biochemical readjustments are often quite shattering. Any extreme emotional state, even joy, can trigger a depressive episode.

There's another factor connected with these particular ages in men and women. They are times of stress. In her mid-to-late twenties, a woman has had the bulk of her children. If she is at home, she is caring for young ones, is taking care of a house, and is involved in community activities such as church groups, PTA, social clubs, or volunteer work. All this requires a great outpouring of energy. And it is usually coupled with financial and security worries. A married woman who has decided not to have children is usually working and undergoing the stress of career building as well as working at a marriage. Single women are undergoing the stress of an active social life (or conversely, the lack of one with its accompanying loneliness), pouring out their energy on work, friends, and romantic interests.

Men in their mid-to-late thirties have the stress of playing the right games at work to get ahead, planning their moves in a jungle of competitors. If they are married, they have the worry of being responsible for wives and perhaps children. The pressures of material achievement are great at this time, since our culture still judges a man's success by what he owns. A man during this period often sees the future as a series of payments and needs which will grow with time, burdens which will never lessen. He sees his life stretching out as an extension of the present, and worries about what he is growing into. If he is unmarried, he usually has a varied social life requiring energy and money—a very stressful combination.

As I mentioned before, stress has an intimate connection with depression. Stress causes certain nutrients to be used by the body at a much faster rate. As a result, there's a higher need for these nutrients, and usually the need isn't met by diet alone. Furthermore, these same nutrients are needed by the central nervous system to manufacture the biogenic amines.

Those lucky enough to escape a case of depression during their vulnerable years face another dangerous time period—the fifties. This period has a physical, biochemical, and emotional similarity to the earlier depression-prone years just described. In both men and women the metabolism slows down once again. Women go through menopause, a time when the greatest hormonal change since puberty occurs. In fact, in many ways the changes of this time of life are the reverse of puberty. Menopause is often physically uncomfortable. The hormonal changes turn some women into screaming bundles of nerves, unable to control their emotions or perceive themselves accurately. In addition, women see the end of their childbearing years and the final end of their sexual attractiveness as females—a similar but more traumatic event than the realization of mortality that comes in the twenties.

Men see their sexual prowess wane. Again, this wouldn't be as traumatic for men if it weren't for the cultural emphasis on that prowess. In our society, a man's image of himself is attached in many symbolic ways to his testicles. His success with women, his ability to "do it" a required number of times for a required length of time, his ability to dominate other men, in fact, the whole *macho* performance attached to the word "man," represent a social standard of value similar to that of beauty in a woman. (When you analyze these two qualities, *machoism* and *beauty*, you can see that they are another cultural way of influencing gender distinctions. *Machoism* is based on what a man *does*. *Beauty* is something a woman *has*. One is active, aggressive. The other is passive and waits to be noticed.)

For both sexes, the fifties is a time of mental and physical stress. Depressions at this age are usually more serious because the stresses are usually greater than at other times. The illness most often becomes chronic rather than acute, that is, it doesn't incapacitate to a large degree but remains constant. This not only is a time of adjusting to the end of physical attractiveness (translated: the utter lack of youthfulness) but it is also a time of adjusting to the end of one's most productive years. In many cases, life seems to hold no future. Those in their fifties, especially those who feel they have not accomplished the things they planned back in their youth, can slip into a depression which will last a lifetime. And while there is no medical connection between middle-age depression and senility, it has been shown that those who are suffering from depression are more likely to become senile, and at a younger age, than those who are not depressed.

Depression in senior citizens causes a much more heartbreaking waste of life and energy. The symptoms of depression and senility resemble each other in many ways. Forgetfulness and loss of memory, loss of ability to concentrate, lack of interest in outside activities, lack of personal hygiene, crying spells, physical complaints where no physical cause can be found—an unfortunately large number of doctors accustomed to senility in aged patients may automatically jump to that diagnosis without checking for depression. In addition, many of the drugs taken by elderly people can produce a toxic depression. Some of the hormones can do this. Drugs used for high blood pressure often cause a secondary depression as a side effect. Older people often don't have the resilience to overcome a drug's side effects, and their metabolisms don't work as efficiently as those of younger people. If you are caring for depression in an older person, or if you see that a senior citizen has changed from a bright, alert being into a dull, lethargic one, check the medicines he or she is taking. Try especially to notice whether the symptoms began close to the time the medication was started. No drug is irreplaceable. Any medication can be changed for another which will do the same thing with different chemicals.

There's another thing: if a doctor has diagnosed senility in someone you know, and the condition seems to have come on fairly quickly—say, within a ten-month period—at least consult with an expert in the field of depression. If the final diagnosis *is* deterioration of the brain, you'll at least know that a human being has not been sentenced to a living death because of a word, when the actual condition is curable and once cured, would allow a return to a normal, functioning life.

Another thing to remember is that depression and senility are not either/or conditions. An older person who is becoming senile may have his or her abilities further impaired by a depressive syndrome. If you have a friend or relative in a rest home and notice a marked deterioration in the condition, don't automatically trust the rest home to spot and treat the illness properly. The special, individual care required where depression and senility are combined, or where depression is diagnosed as senility, unfortunately isn't available in most rest homes. This is not to say that the majority of rest homes neglect their patients. But the medical care available is to a large degree standardized, in the same way that the medical care available from the nurse in a large company is standardized. Certain illnesses are so common that they are treated without further thought. When you have two conditions with such similar symptoms, it's only natural that the more common one will be treated and the second one may be missed.

In a case like that, *you* have to get the extra medical attention which is so essential. But don't expect to take the person you're caring about to just any psychiatrist, plop the person down, and at the end of an hour get back an instant diagnosis.

First, you'll have to find a doctor who specializes in (or at least has experience with) depressions in the aged. The best place to find this kind of help is your local Suicide Prevention Center. Don't be turned off by the name. Suicide is the emergency for which they provide service, but that experience gives such agencies a very specific and detailed referral ability. They will usually know the right doctor to recommend. You'll get more effort from the people there if you go to see them in person, rather than trying to get a recommendation on the phone. People will try harder when they have to look you in the eye.

I cannot emphasize enough the importance of getting a doctor who knows about depression, and this caution will be repeated throughout this book. You see, the field of depression research was actually begun just before the 1960's. To give you an idea of how quickly information from those earlier years became obsolete, compare it to computer technology. The computers of the late fifties and early sixties are today considered so primitive that they are of very little use in today's technology. New discoveries gave birth to more new discoveries until the field grew so rapidly that one had to study all the time just to keep up with the current state of the art. In the late fifties and early sixties there were no such things as liquid crystals, digital machines, and light emiting diodes, at least not for commercial public use. The person who graduated from school with a knowledge in the field of computer technology, and who did not keep up with all the changes, would genuinely be at a loss today working in the field.

The same is true with the field of depression. Those early discoveries were such a breakthrough that the entire medical field was astounded. Some doctors to this day do not believe that depression is a disease. Others graduated long ago and have not kept up with the latest research. These doctors will not treat depression as it must be treated, as a special condition caused by a chemical mixup. And so they will not be able to cure the symptoms. Getting the proper doctor means finding one who is experienced in the treatment of depression, who knows what it is and how to treat it.

Here are some tips for getting a recommendation for a specialist. When you call the Suicide Prevention Center, ask for the chief psychiatrist. You will have better luck getting through to this person if you ask first who the chief psychiatrist *is*, then ask to speak to him or her. You'll need all the "get through" telephone tricks possible when dealing with either government or medical people. A "get through" trick is one which eliminates the need for you to explain yourself and what you want to someone who has nothing to do with your business but who is in a position to decide whether to put you through or not. Usually, people who answer phones are slightly intimidated when you ask for the head honcho by name, whether it's the doctor in charge or the president of a company, so always try to get a name first. You'll have a better chance of getting through to the ultimate barrier instead of having to deal with two or three little barriers.

As an example, when I was a newswriter for a radio station, we had an ongoing story about China. Something mysterious was happening there and no one had seen Chairman Mao for several weeks. I got tired of writing conjecture day after day, so I placed a person-to-person call to Premier Chou En Lai, figuring I had nothing to lose. I didn't get through, naturally. But I did talk to the foreign minister. It gave me a top news story which was picked up by the wire services and run all over the country. Why didn't I ask for Mao himself? Well, that was a little too obvious! So here's another get-through trick: go for the top in small organizations, go for the second-in-command at larger ones. Or if it's a very large organization, try the third highest. You'll never get through if you place a person-to-person call to the President of the United States. You won't even have much luck trying to get the Vice-President. But you stand a better chance with the Speaker of the House.

These are all little tricks one learns in journalism, and journalism is after all the accomplishment of getting the person who has the story to talk to you. The same techniques are useful if you are dealing with the medical profession. Hospitals and clinics can be infuriatingly frustrating when it comes to giving out information. So if you need to find something out, go to the top echelons. The ones in power don't play the secretive game with outsiders as much as the underlings do. Throughout this book you will find more journalist-based hints on getting information from the person who has it.

Getting the Depressive to Accept Help

If you look at every act of kindness, you'll see that very little in this world is totally altruistic. People who do something for others always gain from it, even if it's just the good feelings of doing the good deed or the ego boost of being *needed* to help someone else. So while it may *seem* like just a good deed for you to care enough about a depressive to make sure that professional help is obtained, you have a vested interest in seeing that the help is there and the condition is being treated. If you live with or spend a lot of time wth a depressed person, especially if both of you are older and the depression has come in the second half of your lives, *you* are extremely vulnerable to the illness. I can't repeat this enough. You *must* get medical attention for a depressive. Believe me, there will be resistance to your efforts. You may have to use a bit of trickery or threats to get the person to a doctor. Do it. Get the necessary help.

The only method of getting that help which will do more harm than good is the use of force. To illustrate, a Texas man, concerned about his depressed wife, did everything he could think of to get her to see a doctor. He even had a psychiatrist make a house call, inviting him to dinner as a guest. The wife soon guessed who the "guest" really was, left the table, and locked herself in the bathroom. The psychiatrist went home without doing any good.

Finally, the man could no longer bear it. He made an appointment with a specialist and dragged his wife out of the house by her arm. She was screaming and punching him, but he managed to get her into the car. She was naturally frightened and hysterical, as anyone would be under similar circumstances. But her husband, who believed that depression (or whatever the condition his wife had was called) was actually a mental illness, thought her terror and resistance were due to insanity. He kept hold of her wrist during the drive to the doctor's office so she couldn't open the door and jump out. But the woman, her anxiety and hysteria having reached the point of unreason, reached over and jerked the wheel of the car into the oncoming lane of traffic. Her husband was killed and the driver of the other car seriously injured. The shock was too much for her. The woman's mind, upset already by the depressive syndrome, just couldn't handle this latest blow. What would have been a treatable, relatively brief illness—depression—became an almost catatonic breakdown of all responses, so that the woman required a long period of hospitalization.

Remember that the depressive is already suspicious, convinced of his or her own inferiority and sure that no one really wants him or her around. The illness is accompanied by a complete loss of self-esteem. Our good feelings about ourselves can be measured in the exact degree to which we possess a high opinion of our worth. Without self-esteem, the pain of living makes life a burden. In fact, it would be accurate to call depression the illness of lost self-esteem.

Suicide

Never underestimate the depressive's desire to end the pain in the only way he or she sees possible—death. If you suspect someone you know of having a case of depression, *assume, expect* that there will be overt or disguised suicide attempts. These are not merely calls for attention. The depressive suicide is usually successful; these people aren't fooling around. They want *out*. With disguised attempts, others may not perceive the actual death intention if they are not observing the events carefully.

Disguised attempts can be a sudden series of car accidents, cuts and burns, or nonsurvival behavior such as walking across busy streets without watching for traffic. While it's easy to dismiss a large number of cuts, falls, and other household injuries as just a case of the clumsies, remember that depressed people don't like themselves. An unconscious death wish may manifest itself as strikes against the flesh—stumbles that cause a fall down the stairs, carelessness with a pot of boiling water, lack of attention while using a sharp knife.

In cases of masked depression, clumsiness can become almost a joke. While the illness itself causes a lack of physical coordination, the unconscious mind is also trying very hard to get through. And its message is self-hatred and self-destruction. In a negative way, you could almost call this a healthy sign. You could say that this is the unconscious mind's way of trying to signal a message about the suppressed pain going on underneath.

There are times when an overabundance of small injuries is a warning signal that something destructive toward the self is brewing in emotional areas which haven't yet surfaced. Often these signals come at a time when there is an obvious underlying cause such as a divorce or loss of a job. I recently did a thorough study of the aftereffects of divorce and found two interesting facts. Women were likely to suffer kitchen injuries a lot more often than they ever had before. A slicing knife would slip and cut a knuckle. Bumps on the head would come from collisions with cupboards. Potholders would slip, causing spills and blistered hands and wrists. Men became clumsy with tools. One man, even though *he* was the one who wanted the divorce, told me he spent three months with his thumb continuously bandaged from one injury after another. If he used a hammer, he would hit his thumb. If he moved a piece of furniture, he would manage to smash that thumb. It got so bad that he kept a constant lookout, trying to be extra careful. He told me, "I knew it was more than carelessness the day I was using a drill while squatting down, holding my hand behind me so I would keep my thumb out of harm's way. I overbalanced, jerked my feet back—and came down on my thumb as hard as I could with my heel." Many men told me that after a job loss or divorce, they were suddenly unable to shave with a straight razor without cutting themselves.

Any kind of personal loss can bring on an increase in "accidental"injuries. It's when those accidents continue or become more and more life-threatening that they start being something to worry about. If a case of the clumsies begins with no obvious cause, then it's time to begin looking for a reason. The unconscious mind has many ways of making itself known.

There is one symptom of depression that can be spotted long before the illness starts to progress. In fact, you can use it as an early warning sign. It's a reoccuring mood of irritability. The depressive doesn't notice it. There is no awareness of how irritable he or she has become, though many depressives are aware of feeling more tense than usual long before the disease hits. The irritation may be all out of proportion to the supposed cause of it, so out of proportion that the depressive may frighten those who bear the brunt of that irritation. There may be episodes like a shouting, screaming blowup because the depressive was asked a question while watching a television show. Parents may begin snapping at children for merely walking across a room. Remember, at this time the illness is taking away the stamina to deal with the minor irritations of everyday life, annoyances we are so accustomed to coping with that we hardly notice them. For example, a child who has been out playing will get dirty and a parent will of course notice this when the child comes in to get a glass of milk. But every parent soon learns that there's no sense in insisting that a face or pair of grubby hands be washed at that very moment. The child will return to play, pile up more dirt, and have it all removed at once when playtime is over. Parents learn to accept traces of grime on offspring who have been playing outdoors. A parent who is coming down with a case of depression, though, will yell at the child for being dirty, perhaps order him in to take a bath that instant or insist that the child change clothing. The irritation is usually unreasonable, but there is no way to make the depressive aware of this. That's because depression contains within it a large amount of anger. The anger is most often directed against the *self*, but when it's expressed, it comes out as irritation towards others. (This is true with most people, whether depression is present or not. You have probably met a number of people who are gruff and unpleasant and always act as if they are irritated by everyone and everything. Internally, this person usually suffers from a great *self* anger. But who of us can admit to being angry at ourselves? Stop and think—when you are being your most negative about others, don't you usually feel *your* least confident, or like yourself less than you normally do?)

While suicide in depression is an act of self-loathing as well as an escape, it is usually not done in the irritable/angry stage. One reason may be because the depressive, having made the decision consciously or not, knows that peace is just around the corner. The solution is available. It only needs the pills or gun or razor or fall or other method to bring the completion.

There are certain signs to look for which will indicate that suicide is something the depressive has been dwelling upon. The act rarely comes as a sudden impulse. It *may*, though. With depression as with any other illness, the circumstances depend on the individual. Don't feel secure just because none of the signs of suicidal intent are present. You should approach your watchfulness as the doctor in a hospital approaches post-operative care: an infection may not occur but it *can* happen, and it's something to guard against and keep an eye open for.

Most depressives will give verbal hints of suicidal intent. These are subtle and may be missed if you don't watch for them. Such statements as, *Well you'll be better off when I'm gone*, or *All your problems will be over soon*, are giveaways. If the depressive spends hours writing or typing, acting furtive and secretive about what is being written, look for crumpled sheets in the wastebasket. They may be suicide notes. In cases of masked depression, watch for a sudden desire to get affairs in order or a discussion of how the spouse will carry on should the depressive die. Also look for a desire to "close out," to sell the investments and get the cash or to close a savings account. Look for an increased interest in death during conversations, a wondering if this or that form of death is less painful or quicker. And when the depressive starts making plans, even in a nonserious way, about what should be done with his or her body after death and how the house, children, or personal effects should be cared for, take that as a hint of suicidal intent.

If the person makes an attempt to obtain a life-threatening item, such as sleeping pills or a gun, don't beat around the bush or wonder what you should do. If there's any suspicion, don't hesitate. Come right out and ask, "Are you thinking of killing yourself?" Contrary to the myth, people who talk about it *will* do it. And also, people who are *thinking* of doing it *will* talk about it. By asking if the person has been considering suicide, you create an opening so that it can be discussed. Most depressives want to discuss it. It isn't that they want to die, just that they want the pain to stop. Listen with gravity and sympathy to what they say. Don't ridicule those feelings. To you, in a nondepressed state, the idea of suicide may be ludicrous. To the person suffering from intense emotional pain, it seems like the only solution. Don't say, either verbally or with implication, "Oh, that's nonsense, you have everything to live for." The depressive doesn't see *anything* worth living for. Also, don't humor the person. Depressives may have impaired perception of themselves and the world around them, but they will immediately spot insincerity when it comes to something as important as the taking of their lives. However, just discussing the problem won't resolve it, though it will do a great deal to help. Bring it out into the open, by all means—then take action.

What to Do When You Don't Know What to Do

In discussing suicide with a depressive, don't hedge around the subject. If the person tells you he or she has been thinking of killing him/herself, ask how the act has been planned. Was it going to be done while everyone was away, or late at night when people were sleeping? How? With what? Have the pills or gun already been obtained? Does the depressive have an idea of *when* the suicide was going to take place? Ask your questions calmly and sympathetically. Don't get angry, and above all, don't assure the depressive about things which do not seem to be true to him or her: that her looks really haven't disappeared or that people really do care about him. Your logic will be of no use against the perceptions of depression. Just listen at first.

Now, you may feel that if the depressive gets therapeutic help, the problem is taken care of. Not true. Some 60 percent of all depressive suicides saw their doctors within two weeks of their death. So, once you have an admission that suicide is a probability, start with the obvious. Throw out every item that could be used, such as pills or a gun. (You can give them to someone else to keep temporarily.) Don't just hide it, get it out of the house. Don't lock these things up in a place where you believe the depressive will never get to it. It's not a chance you can afford to take.

Pills and guns are the most common tools of suicide. The car is also one. Dr. Norman Tabachnic of Los Angeles has done considerable research on the number of fatal accidents which are actually suicide attempts. His figures are surprising. A good number of drivers found to be at fault in fatal accidents had been depressed and upset for long periods of time prior to their accidents. In this kind of suicide, the impulse to swing the wheel into an abutment or oncoming traffic may be an impulse, or often the person drinks until he or she is drunk, then drives knowing that the alcohol has taken away the ability to drive safely.

There are only two things you can do when you feel the depressive will take his or her life if allowed to do so: don't let the person be alone, or else hospitalize the person. When I say don't let the person be alone, that means every minute of the day must be observed. The only place the depressive should be totally alone is the bathroom, and you should make sure it doesn't contain any dangerous pills or razor blades. If you have to go somewhere, hire someone to stay with the person. Since it is impossible for most people either to spend every minute with a depressive or always to have someone there, hospitalization may be the best solution. A patient will be guarded in a hospital. And if the desire to commit suicide is intense, this is one of the few times when electroconvulsive therapy (electric shock) may be a good idea. It will provide immediate temporary relief from the depression and give a breathing period in which the thoughts of suicide are lessened or disappear entirely. No matter how rational the depressive is in trying to get you to let him or her alone for a while, no matter how much there is an insistence that no hospitalization is required, you must take action when suicide is a possibility. Even if the person denies that there are suicidal thoughts, keep an eye open. The verbal hints and changes in behavior will give you enough of an indication so that you can use your own judgment. Especially watch for a sudden change in behavior—there's a certain self-assuredness that comes over the person who feels an end to the pain is at hand. It's a quiet aloofness, a poignancy which implies, "Soon I will be leaving all this."

The Contagion Factor

I've mentioned several times that depression can be catching. You may have wondered how a malfunction in another person's chemical system can spread to your own. Well, there are several explanations, and the most obvious borders on the mystical. (I use this word interchangeably with the word *magic* because both have the same basis, in my opinion. There is no "magic," there are only occurrences for which our current state of knowledge provides no explanation. At the moment, people who spontaneously recover from cancer may be said to have "magically" recovered. Yet, there is an actual cause for the recovery. We just don't know what it is right now. The magician who pulls rabbits out of hats may seem to be performing magic; yet that magician knows the trick of doing it, and it seems like magic to us because we don't. No matter how fantastic any occurrence might be, it does have a cause. So it is with occurrences which are "mystical"—a word that has the same root as *mysterious*. Parapsychological experiences such as clairvoyance or telepathy were once the sole domain of self-proclaimed "mystics." "Normal" people experiencing these events soon learned to keep their mouths shut or convinced themselves that they perceived them wrongly. Now, the reality of parapsychology is acknowledged by even the most reputable scientists. They know that there are some things which exist in the real world and for which we have no explanation. "Mystical" things are only those for which the laws of physics have no rules and which have not yet been accepted as commonplace by the public.)

So the depressive has an almost mystical ability to influence the moods of others. You've probably experienced this phenomenon yourself. Have you ever felt perfectly fine, and then run into a friend who was down in the dumps? What happens? You come away feeling drained and a little blue. Your energy level is lower. The most mystical part of this influencing ability is that a depressive has more power to influence than a joyful person. Think about it. Joy is certainly contagious, but how much effect will one happy person have on a room full of people? Nowhere near as much as one depressed person.

At the moment, there are no concrete facts to explain this phenomenon. But whether we are aware of it or not, we automatically grant more power to negative factors than positive ones. As one famous comedienne said about violence on television: "They say that showing violent programs will cause violence in the streets. How come they never worry about comedy programs making comedy in the streets?" We feel on some deep level that bad things have more power to affect us than uplifting things. There have been no real scientific studies to point out a reason or even a definite statement about this, but a number of medical laboratories, including California's UCLA, are working on theories about the influence of depression on others. One theory is the "energy field" idea.

In the past few years, many mystical beliefs have merged with reality in the laboratory. The belief in *auras*, for example, is now taken quite seriously by some scientists, who have discovered an electrical field which surrounds each living thing. In mystical or occult thinking, the aura is a type of energy field which not only surrounds living things but predicts the state of health. According to occult thinking, every human has an aura. The distance it extends from the body, and its color, tell the person's state of health. The aura is also supposed to show the individual's spiritual qualities and present state of mind. Many people claim to be able to see these auras. (Unfortunately, though, none has graduated from medical school. If the art of aura diagnosis worked, it certainly would have revolutionized medicine by now. Alas, the reading of auras has shown little of the promise its practitioners claim for it.) Psychics who make a practice of reading auras tell about seeing people who have no aura at all and who die shortly afterwards. Kirlian photography, which makes strange blurs and lines of light around a photographed object, is thought to be taking pictures of the electrical field, or aura.

Psychics and mystics do not claim that one person's aura can affect other people. But the "energy field" theory of depression is based on the belief that a depressive emits a certain electrical "charge" which is powerful enough to influence the electrical fields of others.

Electricity is actually a mystical subject. Its workings are strange, and even though we know what its effects are, we don't know very much about why it works that way. Electricity is an invisible force which can animate physical matter. It passes along a physical carrier and it can cause chaos if there is a break in the line of transmission. It can cause a thick rope made of metal to jump around and writhe like a snake, but a heavy charge of electricity will make a living organism unable to move.

The machine which measures brain activity is actually measuring the electricity that occurs in the functioning mind.

When this machine reports that clinical death has occurred, it is actually saying that there is no electrical activity in the brain. The cessation of electricity in the body is the ultimate sign of death.

We know that electrical forces can *combine* for greater force; they can also interact to change the various charges that come in contact with each other, and they react with destructive force when a conflicting combination occurs. Two people who dislike each other for no discernible reason may dismiss their mutual dislike as "chemistry." It might be more accurate to call it electricity. The term "electricity" is used to describe a positive attraction between two people. Thus it doesn't seem illogical that the electrical field thrown off by the depressive has enough power to depress those within close range for long periods of time. What does seem strange is that this negative electrical force has more power than a positive one. And there is a relationship between the power of the depressive force and the negative power it has over mass emotions. We're all familiar with the group insanity which can cause a riot or lynch mob. Many of us have felt those same feelings of contagious rage during a bad call in a competitive sport, or in a shared public surge of hate toward an enemy power in time of war. Strangely enough, there has never been an occasion when a mob was incited to run amok doing good. There have been countless times when people have massed together to destroy whatever is in their path. Has there ever been even one time when people massed together in mindless emotion to clean up or beautify everything in their path?

The scientific explanation may lie in the word *mindless*. It may be that the unrestrained human mind is a naturally brutish thing, that it is only the control by the reasoning part of the brain which keeps the brute at bay. If so, then the mind which is not controlling the vulnerability to another's depressive charge is open and receptive to it. If the energy field theory of depression proves correct, then it also proves that it is essential to have a defense against depression *before* one is exposed to it.

Another explanation for the contagious factor in depression is stress. Although the person associating with a depressive may have built up a resistance to the stresses in his or her own life, the stress of dealing with a depressive is usually too much to bear. Take the irritability symptom, for example. Being on the receiving end of another person's constant irritability can wear anyone down. Couple this with the increasing vegetation of a spouse or close friend and you have something frightening and bewildering. If you are in this position, you spend a lot of energy wondering and worrying. Why is your normally responsive lover ignoring all your advances, ignoring *you*, in fact? Why is your uncle who has always kept his home and body clean suddenly refusing to bathe and why doesn't he seem to mind living in a pigpen? What is causing your best friend to cry all the time? You may spend even more energy trying every method you can think of to help the depressive snap out of it, see a doctor, begin a return to normal life and activity. Energy is like money in the bank: you may have a fairly high reserve, but it's not limitless; once you spend all you've got, there has to be some sort of collapse.

Perhaps the best way to describe the depressive's effect on others is to compare it to a vacuum which sucks in energy wherever it comes in contact with it. The more time you spend in the range of this vacuum, the more of your energy is drained. The process is slow but constant. While it's possible to construct a barrier to the energy-sucking vacuum, it requires enormous effort. To even begin the construction, there must first be an awareness that the need for it exists. This is why, in addition to knowing what to look for in a suspected case of depression, it's also important to be in touch with your own feelings before, during, and after your contact with another person. Most of the time, this doesn't take any effort. We are automatically attracted to people who make us feel good, and we automatically avoid people who make us feel bad. But the situation becomes much more difficult if the person who makes us feel down is someone we can't avoid—a spouse, parent, child, or other relative. In these cases we might not even be aware that our feelings are affected because of the other person's effect on us.

A typical example is the case of Roxanne Marsden and her husband Bill. I had been asked to talk to Roxanne by one of her friends who was disturbed at the sudden change in her personality. Over a period of weeks, Roxanne had become withdrawn, moody, and too tired even to converse with others.

Roxanne's husband Bill was ill with depression and had been for about six months. Roxanne didn't know this. She had met Bill five years earlier and married him shortly after their first meeting. Roxanne told me that Bill had always been a negative person. He enjoyed talking about people's shortcomings rather than their good qualities. He liked making moral judgments about the future of this or that person, or about what he felt *should* be their future because of their faults. While he grudgingly gave approval when forced to, his perceptions picked out the negative long before he ever saw the positive in any situation.

Although I knew little of Bill's past history, from Roxanne's description it sounded as though Bill had suffered from a chronic case of masked depression which existed even before she married him. But Roxanne adjusted to the external signs, the negativity and pessimism; she accepted those qualities as part of the man she loved, and she handled them without feeling much stress. When Bill's masked depression escalated into a severe endogenous form, she scarcely realized the difference. He was just as negative, just as pessimistic, but now there was a hopelessness in his attitude. His lack of energy, both psychic and physical, was like a weight dragging Roxanne down. She resisted as long as possible, but eventually her resistance was all used up. At work she began feeling irritated at the extra details added to her work routine when another secretary quit. She was fatigued all the time, even though she was getting a lot of rest and leading a fairly sedentary life. She complained of a "sinking" feeling in the pit of her stomach. It took her appetite away and she began losing weight. The sinking feeling was actually a mild anxiety attack. Roxanne wasn't aware that it seemed to happen only when she was around Bill or thinking of him.

I gave Roxanne a copy of Dr. Nathan Kline's book, *From Sad to Glad*. Kline is the doctor who discovered the first antidepressive drug, and whose often unorthodox theories on depression have proven right time and time again; in fact, his theories have often proven to be the next advances in the medical profession where depression is concerned.

After reading the book, she was aware of Bill's actual condition. Using threats and persuasion, she got Bill to a doctor. After months of therapy and chemical treatments, Bill was stabilized and his symptoms began easing. He was still negative, still seeing the bad rather than the good—but to a far less degree than before. Luckily, Roxanne had taken action before the illness immobilized *her*. Now she had to work on the minor depression she herself was undergoing.

She began protecting herself by a very simple technique: every time Bill would make a negative comment, she would rebut it with a positive one, meanwhile programming herself to feel confident in the truth of her own positive observation. For example, when Bill said: "The Moran boy drives like a maniac. He probably has some girl in the front seat and isn't paying attention. Seems like every kid is like that today." Roxanne would counter with: "Actually, he isn't driving carelessly at all, it's just so quiet outside that his car noise seems louder. And just because he has a girl with him doesn't mean he's paying less attention to his driving. I think you just notice the kids who drive recklessly more than you do the ones who drive safely, because they're so much more noticeable." When Bill made a certain negative remark he often made: "What smells in here?" coupling it with a look of distaste, Roxanne would say gaily: "Sunshine and work . . . I've been cleaning the closet" (or "straightening the bedroom" or something similar). Her rebuttals weren't antagonistic or made to invite a reply. She wasn't doing this to convince Bill so much as she was trying to convince *herself* as a defense against Bill's depressing remarks. It was a hard effort, but it helped Roxanne keep things in perspective. It provided a barrier to her automatic reception of Bill's negativity.

Today, Bill is over his depression and learning to adjust his emotional habits accordingly, though some pessimism will remain with him all his life since it's a part of his personality. And Roxanne can handle that with ease. She has also learned to stay alert for symptoms of a reoccurrence of the old patterns by keeping in touch with her feelings when she is around Bill. That is a hard job, because we get into habit patterns with people we live with and find it almost impossible to keep our awareness of each moment unique to that moment. But Bill and Roxanne's marriage has survived, and so has their love for each other.

That's not the case with most marriages or live-in relationships. Depression does a most thorough job of dividing people. At the moment I am writing this, the marriage of one of my close friends is being torn apart because of the depression of my friend's mother. She wants her mother to spend more time visiting at her house and she herself is spending a lot more time with her mother. The mother is in her sixties and has just passed through menopause. The grandchildren have begun actively to

dislike grandma, because when she's around the television is always too loud, the kids are always too rambunctious, and there
are always a dozen other things she finds to complain about. The
husband, who genuinely likes his mother-in-law, says he can't
stand to see her sitting like a "lump" and he wants his wife to
allow the woman to be hospitalized.

While families may divide and fight for a period of time on
the subject of treatment, the family will usually survive as a unit.
However, one-on-one relationships rarely stand up under the
stress of depression. The victim is in so much pain that it's almost
impossible for others to empathize unless they too have been
there. The depressive becomes wrapped up in his or her own
problems, ending communication. Since communication is the
basis of any relationship, attachments begin to waver under the
effects of bewilderments and misunderstandings. It's hard to live
with someone who becomes little more than a "lump" and
doesn't respond to any efforts on your part to help or change the
situation. You will take it personally, no matter how loving and
concerned you might be. Perhaps the most frightening aspect is
watching someone close to you change so radically. If you are not
aware of what depression is, you find it hard to believe that
another person has no control over what is happening. As time
goes on, you can't help becoming irritated and even disgusted
with the situation. Irritation, fear and distaste, lack of
communication—if these things don't combine to kill love, they
certainly can force one to hold it in abeyance.

The Loss Factor

Throughout these pages I have dwelt on the biochemical
causes of depression almost to the exclusion of underlying emotional causes. But there usually *are* emotional reasons which can
point to a psychological connection between the person's past
and the current condition. The mechanics of depression—the
central nervous system malfunction—have been documented to a
science. But what causes that malfunction in the first place? While
doctors know there is a connection to stress, there is no scientific
answer which explains why a functioning central nervous system
goes haywire. What trips the physiological level which controls
the chemical output of the body's production system?

There does seem to be one factor common to all people who

suffer from endogenous depression. Somewhere along the build-up of experiences which connect the days of a life, an extreme sense of loss has developed. Nearly all depressives feel this loss most of their lives, long before the disease strikes them. It could be something which stems from childhood, perhaps the loss of a parent or perhaps something less obvious—the loss of protection which accompanies the start of independence. When we are infants, our every need is cared for. We aren't even aware that food doesn't automatically appear, that it must be bought and money must be found to pay for it, that it must be prepared and served. We are loved automatically, or if not loved, kept warm and fed. To an infant, love is being kept warm and fed as much as it is being held and crooned to. The complications grow as we do. We must make certain efforts in order to receive positive attention: we must control our bowels, concentrate on eating in ways which get food to our mouths with a minimum of spillage, remember to touch only those things which we are permitted to touch. As time goes on, more complex efforts are demanded. We must learn to share even those things which belong to *us*. We must control our vocal outbursts in content and volume. We must learn to fasten the proper combination of fabrics on our bodies. We begin learning life's hardest lesson; that people will not look inside to see who we *are*, but will make that judgment of our worth as a person by the *style* with which we manifest that personhood. Our thoughts may be beautiful, but how do we hold our fork? The appreciation that once came naturally, merely because of our existence, now has to be earned.

This is an enormous loss, one which is vastly underrated in explanations of psychic traumas. The part of growing up which happens to everyone—the realization that you are not the center of the universe but only one *with* and equal *to* countless other people—is a psychic blow. We all go through it, we all adjust to it. Yet I believe some people never get over their bewilderment that the all-enveloping care they received as infants is no longer there and will never come again. I think some people go on for years, far into adulthood, with a subconscious faith that this kind of care and appreciation will someday return. The belief has no connection with the rational mind. In fact, the rational mind would deny it and isn't even aware of the subconscious wish. But at some point, the person realizes that there will be *no* return to that loved and protected state. Whatever Mommy and Daddy left out of the childhood loving is forever missed, gone, and no one will ever make up for whatever lack there was. At this point, even though someone has managed a very successful career, a family and friends and enviable life style, depression descends like a curtain of hopelessness. In a way, depression imitates many of the states natural to infancy or forced on us by the powerlessness of youth. Infants have a short attention span. They can't concentrate. They do not dress or bathe themselves. They do not make decisions. The loss that comes with growing up is submerged under the excitement of growing up. Decades later, it may resurface as a depressive episode, which actually makes it a *reactive* depression.

Very little research has been done in this area of loss of nurturing. But it may explain another phenomenon which receives little medical attention: postpartum depression in men. Many women, home from the hospital with new babies, are too involved in caring for their infant to notice a fairly common change which their husbands go through, to a major or minor degree. It usually lasts only a week or two and can best be described as an air of disorientation. Some men may react by making subliminal demands for attention from the wife. They may get headaches or other minor physical ills. They may evidence disguised jealousy. In one instance, a woman complained to her doctor that every time she brought the baby to bed for a nighttime breastfeeding, her husband would reach out for one of her hands and place it on his genitals. The doctor told her that this was a common occurrence, that men at this time need reassurance. Part of the reason for that need is that a new being has come along to share the wife's love. But another factor may be that in that surreal part of the mind which never sees the light of day, men believe that in the wife lies the return to that all-enveloping motherhood which was lost as an infant. The wife who allows marriage to turn her into a submissive, passive "little girl" is creating the reverse of that situation—where her husband must simulate at least an imitation of the all-enveloping, all-responsible, parental love. The sub-conscious desire for this does not depend on gender.

Those of us who did not receive the care and attention of loving parents have a different sense of loss. It's not true that we don't miss what we've never had. Our loss is undefined, because we have never felt what it is to have the thing we feel deprived of.

In families that are very restrained and don't make a practice of showing emotion physically or verbally—and also in families where a parent or parents are so busy with adult pursuits that school, television, and friends must substitute for *them*—or in families where parents fit a child into their lives by "making room" instead of creating a space—the child may never even realize that he or she feels deprivation until the feeling emerges many years later in other ways.

About six months before my own depressive episode, I had an experience which to this day still fills me with heated embarrassment. I had gone to the Los Angeles County Fair with a close male friend. We walked around the exhibits, both of us in a good mood, both of us having a good time. Then we came to the exhibit called Storybook Farm, which is a permanent part of the fair. It has live animals which can be petted, a barn with a display of antique farm equipment, a working pump which fills a trough where ponies drink, a real garden with vegetables and herbs neatly labeled so visitors can see what these growing plants look like. It has a mock-up of an old-fashioned farmhouse with the outside wall cut away. Fair-goers walk along a boardwalk where the wall should be, looking at the rooms furnished with artifacts of the nineteenth century, complete with cutaway attic showing stored trunks and rockers. And in this house, for the duration of the fair, a live "family" stays the day and lives as a family of that period would have lived. They cook their meals on the old wood burning stove, get their water from the garden pump, chop wood, and try to pretend that thousands of sightseers aren't standing a few feet away watching their every move.

This was the first time that I had been to the fair. As I crowded along the boardwalk with everyone else, the "family" was at dinner. Mother, father, and three children sat at the table laughing and talking while they ate. Beside the table a dog lay peacefully curled in a half circle. Even though the life style they were approximating was an act, the happiness and unity they radiated was real.

I felt an uncontrollable urge to make some sort of contact. It started in a joking manner—I think I yelled out something to the effect of wondering when those of us watching would all be invited to dinner. The "family" ignored my comment, just as they ignored the thousands of comments they heard every day. I kept on, saying that it was unfair to create such good smells and not share the food. At first I felt as if I were just making fun, joking in a way that would get me a smile or cause them to try to hide a giggle. But then it got more serious. I yelled out, "Hey, how do you go to the bathroom?" My friend stared at me in amazement. He knew one of my personal terrors was being involved in a public scene or making a spectacle of myself. But by now, I was shouting. And I was shouting obscenities. My friend began to put his arm around me and urge me along the boardwalk and away from the exhibit, but my body was rigid and I shook his arm off. People began edging away. I remember some teenage boys yelling and laughing, "Yeah, go on, tell 'em." I couldn't stop what I was doing, even though I didn't *know* what I was doing. I had no control over my mouth as it yelled in anger. At one point, the woman who was the "mother" looked up and caught my eye. Her expression was one of such distaste that it cut me like a knife. I burst into tears, still shouting, with tears running down my face.

The incident lasted only a few minutes and I don't remember moving away, but I remember that afterwards I sobbed for an hour, totally bewildered and wondering what had happened. I was too young at the time to realize what an important clue to the inner workings of my subconscious had just surfaced. All I knew was that for the first time in my life, I had done something horrifyingly embarrassing with no apparent *control* over what I was doing and without being motivated by any apparent incident. What I did was deliberate, but I had no idea why I did it. In fact, by the next day I had blocked the incident entirely from my mind. It came back again later as I was undergoing therapy for the serious depression which occurred less than a year later.

Even in the depths of my depression, I somehow sensed that in that county fair incident lay the key to some important answers. I tried to bring back my emotions of that time. All I could remember was an overwhelming compulsion, an obsession with—what? Finally, I was able to do some thinking along a new angle—not thinking about *how* my parents raised me, as I had always done when thinking of them, but thinking about how I *felt* about how they raised me. I was then able to contact, and make peace with, a sense of deprivation that had been suppressed all my life. One of the important lessons I learned during my depression was that one may "overcome" certain feelings by pushing them far back in the mind and acting as if one were not affected by them. But the feelings are still there. They will fight for expression. They will come out eventually, either in a transference of emotion to another behavioral pattern or, when triggered by some innocuous event, in an expression of surprising neurotic behavior. There is some evidence that people who occasionally get drunk and act outrageously though they aren't alcoholics are actually using the alcohol to release control of suppressed emotional conflicts.

During a case of depression, the fundamental structure of the mind is shaken and disrupted. Even though the cause is chemical, the triggering mechanism can well be something with emotional roots. Because of the biochemical base of the illness, psychiatric therapy alone doesn't cure depression. But because there is also an emotional trigger, whether it be loss, stress, internal conflict, or whatever, chemical therapy alone is often insufficient. When any basic structure is disrupted, a patch job rarely mends the disruption. The mind of the depressive is in a unique state to be rebuilt with care and deliberation. This doesn't mean it is to be rearranged in the sense of changing the basic personality. A human being is not a *tabula rosa*, a blank slate to be wiped clean and written on anew. But think for a moment how the mind grows. Chunks of information are received willy-nilly, to be sorted and filed as experience and perception. Our view of the world is made up of what life has taught us, whether that teaching is based on fact or not. A miser fears being generous. Why? Because somewhere the lesson has been learned that generosity is anti-survival. A promiscuous person needs the contact of sex. Why? Because the sexual act is perceived as being necessary to survival. It doesn't matter what twisted base there is for these perceptions. The reasoning process has decreed these acts, or whatever neurotic behaviors exist, as essential to the well-being of the person who exhibits them. No one deliberately sets out to act in ways which are considered neurotic. The mind perceives its actions as *right*, or at least justified.

We are the total sum of our experiences, colored by the way we perceive those experiences. A spider that frightens us at the age of four years would not have the same effect when we are twenty. Yet the fear ingrained from the age of four will usually affect our perception of spiders for the rest of our lives. It takes a hard, deliberate effort to shake that perception and replace it with something based on knowledge, not the conditioning of the past. The mind grows like Topsy, without being systematically programmed in a logical fashion as a computer is. In depression, when the basic structure of mental "Topsy" growth is shaken and weak, it must be rebuilt. Many depressives find it easier during and after recovery to rebuild with a better sense of order, throwing out old misperceptions and replacing them with thoughts, reactions and opinions which come out of the growth of later experiences. In fact, this is one of the strengths of depression, and one reason why the fully recovered depressive is often stronger, more stable, and better adjusted than those who have never had the illness. The massive effort of recovery leaves the depressive living in the present, without being programmed by the past.

3.

How to Recognize Depression

Help . . . When Do You Need It?

It's lovely when one can be simplistic. Life is so complicated that there are very few basic axioms which sum up every essential about any one subject. So it's very nice to be able to answer the above question about help in one single sentence: *The depressive needs help (and so do those who are also being affected) whenever the illness interferes with the ability to work, love, and enjoy life.*

Period. No degrees. It doesn't matter if depression takes away just a slight bit of energy and the person still functions well. That's as much of an interference as if the case were more serious. The difference between a mild, chronic condition and a severe incapacitating depression is only degree, not difference. There is still interference with the freedom to extend one's abilities to the fullest possible range.

A mild case can continue a lifetime without anyone, including the depressive, suspecting that something is wrong. Dr.

Nathan Kline, the New York psychiatrist who first discovered anti-depressives, says of those who suffer from chronic mild depressions:

"These are individuals who from a clinical point of view are clinically depressed but they don't realize this is what's happened to them. They're also underachievers, they're people with a lot of potential who never quite make the grade, and they will avoid that little extra push which is the difference between achievement and non-achievement."

These low-grade depressions are among the hardest to spot, mostly because those affected never suspect its presence. But what about the serious depressions? How does it happen that someone can sink into a state resembling emotional catatonia before anyone realizes that something is radically wrong and that outside help is necessary?

The change produces alarm without action, as most relatively gradual changes do. Most people who experience the onset of depression in someone they live with or associate with will be aware that something is wrong and try to solve the problem verbally. By the time it dawns on them that professional help is required, the condition has become serious. Even doctors who specialize in treating depression, who know the signs and understand the need for early care, will let the condition get out of hand when they have a prior knowledge of the patient. Why?

The answer can best be explained by examples. Have you ever disciplined yourself into a major change such as losing a lifetime of excess weight or turning from a flighty, happy-go-lucky person into a serious, professional one? Have you noticed that while people remark upon the signs of change, it takes them an almighty long time to *think* of you as other than an overweight person (temporarily thin) or a nonserious person (temporarily going through a serious stage)?

The human mind resists change. We don't like to delve into our mental filing system and recategorize something we're already familiar with. An alcoholic can go on for quite some time with the drinking before he or she (or relatives, spouse, or employer) realizes that something is out of kilter and something must be done about it. A person who is known to do good work can slide on his or her reputation for a long while before reduced or inferior work output changes people's opinions. And a depressive can go on for a dangerously long time before those close can actually *see* what's going on and realize that help is needed.

Notice that I am talking about *others'* realizing that help is needed, if the realization is made at all. In most serious cases of depression, the person affected will go to a doctor only as a last resort. Even then, it's usually because job security or a marriage is threatened or the complaints of others can no longer be ignored. Depression, like cancer, should be caught in its early stages.

That's easy to say, hard to do. We've already talked enough about symptoms, so you will probably recognize when a case of depression has developed to the point where it can be diagnosed. But these descriptions are almost hypothetical because they refer to perfect clinical cases. You can *know* intellectually that if your car skids, the last thing you do is apply brakes. But when a real-life skid comes along, all your knowledge goes out of your head and your foot steps on the brake. In depression, the trick is putting what you *know* together with what is happening. *Anyone* can make an accurate diagnosis once the disease has turned someone into a zombie. The important thing is to be alert for the little changes that allow the illness to be stopped before it causes major damage.

If we are close to someone, we're usually sensitive to their moods. But the depressive often doesn't want to talk about his or her feelings. You might bring up the fact that he or she hasn't been smiling much lately and doesn't seem comfortable and at ease. Your remarks may bring forth a denial, or worse, *Leave me alone*. Continuing to press may bring on an even angrier reaction. Many people, as the disease is coming on, try their best to deny that anything is wrong, frightened of what is happening to them and afraid that others will see the horrible thing that is wrong with them.

If the depressive is noncommunicative, you have to make your own diagnosis without much help. Your first clue, of course, is the noticeable joylessness. Of course, we all go through periods of withdrawal and inability to appreciate the good things. But when this state goes on and on, when the favorite food stays on the plate untouched time after time, when efforts to enjoy and participate in activities seem forced and strained, then you know you have cause to look further.

In an agitated type of depression, there may be mild delusions or fixations long before the typical symptoms of sleeplessness, loss of concentration and memory, indecisiveness, and physical complaints begin. These delusions are often so subtle that they may be missed unless you make a point of looking for them. (One warning: everyone has delusions. If you look for signs of neurotic fixations, you'll find them in anyone you examine, including yourself. That doesn't mean the person *is* neurotic. What you'll be looking for here are sudden, new fixations which are out of character and have no basis. They are usually consistent in that they are repeated often.)

As an example, here's one particular delusion and fixation which occurred in my depressive episode. The fixation came first, three months before the first anxiety attack while I was driving in London. I had left my California home to go to Jamaica, one of my favorite places, for an undetermined amount of time. From there, I was to continue on to England. In Los Angeles I had spent most of my leisure time with a woman friend, who had started out as just an ordinary friend, then became a rival/friend, then an enemy/friend. We were both writers and were both trying to impress the other, and, to be honest, make each other jealous. I'll call her Karen. Karen wasn't working steadily and I was. I was also dating a fairly successful songwriter and record producer, and I would tell Karen all about him but never introduced her. Without telling me, she called him and said she was interested in learning how to write songs. She began visiting his office once a week, with my knowledge, of course. And of course I pretended that it didn't bother me a bit. There was an actor I admired very much, and I was thrilled when a magazine gave me an assignment to interview him. We hit it off during the interview and got to know each other slightly. I was enthralled and enchanted with his way of thinking and his knowledge. Karen called him up to try to get an interview with him too, though she didn't have an assignment; and she didn't get the interview. These things made me feel very superior, and I would drop my successes into conversations in an offhand way. We still pretended to be friends, but our "friendship" had now become a spiteful game of one-upsmanship. And since I felt I was always in the winning position, I rather enjoyed the game.

All during this time, Jamaica had been one place I had raved about, and Karen would talk about her plans to go there too. By the time I finally left for Jamaica and England, the game had ended and we hadn't spoken for several months. She rarely crossed my mind. But after three months on the island, I began thinking I saw her in the area where I was staying. The thought filled me with rage. I would cross a room to see if a black-haired woman there was Karen. One night I thought I saw her driving a car along the road that stretches from one end of the island to the other. It was night, and I was standing by the road at the time. I ran to my car some distance away, spun out onto the road, and began chasing after the car which I imagined Karen to be driving. I was filled with fury at the thought that she had actually *dared* to come to *my* haven! (Remembering this and other pre-depressive incidents, I am still embarrassed. It's hard to believe that the person I am now could have once done those things.)

I drove for more than half an hour, speeding like a demon over a road that curved and twisted. At one point I finally realized two things: this chase was pretty ridiculous, and I would probably never catch up. I knew the fixation wasn't quite, well, normal. Yet, although I did gain control over it, it still would come back.

Later, in England, I suffered from the delusion that I was old and that my face was far more wrinkled than it should be. I was 25. I went to a plastic surgeon to ask for a face lift, and he tried to convince me that I hardly looked twenty. It was no use. I didn't believe him. He wouldn't operate on me, so I went to another doctor to get a recommendation. The doctor refused even to consider a face lift. I wanted to buy heavy pancake makeup at a department store, but the saleslady told me that it was for older women and I didn't need it. None of these expert opinions interfered with my delusion that my face was ugly and wrinkled.

While the fixation about Karen in Jamaica was peculiarly my own, the facial aging delusion is very common among depressed women. A woman in her twenties may be convinced her face looks like an ancient crone's and may say that she's ashamed to go out because of how her face looks. She may spend hours going over photographs taken when she was "pretty"—photos taken only a few months previously. Or she may think her hands have turned ugly or that her breasts are so saggy that she needs an operation to lift them.

A man may have similar delusions. He may believe that his hair is falling out and he is going bald, or that he never looks shaven even after shaving. Another delusion common to both sexes is that of being fat, even when there has been a weight loss. In older people, delusions more often take the form of body deterioration: *My stomach is rotting*, *I have a brain tumor*, *My bones are dissolving*.

No one, not doctors or loved ones, nor even the evidence which should be clear to the naked eye, will convince the depressive that these delusions aren't true. You may get a depressive to admit that he or she is being silly about a particular idea, and may use all the rational thought at your disposal to disprove it—but the delusion will return just as strong as it was before.

Fixations are obsessions which come from individual psychological quirks. There may be a fixation that one person at work is "out to get me." Or a neighbor may be suspected of staring all the time, using binoculars to do so. Most fixations are slightly paranoid and are important symptoms. They will do a lot to tell a doctor what type of depression is at fault and help in determining treatment. And they are also a warning signal, since they begin months before the clinical onset of depression.

I make a distinction between fixations and delusions because delusions are fairly typical in depression, whereas a fixation is an obsession which usually manifests itself only in agitated types of depression. The delusions are most often based on the lack of self-esteem and are expressed as rationalizations for self-dislike—the body or looks are deteriorating or have deteriorated to the point of extreme loathsomeness. The feeling of being old, for example, is connected to the thought that being old is something to be ashamed of. That fixation has no bearing on opinions about other old people, though. The depressive won't feel that anyone else has to be ashamed of being old. One of the most common delusions is the feeling that *No one likes me, they really wish I'd go away, they're only being polite when they act like they are my friends*. And of course, the objective statement here is actually *I'm unlovable; how could anyone like me*?

The loss of self-esteem creates a base for taking the slightest remark or event out of context and using it as proof of rejection. For example, Elaine, a 42-year-old mother of three, usually drove her children to school in the morning. Her husband Dennis became concerned over her pale, haggard appearance and lack of energy. He attributed it to overwork. The couple had been remodeling their home, and for the past several months Elaine had been choosing new drapes and upholstery and painting the rooms. Dennis decided to take some of the work load off her shoulders, so one morning he announced that he would drive the children to school from then on. It was actually far more convenient for him to do this than it had been for his wife; the school was on his way to work and he would only have to leave a few minutes earlier to drive the children there.

Elaine didn't see it that way. She didn't see the concern behind his willingness to take over the driving job. That morning, after her family had gone, she burst into tears and cried for several hours. Then she went into the bedroom and took an overdose of sleeping pills. Luckily, one of the children became ill in school that afternoon and was brought home by the school nurse. The child went to wake his mother, found that he couldn't, and told the nurse. She called an ambulance and Elaine's life was saved.

Why had she done it? She'd been sure that her husband didn't trust her to drive the children anymore. The delusion that she wasn't capable of driving had been bothering her for months, and this was the final straw. Like most families in which the parents are in their most productive years and the children are active in school, everyone would go through periods of time when activities made it hard to pay deep attention to each other. Elaine's depression had existed for months, but she fought it alone. While Dennis thought that Elaine was run down and needed a rest, his work occupied him so much that he felt he could let the problem slide for a time. After all, Elaine wasn't *saying* that anything was wrong, and certainly she would say something if she were having a serious problem.

Dennis didn't know that there was an illness called depression. Even if he had, it probably never would have occurred to him that his bright, wonderful Elaine would have it. He had earlier felt some of her pain and tried to start a conversation about it, but Elaine didn't want to talk about what was bothering her. And Elaine interpreted his concern to mean that he was "just putting up with it," tolerating her, which was why he "made excuses about my working so hard."

Delusions of rejection can be manufactured even out of positive assessments by others. A man in the aerospace industry was promoted to an executive position. He was convinced that the promotion was his superior's way of making fun of him, that he had been promoted in order to make his inadequacies public. If you should cut off a phone call to a depressed person because someone is at your door, the person will usually see that as a sign of rejection. Mention a party you went to and the depressive will be sure that he wasn't invited because no one likes him, even though he may hardly know the person who threw the party. A woman who was an extremely good television producer told the doctor treating her for depression that when she was given a secretary of her own, she took it to mean that her bosses thought she couldn't do all her work herself.

The Need for Communication

Talking to many depressives, or getting them to talk, can be difficult. They may answer in monosyllables or not be able to continue the thread of the conversation. They will probably show little emotion and seem unresponsive to the tone of the discussion. Yet it's necessary, for many reasons, to start a communication flowing. For one thing, it will help you to gauge the degree of emotional pain, and that is your best indication of how serious the depression is.

You may find that the depressive's thought patterns at times are incoherent and inconsistent. Conversation will be constantly interrupted by self-deprecating remarks, and instead of learning more about the person's feelings, you may find yourself dragged into a total effort just to convince him (or her) that people *do* like him, that he *does* have friends, that he *is* worthy. It helps to remember that what you are after is a flow of conversation *from* the depressive, and any judgment on your part will interfere with that flow. That means positive *or* negative judgment. Don't comment on what is said, just try to increase the flow of words.

The technique should go something like this:*

*This is a transcript of an actual interview, part of the first meeting between a patient and a therapist. Later, after recovery, the patient remarked on this particular conversation, saying that for the first time since the illness began, she felt that perhaps the illness was at fault, and perhaps *she* wasn't. It gave her the first hope she had had in months.

DEPRESSIVE: *I've just been feeling like it's no use. I can't get my work done and I'll probably be fired.*

YOU: *What part of your work can't you do?* (The question is specific. You are *guiding* toward specific answers. You're not asking the person to justify the feelings by asking why he or she feels that way. You're only asking for an instance which illustrates the feeling. Remember that the depressive has difficulty concentrating and making decisions. If you ask "why," you're asking the person to concentrate on the answer to the question and decide on one of a variety of possible factors. It's similar to the technique of helping a child decide about breakfast when you're in a hurry. You don't ask, "What do you want?" but instead make an offer: "Do you want fried or poached eggs?")

DEPRESSIVE: *Well, I just can't do anything.* (This is a typical answer. You can expect that answers to specific questions will often be vague at first, so you must narrow the question down until there is no choice but a specific answer.)

YOU: *You get to work on time, don't you?*

DEPRESSIVE: *Yes, but I can't do anything once I get there.*

YOU: *What's the first thing you have to do to start your day at work?*

(Again, this is pinning the answer down to specifics.)

DEPRESSIVE: *I have to open the mail.*

YOU: *Do you do that?*

DEPRESSIVE: *Yes, but not fast enough.*

YOU: *But you* do *it. Then what do you have to do?* (You make no comment on the judgmental statement about the *quality* with which the task is accomplished.)

DEPRESSIVE: *Then I have to start filling out my reports.*

YOU: *Do you do it?*

DEPRESSIVE: *Well, it's really hard. Sometimes I can't get them done.*

YOU: *But you finish eventually?* (You are after a specific answer, not one dealing with *sometimes* or quality judgment. Also, you are asking questions in a way which forces the depressive to state an accomplishment, to admit, "Yes, I finished it . . . yes, I meet my responsibilities . . . yes, I took care of that requirement." In doing so, you aren't going to outside factors where excuses can be used to show how *others* feel about the person.

Here you are sticking exactly to what the depressive does or does not do, and not to other people's reactions to it.)

Suppose the answer is, "I haven't finished them lately." Again, get a specific. Ask what reports have not been finished. Ask for details. Ask if anyone has complained about the reports not being finished or finished correctly. Then get to the part which (in this case) causes the most worry, being fired. Don't ask a general question such as "Why do you think you're going to be fired?" You'll only be allowing room for the person to express a lack of self-esteem. Ask, "What has your boss said or done which makes you think you're going to be fired?" This technique can be used in nonclinical temporary depressions where someone is upset about a job or relationship; it can also be used in self-questioning. It allows the fear to be confronted in a less paranoid, more realistic way.

Talking this way with a depressed person can do two very necessary things. It can help show the depressive that these fears and delusions are not as *serious* as they seem to be, although you must accept the fact that your logic will only lessen them (if that) and not eradicate them. And it will give *you* an idea of what your mate, relative, or friend is going through.

There is another area of conversation which can be even more revealing of the depressive's condition. It works especially well in a case where the person finds it hard to talk about daily events and feelings. This is the area of dreams.

The dreams of the depressive often have unpleasant story lines. They are quite complete and can be very vivid. But it's the theme of the dreams which are the giveaway. The depressive will dream themes of masochism and defeat. A woman may dream that she is being reviled for her ugliness, a man that he has done something which makes him look like a sissy. There may be dreams of humiliation at work. Some of these dreams may come as perceptions only—there may be swiftly changing blurs of color, but the person is upset and frightened by them, or some meaningless sequence may leave an impression in the depressive's mind that it meant he or she had just done something terrible. Sometimes our dreams don't have pictures to match, even though they may be vivid. I know one case in which the person had a recurring dream about a rock. The rock did nothing frightening, it just got bigger in the dream. Yet the dreamer would wake in a state of cold sweat and trembling. In the dreams of the depressive, the masochistic theme is often constant. There are never dreams which make the person feel triumphant or good.

If you run into difficulty when asking the person to discuss day-to-day feelings, don't *suddenly* turn the conversation around to dreams. Wait a day, then casually ask *"What did you dream last night?"* If the answer is *"nothing"* or *"I can't remember,"* bring up the fact that everyone dreams, whether or not they remember. Begin a type of free association: "What was the last dream you remember? Did you ever dream about work? Do you ever dream about when you were a child?" Take it slow and easy. Don't press. Be the oil on a recalcitrant bolt, not the wrench. If you come to a dead end in communication, go to another subject and come back to this later. If the person tells you he or she doesn't want to talk, let it rest for the moment and come back to it a few hours or days later. Keep your eyes open for a pattern so that you can decide the best way to get the person to talk to you. But remember two things: always be gentle in your words and manner, and never be judgmental. Reassurances *are* necessary, but remember you are trying to acquaint yourself with the depressive's feelings and gauge the severity of those feelings in order to find out how serious the illness is; reassurances can end information and become the sole topic of conversation.

One other thing. Don't make the mistake of talking to the person as if he or she were a child or idiot. Remember that the depressive has a fear of rebuff and rejection; a patronizing manner on your part can have quite serious consequences. You may do more harm than good if you can't talk or act normally. If that's a problem for you, you'll have to recognize it as such and either stop trying to have the informational talks or ask someone else whom the depressive trusts to do the talking.

It's hard to achieve the kind of clinical detachment you'll need in order to get the information, and what's even harder is to try remembering it without writing it down. Even though it may seem more efficient, *don't* make the mistake one man made with his depressed wife. When Laura first showed the signs of depression, Dan took my advice to try to get her to describe her illness by talking about how it affected her attitudes and functions. There was no barrier to communication; Laura was quite willing to talk about how she felt. But Dan, who has a rotten memory, was unable to retain more than the vaguest specifics of what Laura told him. So he asked Laura if she would mind if he wrote down what she said on a pad. Laura said she didn't mind. But as Dan wrote and frowned and nibbled at his pen, Laura became convinced that he was "playing doctor" and that he planned to put her into an institution. She did what any sane person would do: she clammed up. Nor would she talk to a therapist when she was finally persuaded to go to one. After five visits, during which she sat without saying a word, Laura finally revealed the source of her unwillingness to talk.

Someone sitting there writing it all down creates a barrier to conversation. How can a person trust you with his or her innermost feelings when you're taking notes? Besides, in hearing the depressive out, you are mainly trying to gain a *feeling* for the illness and its severity. You are trying to gauge whether help is necessary and to make a layman's diagnosis. And you are trying to get the depressed person to lighten some of the pressure and burden by sharing it with someone else. While the burden won't be that much lighter for the depressive, *you* at least will have an insight into some of the major fear and anxiety areas. That will help you deal with the depressive in a more connected way, staying away from fear triggers and situations which are hard for the depressive to handle.

So far, we have been talking about the more serious depressions, the ones which overtly interfere with the victim's ability to function. What about the chronic depressions which are just enough to prevent the person from taking advantage of his or her total ability—and which are bound to get worse as the years go by?

An example of this type is the case of a brilliant composer and musician. You would probably be familiar with his name if you have ever had an interest in pop music. Steve was with a famous group and was well known in his own right as a musician. The group had many top forty records, but when they broke up, Steve's career stagnated. He had been traveling around the world, playing in first-class arenas and auditoriums. From that he went to playing at friends' parties, then to local beer bars. Good musicians would no longer work with him since he was usually paid so little money. His income dropped and he was forced to sell most of his possessions and move, with his wife and child, to a small, rundown house. Even though he spent months without work, he didn't have the assertiveness to go out and look for work in his own field or any other. His wife left him in despair after a screaming fight in which he offered to work at a nearby bar and then refused to call for the interview. He languished on for another few years in this fashion. His wife came back. She was still unable to understand what was going on, and their time together was little more than an ongoing screaming bout on her part; Steve never screamed back. He had fixed up one room as a practice room and there he withdrew from the world. But not to practice. He would sit for hours, fingering his instruments and playing tapes of music he had composed.

One day his luck suddenly changed. A rising recording artist, who remembered Steve from the days of his fame, decided to hire him as one of his backup musicians. For a few months this new status and steady income provided a spurt of psychic energy. But Steve couldn't keep up with the pace of life on the road. He played well—he never missed or was late for an appearance—but he couldn't handle solos and seemed shrunken and insecure on stage. As the macho rock and roll illusion was spun out by the star and the rest of the backup band, Steve radiated nothing. His lack of stage presence might have been ignored, but in the medium of *cool* he always gave the impression that what he was doing was hard work. The other band members demanded raises when more bookings were added to the schedule. Steve didn't, and continued to play at his same pay scale, which was $700 a week less than the others were making. The leader finally let Steve go in favor of another musician who could contribute to the energy on stage.

Steve returned home and picked up the same way of life he had been living before this piece of good fortune. Occasionally, job offers come in, but most of Steve's life is spent fingering his instruments, while his wife goes to the welfare office to ask for food stamps and rent money. After eight years, she is resigned to the situation. Neither one of the couple believes that Steve needs anti-depressants. His wife says: "He's not depressed, he's just passive. I know this because his father used to get into depressed states, and then he couldn't move. But Steve doesn't just sit for hours like his old man did. He's just not aggressive, that's all. But he goes to the store, he takes care of our daughter, he sometimes does things around the house." She and Steve refuse to consider that depression most often takes the form of passivity when it is a chronic condition.

In women, these chronic depressions most often take the form of fatigue. Boyd Cooper, a prominent Hollywood gynecologist told me: "If we doctors did not have the cases of depression-caused fatigue that fill our waiting rooms, we couldn't afford the fancy offices we have. I'd say that many of my patients—at times, almost half—come to see me about fatigue. And I don't see any more of those cases than any other doctor. It's a problem, because unless the real cause of the fatigue is identified, there's nothing we can do."

What does he do?

"When a woman complains about fatigue and there's nothing medically wrong with her, I start asking about the home life. You can spot a depressive environment by her description. Her voice will be uninvolved, flat and dead, unless she has symptoms of agitation, and if that is the case I will hear complaints instead of descriptions. Often, this type of woman will cry while talking, but the crying will also be, well, uninvolved is the only way I can describe it. It seems to have no connection to the emotions caused by her home or marriage situation. She'll tell me that she can't keep up with the housework or that everything seems to be too much for her. This woman will usually have a heavy guilt complex about the quality of her mothering. She'll feel that she's not doing enough for the kids or that she's neglecting them on several fronts. While this probably isn't true, it *is* this kind of person who loses her patience with her kids most easily, yells at them and screams at the slightest provocation. She usually has a sense of being overwhelmed, of feeling that everything is out of her control. She drags around the house, picking up a mop, sweeping for a few minutes, then going on to something else before completing that task. She loses her animation. Actually, she's got chronic depression, but it comes out as fatigue. All the symptoms in these chronic cases come out as not having enough energy to keep things together, as tiredness. She may take afternoon naps or not feel like going out at night. And she comes to me complaining about fatigue and asks for uppers or tranquilizers to ease her anxieties. I can't give her a tranquilizer if she is depressed. I can't give her an upper because there's no medical reason to do so. But I try to get her to see a therapist or specialist and give her a number of referrals. These women though . . . they don't go. I know that if they are going to get treatment for depression, I'd better start it or nothing will happen. A woman *can* go to her doctor for fatigue; but most women (and men) won't go to a doctor because they're feeling blue all the time and can't use their minds as easily as before. That smacks of craziness, and people are afraid of insanity. It still has its "snake pit" stigma. Most of the time the women with fatigue aren't really after a pep pill at all. It's a silent plea for help—they want a magic pill to get them on an even keel again, to kill the mental pain. They don't know what's wrong, but they hope I'll have something to cure it."

Chronic depressions are almost exactly like low-grade, minor depressions. They affect people in the same way. It's only in the acute cases that symptoms get out of hand. A person with a low-grade or chronic case may go through a whole lifetime of muffled promise without anyone's realizing that depression, like a gray film, is clouding every facet of life. You'll find more on the minor depressions in Chapter 8, with some ways you can diagnose yourself to find out if you have a case of it.

When Talking Doesn't Help Anyone

There may be times when the verbal approach doesn't help you gain more knowledge about the condition of the depressive, and also doesn't help the depressed person in any appreciable way. This could be because the person can't *hear* what you're saying. The fact that words cause the eardrums to vibrate and convey the meaning of what has been said to the brain doesn't necessarily mean that the words have been *heard*. The act of hearing requires an essential component: listening. (I know of one reporter for a radio station who had been told all his professional life that he was too hyper, too anxious to "get the story," to be a good reporter. It took almost five years for him to *hear* those words and get himself in better professional shape.)

If a depressive isn't listening, either because you have no power to affect the person verbally or because the illness prevents communication, you're not going to get many useful guidelines to what is happening inside his or her mind. If the symptoms aren't observable on an external level, such as changing sleep patterns or personality disruption, you can proceed without verbal knowledge from the depressive. You can use visual observation.

Even a masked depression will tend to reveal itself facially when the person is not engaged in social interaction. Lines and wrinkles in the face will be more deeply etched. There will be less mobility in the expression. Look at a nondepressed face. You'll see a dozen facial expressions every minute. The muscles of the face move, the eyes change from wide to contracted, there are traces of emotions even in the most composed of faces. During reading, for example, the nondepressed face will move through stages of concentration, involvement with the material being read, shifts of attention which show themselves as facial movement.

The face of the depressive is much more static. The decrease in energy, the actual *depression* of all vitality extends even to the face. Even the unnoticeable effort of using the muscles of the face is harder. You'll observe that a depressed person doesn't change expression in the subtle ways most people do, and in masked depression, while the face may go through changes, the smile or other expression never seems to reach the eyes.

Depending on the biogenic amine causing the problem, a depressive will usually be either nervous and agitated or slowed down and retarded. Since these two traits, hyper action and hypo action (*hyper* means *over* and *hypo* means *under*) are also just plain old personality traits, you have to know a person well before you can use these as visual observation for symptoms. You have to be able to allow for the factors which are part of the personality and notice whether the traits have increased or whether they are unusual and new.

People with an agitated depression are unable to be still. They twist their fingers, pick at their scalp, face, or clothing. They clench their hands, sometimes rubbing the fingers together in a palsied motion. They twitch their feet on their body, move around while sitting. Even in walking, their motions aren't efficient, but use more action than is necessary. When they stop a stride to sit down, there may be several little puttering steps before getting into the chair. Usually, the most observable movement is in the hands. Some doctors have analyzed this motion to be the depressive's defense mechanism, as if bodily movements can somehow fight off the horrible pain. The agitated depressive is not resigned to the condition. It becomes a fight, it can't be tolerated. The movement is an indication of the mind's unrest.

The slowed down, retarded depression shows itself in an opposite way. This type of person is passive and accepts this horrible fate with an attitude of resignation. He or she may express such thoughts as, "I deserve to feel this way because I'm such an awful person," or drop other remarks which justify the illness and explain it in terms of having "earned" it.

These people sit without moving for longer periods of time than nondepressed people do. If you, in a nondepressed state, were to sit absolutely still for longer than a few minutes, your muscles would cry for relief. You would shift your weight slightly, move an arm a fraction of an inch, straighten your back a little. These are very slight movements, designed to eliminate muscular pressure. Even people who practice meditation and can sit without moving for hours will slowly exercise their muscles by changing position in such slight ways that they are almost unnoticeable. The depressive, however, can sit without any movement at all, eyes staring at nothing. There's no tension, no feeling of life in the body.

The illness depresses all activity. The hands and arms don't play as big a part in expressing verbal thoughts. Gestures are minimized: whereas this person may ordinarily hold an arm forward and up when waving, now the arm stays at chest level, held in toward the body.

A normally expressive vocabulary is reduced. There is a lack of adjectives. In listening to tapes of myself recorded during my depression, I found it hard to believe that the dull, dead voice on the tape was mine. I have a very expressive voice and a fairly large vocabularly studded with descriptive words. As my depression began, my language became more simplistic. In one tape made after recovery, I was talking about a friend to whom I had given a gift. I described his emotions as: "He was so happy! He just radiated, and it made you feel good just to be in the room with him." My voice was full of excitement, and the listener could imagine the joy of the man who had received the gift. But in a tape on which I described this same event during my depressive episode, the only words were, "Yes, he was glad."

There is less expression in the voice. You'll notice that the voice of a person with retarded depression will have more of a monotone quality to it than normal, although the degree of change depends on the severity of the illness. Sentences will be started and then fade away. According to renowned depression specialist Dr. Aaron Beck, these vocal changes were noted in 75 percent of severely depressed patients during a study on the factors of depression.

Of course, there are few perfect clinical pictures of every single symptom present according to the lines drawn out for it. We are talking in clinical examples throughout this book, but there will be overlaps of types and degree of depression. In any specific case, some symptoms will be present, some will not be there at all. You will have to take an overview of all the possible factors of the illness. Many times a person will show evidence of *both* agitation and retardation. The type of depression is a deciding factor, but so is the personality. Remember too that you may know the person only during a depressive stage. You may not realize just what a change there has been in his or her personality. If you are wondering how to help a depressed person you have known only a few years, it may help to learn if there was a personality change prior to the time you met. You can find this out from parents or friends who have known your friend for a considerable length of time. And strangely enough, you can also suspect a personality change if there are no friends for you to meet, if the person is a loner and has no contacts.

The depressive is usually a loner. As with Marta's "first impression" facade, these people will be able to hold up a relationship as long as it remains superficial and doesn't have the depth or time involvement which will cause them to drop the facade. The behavior, which is usually letter perfect, according to the book, is actually a studied mannerism. They have learned the "secret." Of course, this type of person is only imitating what she or he considers to be the type of behavior that will gain social acceptance. The behavior is separate from the person, so to speak. Maintaining it requires concentration of an intense kind, and that's why the facade drops after a short period of time. It's hard to find signs of depression in the people whose masks have been developed to such a fine degree. Their act is too perfect, and if you penetrate it, they will deny that you have seen anything. It's much easier if you can be there at the beginning of the illness. Unfortunately, this isn't always possible.

Another word of caution here. The attempt to diagnose depression as it is beginning, and before the symptoms have *obviously* disrupted the person's life, is not a casual undertaking. Here you are, a lay person with no medical credentials, trying to do something that takes the knowledge of a physician, the skills of a psychiatrist, and the tact and finesse of a diplomat. But *you* are fitted to make these observations because you have a personal knowledge of the person in his or her normal state of being. That's something a therapist usually doesn't have. You have to be careful, though (and this should be emphasized) because there are two types of visual observation. One is the concerned, sympathetic, and compassionate "looking after" that a mother will undertake in trying to determine whether her child's quiet behavior means more than a mood, whether it's an indication of an oncoming cold or other illness or whether something upsetting happened in school that day.

The other kind of watching is the "keep an eye on him, he may steal the silverware" type. It's the suspicious, narrow-eyed observation marked by the sideways glance and a quiet wariness. If you are always trying to watch the person out of the corner of your eye, constantly following him or her, and staring all the time, those signals will be interpreted as suspicion on your part or at least will indicate that you suspect something is wrong—but wrong in a way that will frighten the depressed person. The victim of depression may have distorted perception. but it's not dead perception. As open as these people are to rejection and rebuff, even the slightest slip on your part can add to their pain, rather than allowing you to gain the information you need to start easing it. So don't overdo the observation.

Actually, you don't have to depend only on your eyes to concentrate on picking up the facts. Whenever you spend time with a person, your subconscious picks up little mannerisms and feelings from them without your having to try to receive these signals. If you can't relax and be casual about trying to diagnose a case of depression before it becomes obvious, then please, don't try to do it at all. And that's a real toughie, because your natural concern and worry will make you want to jump right in and *do* something. If you feel a depressive episode is beginning and you *have* to find out but don't have the patience to do it gently, try to get the person to go to a specialist for a preliminary diagnosis— and tell the specialist of your concerns. It may be difficult for you to do this, but remember that not only is a cure easier to obtain if the illness is caught at its beginning, but the depressive is less reluctant about getting medical help at that stage. Later, there will be active resistance to the idea of seeing a doctor. Don't be afraid to suggest a doctor if you feel the person needs it. You can take away any sting by saying you have noticed that the person seems run down and tired all the time, and you feel that a doctor you've heard about is good with this problem. Of course, before you say that, make sure you have called the doctor in question and discussed your intentions. The doctor may have some additional advice for you, or may (yes, some doctors will) say this is not a familiar enough field and recommend someone else.

As for finding out the name of a doctor who handles depression, call the Suicide Prevention Center. If your town doesn't have one of these offices or a similar crisis hotline, get in touch with the nearest large university and ask to speak to the psychiatric department. One of the doctors there will probably be able to recommend someone.

You may need to know some terminology in order to discuss the situation with a doctor on a knowledgeable basis. The period in which symptoms appear before the actual onset of the illness is called the *prodromal period*. Its main features are anxiety, tension, and difficulty in making decisions. The prodromal period varies in length, and may not even be obvious in someone with an acute onset. With an *acute onset*, the depression seems to come about almost overnight; symptoms develop over four weeks or less. Prodromal periods are most observable in people who have an *insidious onset*. With this type, the illness takes four or *more* weeks to develop. It is also called a *protracted onset*.

These terms are important for other reasons than allowing

you to talk intelligently to a doctor. The way a depressive episode begins will reveal a lot about its probable duration and severity.

The acute onset usually has a quicker recovery rate. Depressions with a clear-cut prodronal period usually last longer, and usually indicate an insidious or protracted onset. But while the acute onset may mean a shorter duration for the illness, it is also far more likely to indicate a possible reoccurrence later in life. In studies of people who were severely depressed, those with acute onsets were found to have had more than one depressive episode before the age of fifty. Those with insidious onsets were more likely to have experienced only the one attack, and after recovery remained depression free, at least in the clinical sense.

Don't be upset if you are using the right terminology and the specialist you've contacted either doesn't seem to know what you're talking about or becomes hostile that you know how to talk about it at all. For one thing, so little is known about depression that some doctors get a pet theory and treat all cases according to that theory without keeping up with the latest medical discoveries. The field is so new that a doctor who received a degree more than fifteen years ago will have only the most primitive information unless a refresher course has been taken since graduation from medical school. Sometimes a therapist who has a busy practice won't have time to keep up with the latest research and will resent the fact that *you* are aware of it. Even doctors who are up to the minute in their knowledge of this disability may feel that *you* have no right to this knowledge. (Sometimes I get the feeling that a few doctors regard themselves as high priests of a mysterious religion called *health*, and they consider it part of their job to keep the mysteries secret. You've probably come in contact with a doctor who, when you suggested a specific thing which might be wrong with you, poo-poohs your statement and says, "Since when are you a doctor?" In my opinion, any physician or therapist who preserves this knowledge for himself and refuses to admit that you may know what you're talking about does not have the tact, compassion, and empathy to treat a case of depression properly. A doctor should at least listen to your opinions with a show of respect—first of all because you are hiring, and he or she is in your employ; and second because you may be right!)

If a doctor refuses to talk with you in some detail about the depression case you are bringing to the office, or if there is scoffing at the idea that the depression may be biochemically caused, you might be better off with another specialist. Depression has been considered a disorder solely of the mind for so many years that many therapists and physicians still think of it that way. They may even go so far as to disbelieve in the results obtained from anti-depressants and refuse to prescribe them. You must question the doctor about his or her theories of depression, how the patient will be treated, and what special training makes this doctor a specialist in the field. If it's just the fact that hundreds of cases have passed through the office, don't discount that. A good doctor can learn as much from his or her patients as can be learned from even the best papers and studies on the subject.

When to Start Looking
Once you notice signs of a personality change in someone close to you, there's a natural tendency to want to find out what is causing it. Don't automatically jump to the conclusion that depression is the answer. It could be a variety of factors: the person may be preoccupied by job pressures and responsibilities, or may have some other organic illness without realizing it. Hypertension will often imitate an agitated depression, with its symptoms of irritability and tension. Hypoglycemia and thyroid illnesses will cause a toxic depression which may be treated with anti-depressives for years without bringing relief because it is not the biogenic amines that are causing the illness, though they are affected. And to be honest, the personality change may be caused by the person changing his or her feelings toward *you*. There are a few checkpoints, however, that will indicate if the symptoms are actually caused by a clinical case of depression. So, if you suspect but aren't sure, ask yourself these questions:

- Has the person been under stress lately?
- Has the stress been prolonged, say, for a period of three months or longer?
- Has there been a radical change in the person's life or life style, such as losing or changing jobs, a divorce or death in the family, a move to a different locale?
- Have the children recently left home?
- Is the person at the depression prone-time of life (mid-twenties, late forties for women; mid-thirties, early fifties for men)?
- Is the person over 50 years of age?

These things have known connections to depression, although scientists don't know yet what that connection is. If the answers to at least two of these questions are *yes*, that is a sign that the personality change is likely leading to a depressive episode. But—don't discount other causes until you know for sure that depression *is* the answer.

On the next few pages is a very important diagnostic tool. It's a depression check list which allows you to gauge whether the symptoms of the illness are present and to what degree. It also will tell you if these are personality changes (indicating a depressive episode) or normal patterns (indicating a chronic case).

There's no *score* on this test. There's no right or wrong answer. You will know if the chart indicates depression from what you have read in this book so far. But if you have only skimmed or skipped up to this part and can't resist using the chart, even though you have not read the information you need in order to analyze the results properly, here's how to gauge the answers. Suspect depression if:

There are two or more *never* or *rarely* answers to the first section, and

Four or more *almost always* or *often* answers to the second section.

Two or more *never* or three or more *rarely* answers to the third section.

Seven or more *no* answers to the last section.

If the answers to the first three sections show that there has been a change in normal patterns, and especially if the change has appeared over the previous six months, you can accurately diagnose a depressive episode as existing.

You can if you wish, give the chart to a person you feel is depressed to fill out him/herself, but you may have to compare the results to see if the answers match your perception. It might help if, after the depressed person has filled in the answers, you fill in the chart too in order to measure your observations against his or hers—but do so discreetly. If there's a great difference, you may have to recheck your perceptions for accuracy, or perhaps understand that the depression has interfered with the person's ability to answer the questions accurately. If the person is unwilling to take the test at all, you will have to fill in the answers as best you can from your own observations.

DEPRESSION CHECK-LIST

	Almost always	Often	Rarely	Never	Is this a change in normal patterns?	Has the change appeared in the last six months?
Physical Symptoms						
Sleep comes easily, lasts the whole night, and results in a rested feeling upon awakening.						
Health is good with few physical complaints.						
When there is a physical complaint, it's due to an obvious and diagnosable cause such as virus, over-exertion, or lack of sleep						
Energy level is sufficient to accomplish all desired tasks.						
Behavior Patterns						
Easily irritated						
Periods of anxiety						
Inability to concentrate						
Crying spells or urge to cry						

DEPRESSION CHECK-LIST (Continued)

	Almost always	Often	Rarely	Never	Is this a change in normal patterns?	Has the change appeared in the last six months?
Behavior Patterns (Continued)						
Moods of sadness						
Quick swings in feelings and moods						
Feelings of confusion						
Forgetfulness						
Personality Patterns						
Makes firm decisions						
Makes plans and carries them out						
Makes choices quickly						
Instigates and welcomes communication with others						
Completes jobs or tasks						
Gets together with friends or goes out to socialize						

Keeps clothing and body groomed and clean

Takes care of household chores

Maintains personal responsibilities such as paying bills, keeping appointments, etc.

Eats well with regular appetite

Handles frustration without becoming overwhelmed by it

Feels sexual desire

Remains alert without periods of drowsiness during the day

Feelings and Perceptions	Yes	No
Life is interesting and worth while		
I'm glad I'm alive		
My friends like me		
I'm as intelligent as other people		
I'm a reasonably good person		
I am of average or above average intelligence		
I am of average or above average competence		
I have at least three likeable qualities		
My looks are okay		

85

DEPRESSION CHECK-LIST (Continued)

	Yes	No	Is this a change in normal patterns?	Has the change appeared in the last six months?
Feelings and Perceptions (Continued)				
If people knew what was inside my head, their opinion of me wouldn't change very much				
I feel involved and concerned with life and living				
If I died, at least one person would be sad				
I am interested in a number of different things				
I feel pretty good most of the time				
If I think something is funny, it makes me laugh				
There are people I feel very close to				
If I feel down about things, I usually feel they'll get better				

Most of the people who were my friends a year ago are still my friends

People like me well enough to do things for me

I look forward to certain days and occasions

My mind works as well or better than it always has

Sometimes I feel very loving

I feel calm a good percentage of the time

I rarely feel afraid

I can decide what I want from life and will have a good chance of getting it

I am able to become interested in things outside my own personal concerns

I have certain goals I'm working for

Sometimes I like to wear my best clothes and go somewhere special

I may not be the most saintly of people but I'm not the worst

Once this chart is filled in, it should be kept. It's an invaluable aid to the doctor who will be treating the illness. In fact, you may wish to use it more than once, so it might be a good idea to make several copies of the chart instead of writing on it in this book. Furthermore, remember that if you live with a depressed person, you are in an extremely vulnerable position yourself. You may slip into a depression without being aware of it. So take the test yourself periodically. Even if you have no depressed friends (that you're aware of), you should still fill in this chart every once in a while. It will give you more self-knowledge about your own moods and feelings, and it will let you know if you're coming down with a case of depression even if you have no one close to you who can act as an observer and help diagnose the illness.

4.

Stress and Depression

The faster mankind moves forward, the harder it is on the individuals involved. It's analogous to a car, which will last for years in good operating condition when consistently run at low speeds. But if the car is always pushed to its limits, it wears out faster. It needs more maintenance than one driven more slowly. The high speeds cause more friction. There's a greater degree of vibration in all the parts, and they become loose faster and wear out more quickly. The car will burn oil at a higher rate. And then there is always the greater risk of an accident, not because the driver pays less attention, but because the higher the speed, the less the ability to control the car and react quickly enough to events happening on the road.

Anyone with even a primitive knowledge of biology knows that no organism can live in an environment of its own waste products. Stress, which is a waste product of the unavoidable pressures of our culture, thus becomes a life-threatening syndrome. In fact, the stress-related illnesses—heart disease, hypertension, and cancer—are the top killers in the country. Primitive societies, which have little technology, have none of these diseases. Even tooth decay is unknown in cultures which don't have the refined food products that are part and parcel of the diets of progressive, more "civilized" countries.

But stress is more than a reaction to a pressured environment. Obviously it must be, if it can produce illnesses. There is a common misconception that stress is an emotional reaction only. But any physical thing which affects us is also stressful and causes the same symptoms as emotional stress. For example, stress eats up certain nutrients in the body, particularly vitamins B and C. This will happen in someone who is worried about a job, who is recovering from an operation (also a stress), or who has pushed his or her body to its limits by going without sleep or food.

One of the biggest fallacies in Western medicine is the idea that the mind and body are separate from each other. More and more doctors are beginning to acknowledge that mind and body are a united front, and when one is affected, the other reacts. The very idea that the mind can cause symptoms of physical illness while remaining in an apparently healthy state itself is a major change in our way of thinking. Psychosomatic medicine, which is the study of physical illnesses caused by the mind, is one of the most rapidly developing fields in health care. While we've found cures for the minor stress illnesses, such as ulcers, the major stress diseases still baffle medical scientists.

There's a correlation here. Humans pay far more attention to tangible data picked up by the five sensory organs than we do to our instinct or any other form of nontangible information. If we can't see it, smell it, hear, taste, or touch it, we tend to pay little or no attention. That's why, with all we know about the body and with all the miracles doctors are capable of performing, such as severed limb reattachments or organ transplants, we're practically helpless when it comes to an illness which isn't produced by a tangible factor. This is especially true of those illnesses which affect the mind or the way of thinking. Until recently, we haven't paid much attention to the brain because we couldn't *see* how it functioned. When you come right down to it, it's amazing that we know so much about the physical being and so little about what's inside that being's skull.

At this moment, we have *some* idea of what causes heart disease, hypertension, and cancer. But most of that knowledge is rudimentary. And worse, we know a lot more about curing the symptoms than we do about preventing the illness in the first place.

The same is true of depression. There are many theories about what causes it and all of them seem valid and provable. But we don't know how to prevent depression in our population.

There is one factor here which has been overlooked by most specialists in the field. That's the fact that many people who once became vegetables from a serious depressive episode become stronger, more stable after recovery, and once they recover, they never again suffer from depression. Most of these people have "found" something. Their entire way of thinking has been changed. And strangely, they no longer react to stress in quite the same way they did before their illness.

Doctors are aware of the connection between stress and depression, as they are aware of the connection between stress and those illnesses which affect blood pressure, the heart, the digestive system, and the endocrine glands. There are many explanations about why stress affects these parts of the body, and perhaps some of them will lead to better preventive medicine. In the past decade, we have gained enormous knowledge about how the human being reacts to stress—a science which was previously ignored in medicine.

Once the brain perceives a thought or external event as being a stressful stimulus, the first part of the body to react is the adrenal glands. There are two of them, one perched above each kidney. They produce adrenaline, a hormone which helps regulate body metabolism. (*Metabolism* refers to the speed and efficiency with which the body performs its life functions—digesting food, taking the nutrients and energy from the food, distributing those nutrients to the organs that use them, and disposing of the part it can't use. It also refers to the efficiency with which those organs use the nutrients and do their job.)

Adrenaline is necessary for life. It helps increase body resistance to disease, but more important, it provides the "fuel" needed for our *fight/flight* reactions. This is a system that creates the anxiety and urge to take action in a threatening situation while providing the extra energy we must have to take that action *fast*. Stress and tension react on the adrenal glands by calling for the release of more adrenaline. Adrenaline speeds up the heart, contracts the blood vessels, and raises blood pressure. Suppose someone frightens you by suddenly appearing out of nowhere, or you have to slam on your car brakes to avoid a collision. Afterwards, your heart is pounding and your breathing rate is increased. You may hear a throbbing in your ears because your blood is moving through your body faster. In the first example, you reacted with fear to what *may* have been a threatening situation; in the second, you reacted with action as a flight away from danger—stepping on the brakes. Adrenaline also effectively kills the appetite for food; that's why you don't normally feel like eating when you are tense and nervous—a state which increases the production of adrenaline.

The adrenal glands are the primary reactors to any kind of stress, but the entire body revs up to help you survive a stressful situation. The reaction is primitive, going far back into the beginning of the species, when we were cave people. In those days, stress was generally a life-threatening situation—facing an animal attack, running from an enemy or a fire, crossing a dangerous river, or moving over other treacherous terrain. It's not a *gray brain* reaction (from the logical and reasoning centers of the mind), but an instinctive, animal response, and it helped survival in the days before civilization. But today life requires the use of the gray brain for survival. Yet under pressure, we still react as if to a tangible stress. That reaction creates a situation in which the conscious is fighting the subconscious, and the mind is fighting the body.

A less subtle analogy would be an instance where your house is on fire and you rush back in to save your child. Every instinct, every subconscious impulse, would tell you to get as far away from the fire as you need for safety. Yet your reasoning mind overrides this and uses sense and logic to allow you to go into the fire, decide how to grab the child, and figure out how to get away. The whole time, your brain is fighting not to give in to panic and fear. So, as adrenaline rushes through the body as the first reaction to stress, the brain begins putting up a fight to overcome any animal reactions and reacts in a way which is suited to civilization. Your boss is unfair—you smile and take it instead of using the rock-on-the-head method of removing this stress. An elevator makes a strange sound—you disregard it and stay on until you reach your floor instead of rushing off in a panic.

Since the entire body operates faster under stress, more energy is used. The principles of energy are always the same, whether the energy is operating the body or a vacuum cleaner. The first principle of energy is that it can't exist without a source. This can be a waterfall, petroleum, or nutrients in the body. The second principle is that energy needs a power plant to convert the source into a usable or predetermined form. This can be a generator or a central nervous system. They are equivalent in terms of function. Another principle is that if any of the parts of the process don't work efficiently or if any part gets worn down, whether it be the source-gathering part, the conversion part, or the distribution part, the energy quotient will be lowered.

Long-term stress wears down the parts. Stress is one of the most wearing states in which the human body can exist. It depletes vital nutrients and decreases metabolic efficiency.

Long-term stress is very different from the quick over-in-a-moment event such as an earthquake or fall, robbery or auto accident. In the isolated stressful event, the body reacts suddenly and all at once, peaking instantly and then returning to a normal state. To facilitate this return, the body begins compensating for the havoc wreaked upon it by the stress reaction as soon as the threat is removed. You become weak and have to sit or lie down so that you are in a calmer and more restful position. You may close your eyes to dull the sensory input, compensating for the sensory overload which just took place. You may feel the need for comfort from others, a soothing arm around you or the presence of a concerned human. This gives you a feeling of protection and safety, overcoming the fear and feeling of being threatened. You don't want bright lights, noise, or a lot of activity around you. Your instincts are to place no demands on your body whatsoever so that it can use all its energy for repairing the effects of the reaction to the sudden sharp stress.

With long-term stress, you never have the opportunity for this repair. The body can't replenish itself. Mechanisms which prepare the body for dealing with stress have negative effects when they work overtime. For example, continuous stress has a noticeable effect on the digestive system. Instead of resting between snacks and meals, the digestive system may keep working, trying to keep the stomach empty so there will be no hindrance to the fight/flight reaction. This causes a frequent or even constant production of the acid juices which dissolve food so it can be metabolized. If there's no food to work on, the juice has nothing to neutralize itself with, so it begins working on the lining of the stomach or the intestine. Eventually, a hole is worn in these tissues and, if you catch it in time, your doctor will tell you that your stomach discomfort is caused by an ulcer. Then you may, for your health's sake, begin making an effort to deal with stress in a different way. Sometimes it's not caught in time and the hole goes right through the tissues. It's then called a perforated ulcer. The raw wound bleeds and may cause death from a massive internal hemorrhage. Or bacteria from the stomach or intestine can spill into other parts of the body, causing peritonitis.

Aside from *this* serious stress illness, the digestive system produces other symptoms. Flatulence and constipation or diarrhea are the most frequent. The entire gastric system is moving, sometimes so fast that food isn't fully digested. There's a correlation here between depression and the *type* of bowel reaction resulting from stress. Diarrhea is a panic response—the body evacuates its waste in preparation for flight. In fact, psychiatrists know that a patient who frequently has loose bowels is expressing a subconscious desire to get away from a troublesome situation. Constipation is an immobilization response, a depressive reaction. The person who reacts to stress with loose stools will be the kind to get an ulcer. The person who reacts with constipation is more likely to get depression.

In depression, all systems slow down, including the digestive system. Food may stay in the stomach so long that it begins to ferment, causing gas and bloating. In addition to the fact that depressives lose *all* appetites, including interest in food, the very act of eating often causes discomfort. The stomach doesn't produce *enough* acid, so it takes a longer time for food to be digested. In autopsies of depressives who have committed suicide, the stomach lining has been found to be paler than that of nondepressed people; not as much blood flows to the area.

The digestion of food takes a lot of energy, something which is limited in supply to the depressive. You may have noticed that you feel cooler, sometimes chilled, after eating. That's because blood is rushing to your abdomen to aid the gastric system. In depression, every function is lowered and works less efficiently; the process of turning food into fuel just doesn't go as smoothly.

That's why one of the most common physical complaints in depression is gastric distress. Many depressives become almost preoccupied with their bowels. When you understand what's happening to them internally, the obsession is not surprising.

Stress and "Brain Food"

Did you ever drink too much and wake up the next morning with a hangover? While the headache and sensitivity to noise are the most overwhelming feelings, you also feel dragged out, low on energy, and slightly depressed. Much of what you are feeling comes from a vitamin B deficiency. Alcohol destroys much of the body's supply of this vitamin, and it is this vitamin which is most needed by the central nervous system.

Vitamins B and C work together with a synergistic effect. One can't be metabolized without the other. Even if there is sufficient supply of *one* for the other to be used by the body, it still won't function efficiently without a large enough supply of the supportive vitamin.

Vitamin C is essential to the body's immune systems. It's the major nutrient used to manufacture collagen, the glue which holds our cells together. Without it, we get scurvy, an illness in which the body literally falls apart—it comes unglued. Vitamin C helps body tissues to repair themselves after exhaustion or injury. The B vitamins have a similar function in the brain and nerve cells. (There will be more on how these vitamins work in Chapter Nine.)

Stress causes both B and C to be used by the body at a faster rate. Health food stores sell a "super stress" vitamin formula which is mainly vitamin B with sufficient C for metabolism. (Don't buy B vitamins in this form, though. The super stress is an expensive vitamin, and it's cheaper to buy vitamin B straight and get your C separately. C is a relatively cheap vitamin.) B is so important to the brain cells that without it those cells will die off. And the brain, like the liver, does not regenerate. Once it has been damaged, it can't be repaired.

A depressive will usually test out on metabolic function tests as not having enough B in the system. There are some thoughts now that the connection between depression and stress is based on the fact that stress uses up vitamin B so fast that it causes a deficiency. After this deficiency has continued for a period of time, depression results as a natural reaction. It's a way of slowing the organism's reactions so that there is a lessened reaction to stress, and this is nature's logical way of conserving what little supply of this vitamin is still available to the brain cells so that they stay alive. While this theory has yet to be proven, the connection between stress and depression is too well established for medical science to be as yet unable to prevent depression by treating stress as a cause of disease.

Stages of Stress to Depression

There are three aspects which almost always precede a case of depression. First is a period of prolonged stress. This is of course a subjective matter. In one person a three-month stressful period may be considered prolonged. In another, there may be no signs of strain after three years of stress. But eventually, the body will react in a negative way.

The second aspect—one could almost call these aspects *stages*, because they come in sequence—is a feeling of being overwhelmed by all the pressures and things to be done. This can result in what could be called "circling" activity, the kind of thing one sees with a mouse caught in a trap. First it tries to get out, then it begins running around in circles. The circling activity of the person facing a mountain of things-to-be-done may consist of getting on the phone and talking for hours before tackling any of the work. One woman in Los Angeles always feels great pressure when it comes time to fill out her income tax. She'll lay out all her papers and receipts, get the form ready to be filled out—then go to the store, decide that she *must* visit a friend she hasn't seen in a while, realize that she hasn't done the mending for some time and she just *has* to do it right now. In other words, circling activity is trying to push the mountain out of sight by running all around it picking weeds.

The third stage is a feeling of powerlessness. It's a sense of helplessness, a sense that one has no control over one's fate.

Ron Stallmun is a good example. At 32, he was a perfectionist (as many depressives are) who was a salesman for a business machine company. But during the mini-recession of 1975, people weren't buying many business machines, especially the expensive ones made by Ron's company. At the same time, the entire field was changing. Computers had become less expensive and so easily available that Ron's company was in danger of having developed a line which would soon become obsolete. Ron's boss became testy and hard to get along with. Ron's customers became fewer and fewer. At the same time, his wife became pregnant with their third child—and the oldest one, a boy of 10, was expelled from school after getting into several violent fights. Ron now had to take time from his job to see that the boy was given proper psychiatric counseling. His wife couldn't drive the child to the therapist; the pregnancy made her carsick. Because of the company problems, the raise Ron had expected—had counted on—was delayed. Then came the news that his mother had had a stroke and would probably require medical care for the rest of her life. This happened just at the time Ron was trying to close a deal with a client for the largest order he had gotten all year. He had to interrupt the deal to fly across the country to see his mother.

When he got back, he noticed that he was low on patience. He would be sitting at his desk, calling potential clients for appointments, when he would get (in his words) "a spasm where I had to move." He would end the phone call and get up and move around. Then he found that, while speaking, he would lose the thread of what he had been saying and not be able to complete a sentence. He kept thinking that he was having little blackouts, because in the middle of a conversation he would not remember what the other person had said.

"I found I couldn't read the business reports. I'd start to, and really be interested—but then my mind would go to sleep or something, because I'd suddenly realize that I had no idea what I'd just read. Then I began getting clumsy. I'd knock over an ashtray while reaching for the phone, or trip over the edge of a rug. These things grew so frustrating that I'd feel tears come to my eyes. A few weeks later, the tears wouldn't just come, they'd be pouring down my cheeks. I remember thinking, a grown man crying because he spilled a glass of tomato juice! But I didn't know anything was wrong then."

Ron started missing appointments. He would "circle"—straightening papers on his desk, going through the files—until he was late. Then he began driving up to the place he was supposed to be and find himself unable to get out of the car. "I couldn't take another rejection. If they didn't want to buy from me, they were rejecting *me*, not what I was selling. I'd walk into a place with my shoulders slumped, just knowing they'd say no. When one firm wanted to order a series of machines, I couldn't believe it. I had my case out with all the books and they were saying yes and I was saying, 'You really want to buy this machine? But what if it doesn't work?' I didn't realize until later that I was trying to talk them out of the sale. I was feeling that if *I* was selling this machine, it couldn't be much good. And I was afraid it would break down or that the company wouldn't live up to its repair agreement and that these people would blame me. I know that sounds insane now, but at the time it seemed . . . *right*."

At home, Ron grew so irritable that his family started tiptoeing out of the way when he came home. He began waking up at three or four in the morning with anxiety attacks. He couldn't stand the feelings of dread which sometimes bordered on terror.

"It was like a sinking feeling in my stomach, so bad that it was almost like a physical pain. I'd go downstairs and start smoking. I'd usually go through a whole pack in a few hours, by the time it grew light."

The heavy smoking caused a cough. Ron became convinced he had cancer. He started dropping vague exit hints to his wife: "Your troubles will be over when I'm out of the way." "I don't deserve you, so don't spend time mourning if I should die."

Ron's wife is a loving, gentle woman. But her mind was on the coming child and she too was involved in the problems which beset the family. She realized something was happening to her husband but didn't know what and had no idea how to cope with it. So she responded in the usual way mates and relatives respond to a case of depression. First, she showed her concern and tried to drag Ron out of it by "cheering" him up. That didn't work. She poured her heart out to her parish clergyman, who asked Ron to come in and talk with him. But while this man was compassionate and understanding, he knew nothing of the illness. He advised Ron to turn to God and come to church more frequently. This had a negative effect on Ron. He interpreted the clergyman's talk as confirming his own secret opinion that he was the worst of guilty sinners. On the way home from the talk, he said to his wife, "Even God doesn't want me." And his wife, Sandi, blew up. She told Ron that he was feeling sorry for himself and that if he didn't pull out of this funk she was going to scream. Of course, Ron took this as just more of the same rejection he felt he was getting everywhere else. Sandi's patience was gone by now, and she reacted as most people do to a continuing case of depression—with anger and hostility.

Ron still went to work nearly every day. But his frequent absences and lack of efficiency became too noticeable to be ignored. His boss called him in and suggested he take a vacation. And of course, Ron saw this as an attempt to ease him out of his job.

By now, the situation was in its second month. Ron saw nothing ahead for him, no future, no hope. He decided to commit suicide.

He made his preparations carefully. Because of Sandi's carsickness, she rarely left the house except to see the obstetrician once every two weeks. Ron arranged for Sandi to go to the doctor with a neighbor, told the children to go to friends' homes after school, and wrote out a short will and suicide note. He had heard that a combination of tranquilizers and alcohol is lethal, and Sandi had been taking tranquilizers for a few weeks—a full bottle was right there in the medicine chest. Ron took half the bottle, then couldn't swallow any more. He poured himself a glass of whiskey, gulped it down, then poured another. The whiskey bottle wasn't full, but Ron finished what there was, figured it would be enough, and staggered over to the bed in a bleary haze, waiting for death. He remembers that his last thought was wishing he had gotten under the covers because the house was cold, but he didn't have the strength.

Sandi, in the meantime, grew more and more uneasy. As she and the neighbor pulled into the parking garage of the medical center, she had an overwhelming urge to go back home. At first, she tried to ignore it, but the feeling was too insistent. Finally, she told the neighbor that even though it seemed crazy, she wanted to cancel her appointment and go back.

Sandi later said: "I'm not the kind to be superstitious, but I have learned that sometimes it pays to play your hunches. I felt a pressure to get back home *right now*. I didn't connect this with Ron in any way. He had told me he was going to spend the day in the park. I thought maybe there was a fire or a break-in or something. All I knew was that I had to be there."

All the way home she kept pushing her neighbor to hurry. As the car reached the driveway, she rushed out and inside. But there was no feeling of relief when she saw that nothing was disturbed. She looked into each room, and found Ron in bed, with the covers twisted around his body. As he passed out, he had evidently tried to cover himself.

The suicide note was on the night table, but Sandi *knew*, without having to open it, what the subject matter was. She ran to the phone and called an ambulance.

Ron was in a coma for two days. When he came out of it, he was still groggy and spent most of the week sleeping. The hospital kept him for observation and one of the doctors diagnosed depression. Nine days after Ron had tried to end his life, he was put on anti-depressants. He left the hospital and for the next three weeks he was like a zombie, sleeping most of the time and feeling like a vegetable even when he was awake. (Anti-depressives often cause a drugged feeling in the patient for a short time. The feeling can range from that of being slightly sedated to that of trying to function while under the effects of a sleeping pill. It passes as soon as the body adjusts to the medication, usually in a week or two. In Ron's case, it lasted nearly three weeks.)

Sandi did a smart thing during this period. Realizing that she could not give Ron the support he needed and still take care of the children and house, she hired a nurse for him. The nurse bathed and cared for Ron and was able to suggest a therapist who specialized in depression, so that Ron didn't have to go to the hospital psychiatric clinic. After the groggy effects of the medication wore off, Ron began seeing this doctor twice a week. His symptoms lost most of their severity in six weeks. But the depressive episode lasted for about five months. During this time he was able to keep things together and function, even though it was minimal functioning. But he learned to take things easier. He stopped making three or four appointments a day and learned to make only one. He learned to tell himself that a nonsale was not a personal rejection, and after a while he began to believe it. The baby was born two months before his depression lifted. At first, Sandi was worried that the baby might upset Ron's precarious equilibrium, but both she and the therapist were too aware of Ron's illness to let him succumb to regression. Sandi again hired a nurse to help her care for the baby and spent as much time as she could giving loving support to Ron. The birth didn't seem to affect him negatively, but Ron remembers feeling a sense of panic when the baby was born.

"I wondered if I could support him. I didn't feel anything else, not good, not bad. He wasn't quite real to me. I felt separated from him, and didn't begin feeling any emotions about him for a couple of months."

Ron had been sleeping the whole night through since he began taking the anti-depressants, though he woke up earlier than he had before the illness hit. One morning, five months and eleven days after he had begun treatment, he woke up "feeling that something was different." It was on the way to work that he realized what it was. He had an appointment with a long-time client and had always enjoyed talking with one of the executives of that company. He was looking forward to seeing him when he made the call.

"This hadn't happened since I got depressed. I never looked forward to anything, I was just thankful to make it through the day. For some reason, being able to be enthusiastic about a meeting gave me a feeling of confidence. It was so noticeable that a couple of people in the office remarked on how happy I looked. In retrospect, I see that I wasn't *happy*, I was just normal, normal for me. I knew I was walking differently; instead of slumping around, I was walking the way I used to—quick and bouncy."

The next day, when Ron saw the doctor, he remarked on how good he had felt for the last two days. He wondered if he was "cured." The therapist told Ron that "cure" is a relative word in depression, but it was quite possible that his central nervous system had once again returned to its proper function. He advised Ron to continue taking medication for a while and adopted a wait and see attitude, asking Ron to do the same. And while there were still some days when Ron felt blue and alone, he could cope with them. Four weeks later he stopped taking anti-depressants. Aside from one minor episode five years later, Ron has never been pulled down into depression again. Even the reoccurrence didn't incapacitate him; he continued working and dealing with his everyday problems.

During his *severe* depression, Ron and his therapist had worked out a diet and sleep regimen especially suited to cyclic depressions. The diet was high in protein and B vitamins—liver and other organ meats were on the menu twice a week—and low in sugars and fried foods. Ron stayed away from candy bars and processed snacks such as potato chips. He planned his evenings so that he got a minimum of eight hours sleep a night. And he developed a process of conscious relaxation, almost like meditation, which consisted of deep breathing and muscle relaxation. (This relaxation method will be detailed later.)

Ron and Sandi were extremely fortunate. They received an accurate diagnosis, found a specialist who could treat the condition, had the money to hire outside help, which removed enough strain from Sandi so she had patience to give Ron the loving support he needed to see him through the illness. But you don't need to have all these factors to help someone you love through a depressive episode. Sandi was working from ignorance. Not as much was known about depression then as is known today. If Sandi had been able to see what was happening with Ron, the situation would not have become so extreme and Ron would have been helped before he got to the point of wanting to take his life.

Measuring Stress

Reactions to stress vary as much as reactions to food. One person can eat two candy bars a day and never gain an ounce. Another can eat one once a month and gain five pounds. One person can undergo a sequence of negative events without feeling the stress. Another can have a slightly bad thing happen and reverberate for days. So how can you measure stress?

To be honest, figuring out a stress quotient is not so much measuring as estimating. First of all, any extreme is stressful (we're talking now about mental stress, not the physical stress of injury, operations, or disease). Boredom is a stress. Many healthy people who have spent a productive life, active and involved, look forward to retirement as a time of reaping the rewards of an industrious life. Now they can relax, now they can begin achieving all their leisure dreams. But after retirement, they seem to get smaller. They fade. Many sink into depression or become ill with other diseases. These people made no plans for all this free time, or the plans they made were of short duration and were quickly accomplished. Boredom preys upon them. They become fidgety, irritable, and restless. The lucky ones will realize what the problem is and take another job, one chosen for pleasure rather than income, or chosen for challenge or to build up a sense of being needed in the world again. The unlucky ones will keep their retirement and after a few years, suffer from one of the diseases of the aged, such as stroke or heart attack. Or they will vegetate from depression. They may even die from a flu or other minor illness. Boredom, like inertia, is a stress.

Its opposite, overactivity, is also a stress. Trying to do three things at once and excel at them all, trying to meet deadlines under pressure—that is wearing on every part of the system. It doesn't matter whether you're an executive who has to fill out a report, keep an appointment, and make some heavy decisions all within a short time; or a housewife who has to clean the house, plan dinner, pick up the children and drive them somewhere all within a few hours. Extremes are stressful.

Change is also stressful. When we get used to something, our mind files it and allows us to think and act in mental shorthand, rather than thinking everything out thoroughly over and over again. Take driving as an example. Your mind can be thinking about work, reliving a memory, or doing your income tax while you are involved in an activity upon which your life depends. As you play out scenarios or finalize plans in your head, your hands automatically shift gears and turn the wheel, your feet automatically step on the accelerator or the brake or the clutch. Your eyes and ears are alert to what is happening on the road, sending signals which tell your hands and feet what to do. Yet all this time, you can be thinking about something else so intently that you might look up with surprise when you realize how close you are to your destination.

Yet if you suddenly found yourself behind the wheel of a truck or other vehicle you never drove before, you couldn't afford to shift your mind to other places while putting your driving on automatic. The truck would be a change and you wouldn't have automatic responses yet. You would have to devote your full attention to what you were doing until you grew used to it.

It's the same with any change. We depend on certain mental codes which eliminate the necessity of thinking each situation anew. Example: Here comes Joe. You know Joe. You know he's a friend, and you don't have to put your guard up. You don't have to *think* about Joe because you have already done that. He is categorized in your mental filing system. Your thoughts and responses to him, while personalized, are somewhat automatic, based on your knowledge of him. Because of it, you are at ease with Joe.

But suppose Joe, normally quiet and reserved and conservatively dressed, shows up in a loud checked suit which is dirty and rumpled. Instead of his usual low-key manner, he is loud and aggressive. At first, you would be concerned and alarmed. You might ask him what's wrong. If he tells you "nothing," and shows no signs of returning to his former personality, you would find yourself shying away a little. *This* isn't Joe, not the Joe you know. This is someone different. You would find it hard to accept this person. In time, you might grow used to the change, but it would mean rethinking Joe, replacing the old image you had of him with a new one.

This mental refiling is hard work. It's the reason that most people are so resistant to change. The older we get, the longer we have usually held our ideas, so rethinking them is even harder. This is the reason that the young are more adaptable to change, while the older one is, the less he or she likes change.

There's actually a stress scale which uses change as a basis of measurement. In 1972, Dr. Thomas Holmes, a professor of psychiatry at a medical school in Seattle, wrote an article about a 25-year-long research project on stress-producing experiences. He developed a scale of points for each stressful change. During his research, Holmes had discovered that many physical illnesses were preceded by a combination of these stresses—good and bad. The Holmes scale is used today by many doctors to predict an illness potential based on a patient's current life events. Although Holmes didn't use his scale to predict depression, nearly everyone with a case of depression can point to a number of the experiences used as a measurement of stress on this scale.

The Holmes scale is reprinted here so you can use it to gauge the level of stressful changes in the life of someone close to you, or in your own life. Each event has a number after it; this is the stress quotient for that event. When you have checked off the events on the list which apply to the person you are concerned about, add up the number and compare them to the scale. Use a one-year time period to measure an inclusive stress score. You will then get an idea of how much stress the person has been under. The Holmes scale predicts that a major illness will occur within two years of collecting a high total and lesser illnesses within a two-year period of a medium score. It is Holmes's theory that the crises listed in his scale actually cause illness. But considering the relationship between stress and depression, the scale might be a better predictor of a potential depressive episode.

The Holmes Stress Scale

1.	Death of a spouse	100
2.	Divorce	73
3.	Marital separation	65
4.	Jail term	63
5.	Death of close family member	63
6.	Personal injury or illness	53
7.	Marriage	50
8.	Being fired from job	47
9.	Marital reconciliation	45
10.	Retirement	45
11.	Change in health of family member	44
12.	Pregnancy	44
13.	Sexual difficulties	39
14.	Gain of new family member	39
15.	Business readjustment	39
16.	Financial change	39
17.	Death of close friend	39
18.	Move to different type of work	36
19.	Change in number of arguments with spouse	35
20.	Mortgage over $10,000 (this was pre-inflation sum, today change to $28,000)	31
21.	Foreclosure of mortgage or loan	30
22.	Change in work responsibilities	29
23.	Departure of child from home	29
24.	Trouble with in-laws	29
25.	High personal achievement	28
26.	Spouse's beginning or stopping work	26
27.	Beginning or end of school	26
28.	Change in living conditions	25
29.	Change in personal habits	24
30.	Trouble with boss	23
31.	Change in work hours or conditions	20
32.	Change in residence	20

33. Change in school	20
34. Change in recreational activity	19
35. Change in church activities	19
36. Change in social activities	18
37. Mortgage or loan under $15,000	17
38. Change in sleeping habits	16
39. Change in number of family get-togethers	14
40. Change in diet or eating habits	15
41. Vacation	13
42. Christmas	12
43. Minor violations of law	11

I would make a few additions to this scale: I would change number 22 to read, *Any change in responsibilities*, and in addition add the following stress factors: 40 points for any serious *Personal setback or failure of plan or goal*; 39 points for *Affair*, whether you or your spouse is having one; 30 points for *Destruction or serious damage to home or car*; 15 points for *Loss of close friend*.

According to the Holmes scale, you have a fair chance of getting ill once you accumulate over 150 points. Up to 200 is low. From 225 to 300 is medium, which means you have a 50–50 chance of becoming ill. A total of 325 or more is high. If you have accumulated any of these score totals in a relatively short period of time—say, within one year—you should very carefully watch for a reaction to the level of stress you have suffered. If you are testing another person, remember that everyone's response to stress differs; Dr. Holmes' scale predictions, based on a 25-year research project, have reference to the *average* response to stress.

Unavoidable Stress

If you listen to most advice given about stress, you'll usually hear two flat statements: (1) that most stresses are avoidable and (2) that you must get away from the stressful situation. Well, in a way that's true. If your job is stressful and you've tried but can't get another position at the same level and salary, you can always be a beach bum. And of course, it's possible to leave a marriage after several decades and run away. These are not solutions. Unfortunately, people who make those cheerful statements fail to give individual instructions. Yes, some stresses are avoidable.

However, if they *were* so easy to get away from, most people *would* take the fastest exit. No one likes feeling tense, nervous, and haggard from being under a strain. While I would like to give lots of Pollyanna advice on how you can get rid of stress in your own life or help someone else to do the same, that kind of hogwallop doesn't do much good. It may inspire someone to action or the intent of action, but the pressures we develop in life have their own momentum and inertia. They persist.

Granted that there are certain personality traits which create the same stresses over and over again, regardless of what new person or place arises and offers a chance to start over with a clear slate. But no one is going to rid him/herself of these traits merely by hoping to do so. Furthermore, some stressful situations come of themselves, without the person involved having any conscious control over them. Since the stress is impossible to avoid without making major changes which in themselves would cause stress, the only alternative is to change the method of *reacting* to the situation.

Lisa Goodman is a superb example of a person who changed her reaction to an unavoidable stress. Lisa is a radio reporter in Los Angeles, and we met while covering various stories for our respective radio stations. Even though Los Angeles is perhaps *the* major radio and television market in the country, the electronic media people there are like a small community. They know each other and know all about the executives and operations of all the other stations.

Lisa's station was renowned for the bullying tactics of its news director. A bigoted, irrational man whose conservative attitudes were so far to the right and so rigid that everyone wondered how he kept his job, the news director (call him Dan) was such a bully that he was actually a joke among the other reporters in town. The main target for his fear-provoking and intimidation tactics was women. Dan didn't believe women should be employed in news. He was also an insecure man, and the more competent a woman was, the more insecure she made him—and the rougher he was on her.

Lisa loved her job and had no desire to leave it. But somehow, she became the focus for the news director's cruelties. After several months of this kind of pressure, she started looking around for a job at other stations. But getting an on-the-air job in

Los Angeles is hard, and there were no doors open to Lisa. She complained to the general manager of her station, but nothing was done. So she had a choice: give up her job, stay in Los Angeles, and work in some other capacity; move to another city where on-air jobs were more readily available; succumb to the situation and let it drag her down; or change her way of dealing with the stress of the situation.

Lisa chose to deal with it in a different way, but not at first. At first she spent each day at work tense and unhappy, trying to defend herself against unfair accusations and vicious attacks from Dan. This went on for almost a year. Then she decided to try befriending him by playing to his ego. She flattered him at every opportunity, asked his advice about her work, and played out a scene which she now sheepishly calls "little girl to big daddy." That went fine and for a few months Dan was off her back. But a combination of circumstances happened to place Lisa in the way of one of Dan's frequent irrational outbursts. The man always lost his cool during a big story, trying to keep such a tight control over everything that there would be many mistakes made in getting the story on the air. A large brush fire had broken out earlier in the day, and toward the afternoon it looked as though it was moving in on a residential area. As usual, when a story of this importance broke, Dan was running around yelling and giving orders, then counteracting them and generally creating chaos. Lisa made a suggestion about handling the story differently.

Dan turned on her, threatened to "rearrange" her face, called her several insulting names in front of the whole newsroom, and told her that if she said one more word she would be fired.

Lisa understood for the first time that nothing would work with this person, whether she did her job well, became his bosom buddy, played every ego game possible—none of it would matter. She realized that you can't predict or control the actions of an irrational bully (of which there are many in the business world, though few are as obvious as this one).

For a few months Lisa became so discouraged that she no longer cared how well she did her job. In fact, she was danger-ously close to descending into a "broken" air person, a common phenomenon in this business. They go about their jobs routinely, with little energy or verve, accepting the most obvious angles and not looking for the different spark which will make their stories special. She lost the pride in her job that had made it a pleasure, stopped putting in the hours of free overtime she used to spend rewriting and recording a piece until it "felt" right. The stress continued, though, and Lisa felt depressed about her job and herself.

We talked about the situation often, and several times she broke into tears. Her vacation was coming up, and mine followed soon after she returned, so I didn't see her for a while. One day she called and asked me to have lunch. When I saw her, I was amazed. Instead of the pain-filled eyes and little worry wrinkles which had aged her face the last time I had seen her, Lisa was sparkling and vibrant. I hadn't seen her this way since Dan became news director two years before. And she couldn't wait to talk about the change.

While on vacation, Lisa had spent most of her time thinking about her work situation. She also bought a copy of a Los Angeles newspaper every day, and it was an article in this paper that had sparked her turnaround. The article dealt with the reasons why people couldn't hold jobs, and among the list of firable flaws, the top one was not getting along with others. That started a whole new train of thought. She knew she wasn't the only one having a problem with Dan. In fact, the other women reporters and anchorpeople had even had a meeting about the personality problems the man was having with nearly everyone in the news department, but it was a bell-the-cat solution and no one wanted to be the person who went to management with the problem. The other newspeople at the station weren't organized or involved enough with each other to act constructively to resolve the situation, and Lisa knew that while her workmates would be sympathic, she could get no help from them.

Lisa said, "I knew I needed two things; hope that the situation would change and some proof that would be valid to me that it would change. I had been hoping that Dan would change toward me. Then I realized that wouldn't happen. And in thinking about it, I also realized that I had let the problem obsess me. It was all I could see. So while I spent less mental involvement with my work, I hadn't involved myself with anything else as a release."

The *hope* Lisa needed came from the newspaper article. Knowing that Dan had a problem getting along with others, and that even though higher management tried to ignore the problem they were aware of it, Lisa began thinking, "It's only a matter of time until he reaches a point where even the general manager sees that he's having a bad effect on morale—and that because of his problem, the station isn't operating as well as it should be or could be." She laughed when telling me about this part of her change. "Maybe I'm feeding myself a line, but it's a line I can believe and wait for, no matter how long it takes." She then could state her problems with Dan in a way that made them bearable and easy to handle: "Every time I looked at him, I kept one thought in mind: that they would have to let him go eventually and that my only priority was to mark time and stay there until he was gone. But in the meantime, I still will look around for a job at another station."

Lisa's state of mind was such that she couldn't relax and forget about the situation by spending more social time with friends. So she looked around for something that would get her mind off work and act as therapy for her stress. She tried jogging but found it much too active. So she started a garden.

"It gave me something to be involved in. Working in the earth, making things grow, gave me a sense of accomplishment that overcame a lot of my sense of diminishment at work. I made it a discipline. I would get up every morning an hour earlier and go out and grub among the plants. It gave me a sense of serenity that was like a shield at work. Even when I was devastated by some injustice, I would think of my garden, and the frustration would stop goading me into taking some verbal stance I knew I would regret. The garden became a symbol, as trivial as that sounds. But I needed hope and I needed a symbol to help me keep in mind that although this was *happening* to me, it was outside of me, the situation *wasn't me*, but a passing negative event in my life. And my life would continue long after it was over."

I have gone into great detail about Lisa because her solution is one of the best I have ever heard for dealing with unavoidable stress. The key phrase is: *This is a situation I am passing through. Even if I do not pass through it to a desired outcome, there will come a time when the pain will be past, and I will feel good.*

If you know that your mate or other loved one is undergoing

a stressful time, you may have to do more than provide verbal comfort. You may have to be the one to provide the realization that all things must pass, including the tension of the present situation, and of course, that is best done verbally. But you will further have to work at getting the person involved in something that acts as therapy. If, for example, a son or daughter is working on a project, a temporary stress, you might be able to take a weekend trip. Bring the project if the youngster insists, but talk him or her into getting away. If the stress is a continuous one such as a job problem or financial upset, think carefully about the person's interests and figure out what new hobby might be appealing. Use more than gentle persuasion to get the person involved on a daily basis with that hobby; make plans and, if necessary, buy the equipment needed for that involvement. One woman who was concerned about the stress her husband was under borrowed an expensive camera from a friend and bought twenty rolls of film. She suggested going out for a walk and photographing the ordinary things found in the neighborhood. He muttered something about not having the time or energy, but she persisted, finally buying an inexpensive camera for herself and asking him to accompany her. She made sure to have every roll he shot developed immediately, and they would spend hours looking at the shots. She made these photo sessions so much fun that soon even she forgot their original purpose. The man grew interested enough in photography to begin investing in equipment.

After hearing of this and many similar experiences, I believe there's a rule which can be applied here: There's no time like a negative, stressful period in one's life to get involved in a new hobby. An outside interest having nothing to do with the other troublesome aspects of one's life can be therapeutic, helping repair the drain of energy caused by stress. This technique is derived from a scientific approach to problem solving. When scientists are working on highly technical problems, they often hit a snag where, because of their closeness to the problem, they can no longer think creatively about it. When that happens, they will stop trying to get the answer and turn to something else. When they have given their minds a chance to rest from the single track it was running on, they will return to the problem with fresh vigor. That same approach, when used to handle daily stress, will often give the breathing space necessary to keep one from succumbing to it.

The Biggest Excuse

As you read this, you might be saying, "I don't have time to get involved in something new." This is the same response you will probably get when you try to involve someone else in something new. Nonsense! You have all the time there is. When anyone is under a lot of pressure, they very rarely approach every second of their time with direct efficiency. No matter how you deny it to yourself, or how someone else will deny it to you, stress creates a lot of circling activity. No matter how busy someone is, you can be sure that he or she isn't devoting every single moment to finishing everything that has to be done. First of all, *no one* has that type of concentration. Second, the reason no one has that type of concentration is that it's not humanly possible to spend all of one's time directly involved in one single pursuit. Even the most obsessed mind will wander. The mind will *take* the break that the consciousness tries to deny it; attention will stray, repetition and inefficiency will prevent progress if one pushes the mind in one direction too hard.

The problem is finding the time among the hours you have available (or someone else has available). This is why, if you are observing someone else, you are in a good position to find the time for that person. We can see the circling activity of others better than we can see our own. In fact, if you're using this book as a guideline for yourself rather than for someone else, use a piece of paper as your observer. Make a list of everything you did during one day, no matter how trivial, from driving to work to picking up the paper. Let's say the day began at 8:00 A.M. and ended at 10:00 P.M. That's fourteen hours. With sixty minutes to each hour, the day consisted of 840 minutes. Divide the total number of activities into 840. You'll get an idea of the average time it took to perform each activity, including the trivial ones. A shock, right? How could you have spent all that time doing—what? When you look at your day divided up like this, you can see how much time you really have and how much of it was spent in circling activity. You won't be able to convince yourself that you "don't have time" to take a few minutes, even an hour, to do something that makes you feel better. And, if you're trying to get someone else involved in something to make *them* feel better, neither will they.

Time isn't something you have, it's something you make. You can look at time as a lump of steel. As a lump, it's worth a few dollars. Made into the body of a car, it's worth a lot more. Made into watch springs, it's worth ten thousand times what it was as a lump of steel. Neither you nor anyone else is going to be able to use every moment of the day getting necessary things done. The area to attack is the time spent circling around the getting-things-done activity.

If you spend circling time having a conversation with the supermarket checker while the mind stays involved in the daily stresses, that is again circling. It's better to say, "This conversation is what I'm doing with my spare time, and I'm doing it to make myself feel better and lift myself out of the stress feelings of the day." Then, if you see that the conversation isn't what you want to spend your spare time *on* (time being money in the sense that it is your decision how you will spend it), you will have the perspective to spend your time in a way which will give you more value for it. So if you're saying you don't have time to escape from your stress, or if someone else tells you the same, *take* the time at least to figure out exactly what all those hours of time are buying.

When the Mind Is Too Cluttered for New Input

Sometimes, especially in pre-depression cases, the mind is racing too hard to settle on any one thing. It can be compared to a car set in neutral gear when a foot presses down on the accelerator. The motor is revved up, the fuel is being consumed, but there is no real activity. A lot is going on in the car, but the main function of all this activity—motion—is not being performed. There's an even better analogy for this mental state. When we experience various events, we tend to file them away, making mental codes that give us data for the future and integrating the experience into the other parts of our reality. A mind that is busy with circling activity, rather than with forward motion, will usually be crowded with a hundred little details which remain unfiled. The human dynamos, the hell-bent-for-success types, can rush right along ignoring all the details that aren't directly concerned with business. Then, later in life, these people have so lost touch with themselves that they are adrift, with no awareness of who they are. In a way, their forward motion has the same long-term effects as the "circler"—they neglect to put the contents of their mind in order. It's similar to the car analogy used before. There *is* forward motion—but there is far more "revving" and fuel consumption than necessary—or, in the long run, safe. True mental health depends on filing everything we think and experience, thinking about things enough so that they aren't just floating around in our minds, unconnected to anything else.

However, there are instances when a new activity should *not* be considered. People who have allowed their minds to become cluttered with unfiled details—in other words, who let the pressures of things undone and problems not resolved overwhelm them—are creating minds which constantly race without going anywhere. The agitation of the prodromal period of depression usually stems from this cluttered feeling in the mind. There's too much happening for the mind to focus on any one thing. There's a state of rolling confusion as thoughts skip from one thing to another, touching on worries, problems, things to do, past mistakes, and a myriad of other draining thought patterns. In this type of pre-depressive, starting a new activity is the worst thing that could happen. The person is already in a state in which one detail, one new thing, can be the straw that breaks the camel's back. What is needed is not a new activity, but rest. If you are trying preventative care on someone you care about, or if you recognize these descriptions as fitting your own mental state, you have to find a way to create an environment for that rest. It may be something as simple as lying down in a dark room with no disturbing sounds for an hour before dinner; it may be being closely held by a caring, comforting friend. One good method of easing a busy brain is a massage. When muscles tight from tension are kneaded and rubbed into relaxation, the mind follows. Remember, mind and body are inseparable. This is why we often feel so good after working out tensions in hard physical activity. The body that exhausts itself physically does not have the energy for tension. It needs to rest. And when the body is exhausted, the tensions of the mind often flow out too. One is just too tired to give the energy needed mentally to race madly through all that clutter. If stress and tension are beginning to wear on you or a loved one, try relaxing the body, either through conscious effort, massage, or physical activity.

If you are looking out for someone else, you will have to use a discerning eye here. How does the person react to new details? Do his jaws tense when he is faced with another thing to deal with? Does she complain about not having "time to think"? If the person constantly seems to be racing the clock, suggesting a new hobby or activity is not indicated. But if stress results in meaningless circling activity, and you can see that the problem is not too little time but lack of using that time efficiently, you might have to help the person look at the time more objectively, thus eliminating the stress of too little time and creating time for an activity which will help get the mind off the stress. What this means is that time spent in circling activity—that is to say, non-productive time—must be directed toward accomplishment activity—either the accomplishment of tangible productivity or of much needed rest and relaxation.

5.

Chemical, Electrical, and Verbal Therapy

Depression will many times go away by itself. The same is true of many illnesses. Pneumonia will go away, if the patient lives. So will diphtheria and colitis, if the case is not too serious and if there are no complications and if death does not come before recovery. But immunization can prevent many of these illnesses, just as the right kind of precautions can prevent depression. And, once the illness has begun, therapy will make it go away.

In illnesses caused by bacteria, the therapy is in the form of drugs. But there are three main kinds of therapy for depression. One is verbal, administered by a trained therapist. Another is a wide range of anti-depressant drugs, and these are usually given in conjunction with verbal therapy. And the third is ECT, electro-convulsive therapy, or shock treatments.

In shock, the patient is restrained, usually through drugs (though in earlier years shackles were used). Electrodes are applied to the temples, and doses of electricity are applied to the brain.

This is one way of curing depression. Unfortunately, it is not a very good or often very lasting way.

ECT creates horror in most people's minds because of how it was administered in the past. Formerly, the current caused the entire central nervous system to convulse. The convulsions were occasionally so strong that the bones in rigidified limbs would break under the muscular strain. When the patients came to (ECT produced a loss of consciousness and still does), they would not remember the pain of the shocks. In fact they wouldn't remember anything about it and often could not remember anything that had happened for several days before the treatment.

ECT today is more gentle. There are no wild convulsions. Gags do not have to be put in patients' mouths to keep them from breaking off teeth by the force of a clenched jaw, though precautions must still be taken to see that the tongue isn't bitten or swallowed. The patients receive two injections; a barbiturate which knocks them out and a muscle relaxant which eliminates the convulsions.

The patients usually recover consciousness within about fifteen minutes after ECT treatment. There is often a headache, and sometimes the jaw hurts from having been clenched during treatment. At first they don't recognize their surroundings or anyone in the room. Gradually, recognition returns and the grogginess and headache go away. Memory of the treatment and of the hours or days prior to the treatment *never* returns.

ECT treatments vary. They can be given three times a week for a month, or a few times a week every other month. But after around six or seven series of treatments, a memory loss (or an impairment in the memory function) begins to develop. There may be forgetfulness of an appointment or a telephone number or even the name of a friend. This memory loss is much worse during the course of the treatment, and clears up quite a bit after the ECT course is finished. Many doctors say it clears up totally. However, I've talked to a lot of people who have had anywhere from 5 to 25 ECT treatments. Most of them did recover from depression very quickly (within two months) after ECT, but all had the same two complaints: their memory was never as good as it was before the ECT, and they themselves were changed by the treatment.

Though doctors argue about the degree of memory loss incurred by ECT (no one has ever measured the percentage of intelligence which depends on memory, but it is considerable), all doctors admit that this type of therapy alters brain function. Those in favor of ECT say that it alters the brain toward a positive, rather than a negative, response. But in interviewing more than 25 people treated by ECT, I found one thing in common: they had dulled. Although I knew fewer than half of them before their treatment, the change in those individuals was remarkable. Yes, there was a serenity that was absent during their depressions, but it was a bland serenity. In one person, whom I had admired for his creativity, the creative spark seemed extinguished. He was normal in the traditional sense of that word—he held a job, was interested in establishing financial security for his family—but he no longer had the spontaneity that had made him a charming and popular person. Where once he had written moving poetry, he no longer showed any interest in writing.

Most of those I interviewed in the ECT group also showed the same lack of spontaneity. They seemed settled, almost vague. One woman told me that she would rather have her depression than to have gone through the ECT; her mind felt like a stranger's and she seemed to have lost the thrust that made her a real go-getter.

This is not to say that ECT is a totally bad therapy. It's quick. In the case of someone who has deteriorated to the point of being intensely suicidal, it's probably the best form of treatment. Every doctor can tell you stories of patients who were given other forms of treatment during a suicidal period and who managed to take their lives regardless of constant observation. However, the benefits should be measured against what may possibly be permanent effects. While not everyone suffers from these side effects, the element of risk is great enough so that ECT should not be taken as an easy way out unless the condition is so serious that there's no other choice.

If a doctor has recommended this treatment for a relative of yours (this is usually the only circumstance in which you will be involved in making the decision), you have to weigh the decision carefully. If you have serious reservations, say *no*. It will be worse on the patient if you are apprehensive. The depressive will pick up this anxiety and resist not only the treatment but possibly the benefits from it. Side effects will be exaggerated and your reserve may cause a traumatic reaction in the depressive. If you *do* decide that ECT is the best course, you must put yourself and your relative totally in the doctor's hands.

One factor may cause trouble: no food must be eaten for at least four hours prior to treatment. There is almost always an order that no liquids be consumed. You will have to keep a close eye on your relative to see that these orders are obeyed. The person may feel paranoid or resentful that he or she can't have anything to eat or drink, and there may be a pathetic reaction of being persecuted. You will have to deal with this. If liquids or solids are in the stomach, it may be vomited up during treatment and, because of the anesthetic, inhaled into the lungs. The result may be suffocation, unless emergency treatment is given immediately. Of course, any hospital (where treatments are always given) will have equipment to deal with the situation, but it's still risky. So obey the doctor here. No water means not even a sip. Afterwards, create a calm, restful environment for the person. Keep talk and loud noises at a minimum. The patient may wish to sleep for a few hours. Let him.

The ECT patient can't drive for a day or more after a treatment. Most doctors will categorically state that a patient shouldn't drive for the entire period ECT is being administered. Also, few patients can continue to work at their regular job during a course of ECT treatments. This is why this type of therapy is usually performed on hospitalized patients. Normal life, that is, driving and working, can usually start within two or three weeks after the entire series of ECT treatments has been given.

Drug Therapy

There are dozens of different brands of anti-depressants, and more are created every year. It's a very profitable field. There are four main categories of these drugs used in treatment, and each is applicable to a specific type of depression.

As we've already discussed, the subtleties of symptoms are what separate a retarded depression from an agitated one, or indicate a case where distortion or paranoia is predominant. Each of these symptomatic qualities indicates that a different hormone or combination of hormones is at fault. The doctor has a difficult choice: he or she must balance the patient's need for immediate relief against the time span necessary for proper diagnosis. This takes skill bordering on brilliance. The differences in symptoms are often so slight that the need for urgency causes a misdiagnosis. In addition, some doctors play guessing games with drugs. A doctor who has not kept up with the latest research, who received a degree before the early 1960's, will often not be aware of the latest discoveries in the field of anti-depressant therapy. This kind of doctor may begin with one type of drug, see that it's not working efficiently, switch to another class of drug, and so on until the right chemical help is found. It's a trial-and-error method which eventually works but can prolong a patient's agony while doing so.

Fortunately, many more doctors today are thoroughly trained in accurate diagnosis and prescription service. But it is still a good idea for you to be able to discuss drug therapy intelligently with your doctor. If there is a reluctance to answer your question, or an arrogance and disdain that *you*, a lay person, should even try to talk about the type of help being given, take a second look at this doctor. The medical attitude, unfortunately so common, that doctors are high priests of some mysterious religion called *health*, and that they are the only ones capable of understanding the mysteries involved, is especially damaging to the loved one of a depressive. If you are informed and know what you're talking about, there's little reason for a doctor not to discuss the problem with you. Any doctor who puts his or her own ego before the help needed by both patient and family is certainly incapable of treating an illness in which compassion is largely related to the cure. (This of course doesn't mean that a doctor is required to remain polite when a patient's relative who has a slight smattering of knowledge demands to be treated as an equal in knowledge by the doctor. Nobody likes a know-it-all.)

The MAO Inhibitors

Probably the most common type of endogenous depression seen by therapists is caused by the overproduction of an enzyme called *monoamine oxidase*. Here's an oversimplified description: An enzyme is a chemical that brings about certain reactions in the body by dissolving or "eating up" something else. The enzymes produced by the central nervous system 'oxidize' certain brain chemicals used in triggering electrical impulses. In other words, the enzyme causes those chemicals to react with oxygen so that the electrical impulses from a group of brain cells do not repeat. The name of the enzyme is an accurate description of its function, because the particular chemicals it effects are called *monoamines*. (another name for them is *biogenic amines*, and they are part of the same chemicals we talked about earlier). Here is a more detailed explanation of the process:

Each brain cell produces an electrical charge when stimulated. The combination of cells which fire electrical bursts depends on the particular stimulus, be it a perception, an action, or thought. The end result is a usable piece of data. In other words, when a group of cells discharge their contents in the form of minute bursts of electricity, the organism becomes aware of whatever the stimulus is and reacts to it. The nose perceives an odor, for example, which triggers certain brain cells and the odor is translated. The person becomes aware that the smell of flowers is in the air—or conversely, the smell of excrement. This perception triggers other cells to fire based on the reactions to the odor. Smelling the flowers may bring back a pleasant memory or cause a visual scan for the source. Smelling the excrement may cause disgruntled feelings toward a pet dog and also a visual scan along with the flash thought, "I hope I haven't stepped in it."

Each stimulus, when perceived, is filed. One may continue to be aware of it to a greater or lesser degree, one may incorporate it as a memory. But the stimulus becomes integrated into the person's reality. You don't normally go through the entire sequence over again as if for the first time.

The reason for that is *monoamine oxidase*. This enzyme dissolves the chemicals (the monoamines) which trigger brain cells to fire when stimulated. Without it, a sequence would continue to repeat itself long after the signals to do so have disappeared. To illustrate, when you feel a slight pinprick, the sequence that occurs causes the proper group of cells to fire, causing you to identify the pain and its source, and resulting in an action—you move away. If there were no enzyme such as monoamine oxidase, you would continue to feel the pinprick as if it were just occurring. There would be no cessation of stimulus and the brain would quickly be overwhelmed.

Unfortunately, there is a frequent problem with an overproduction of this enzyme, so that the chemical signals which trigger a brain cell to fire are stopped before they have a chance to function. The result is that some of the cells which are part of the resultant thought or action are missing. The part of the brain which translates these hundreds of thousands of cell firings into a unit of information has no power of judgment. It presents the information it has translated without any indication that something is wrong with the message, and *we* have no way of knowing that the presentation isn't accurate.

The overall effect of an excess of monoamine oxidase is almost exactly the same as an underproduction of the biogenic amines used to carry the electrical brain cell charges to the cerebral cortex, the brain's translator. This is why a doctor must be able to tell whether the problem is one of *underproduction* of these chemicals or *overproduction* of the dissolving enzyme. The basic mental problems in depression are caused by a lowering of emotional and intellectual response ability in the brain. If too much monoamine oxidase is causing that problem by eliminating some of the cell transmissions needed to complete a unit of thought or action, then the solution is obvious—cut down on the central nervous system's production of monoamine oxidase.

This is what the class of drugs known as MAO inhibitors do. As a matter of interest, this class of drug was the first breakthrough in discovering a modern treatment for depression, which until that time had been regarded strictly as a mental illness. Its discovery led to the development of other anti-depressant and depression-aiding drugs, and for that we can be grateful to the man who can be considered the father of all of today's advances in the field of depression. He's a New York physician and the discoverer of the first anti-depressant: Dr. Nathan Kline.

Dr. Kline made his discovery through a combination of research and accident. In researching a drug given to schizophrenics, one which lowered extreme emotional excitability, Kline reasoned that if there is a drug which lowers the brain's activity, there must also be another to heighten it. He and another doctor, Mortimer Ostow, came up with a theory of how this drug would work, even though there was no such drug in existence at that time.

Not too long after, Dr. Kline became aware of a drug called Marsilid, which was an experimental treatment used for tuberculosis. It had an unusual side effect: it created a feeling of well-being, almost euphoria, in patients who took it. While that effect had been noted, its potential was practically ignored, even though at the time, biochemists were studying a possible relationship between Marsilid and brain function. Dr. Kline decided to do some experimental work based on that research. He gave the drug to a number of severely depressed patients in his practice. A little more than a month after treatment began, he noticed improvements in most of the patients. As his work continued, he saw that many of those treated with Marsilid completely recovered from depression in a relatively short time. Dr. Kline, who was then chairman of the American Psychiatric Association's committee on research, wrote a paper on his findings in 1955. Within a year there were nearly half a million people being treated for depression with Marsilid, and a new field was born—chemical therapy specifically for the central nervous system-caused depressions.

Marsilid is no longer used in America because of the side effects it caused in some patients, but it created a host of other MAO inhibitor drugs. While they all affect the monoamine oxidase enzyme in the same way, each performs a little differently. Even when a doctor correctly analyzes the *class* of drugs indicated in a depression, there is still often a need for trial and error regarding the particular type, since one drug's approach may be right for one patient and another for other patients. This is why you shouldn't lose faith if a doctor seems to switch prescriptions after deciding on one class of drugs. He or she may just be testing the various approaches of each drug in a particular class to achieve the best effects. But, if you do know something about the classes of anti-depressants, you can judge if the doctor has at least decided that one class of drugs is the solution to the problem.

There are certain precautions necessary with MAO inhibitors that don't apply to other drugs; certain dietary restrictions *must* be obeyed, and there are certain other drugs which must not be taken because of a possible injurious side effect. Doctors will almost always be explicit about which substances, food or drugs, to avoid, but just in case you hit upon the rare doctor who might prescribe and forget the warnings, here's a list of proscribed foods. This doesn't mean, by the way, that one taste will cause damage, but normal eating patterns must be altered to eliminate these foods: cheese (especially strong cheeses), pickled herring, chicken liver, yeast, beer, Chianti wine, whipped cream and regular cream, chocolate, and fava beans, which are used in some Middle Eastern dishes. Also on the stay-away list are medications containing amphetamines and antihistamines (which are found in over-the-counter cold preparations). Whenever anti-depressant medication is taken, whatever the class of drug, tranquilizers and narcotics as well as stimulants may be dangerous, so professional advice must be obtained before any experimentation is done with these. Since you as a relative may be in a better position than the depressive to watch over the diet, always make sure you ask a doctor who prescribes anti-depressants if there are any drug or diet restrictions. If your relative is going alone for treatment, a phone call to the doctor won't be out of line.

The Tricyclics

Every new discovery is received with some skepticism, and the field of medical drugs is more prone to this problem than most. In fact, when Nathan Kline presented his first report on the unexpected benefits of Marsilid, he got an argument that he was wrong—from the director of the company which produced the drug!*

In the case of the tricyclics, we have a Swiss doctor to thank for these valuable drugs. Dr. Roland Kuhn spent nearly seven years researching a chemical therapy for depression, and he made his discovery a few years after Kline presented his documentation on the effects of Marsilid. But Kuhn met resistance every step of the way. When he began his research in 1950, there was resistance to the very idea of a chemical treatment for depression. He couldn't get the research grants needed to pursue the studies because his goal was unacceptable to both drug companies and medical technicians. Dr. Kuhn didn't give up. With a group of other researchers who also believed they were on the track of a radical new treatment for one of humanity's oldest ills, a chemical compound was finally proved to have active results. It was called *imipramine*. Its effect was basically the opposite action of an MAO inhibitor. It *increased* the availability of certain biogenic amines to the brain. (By the way, a small dissertation: medical people, like

*Kline, *From Sad to Glad*.

bureaucrats, are nuts for names. That may explain why there can be up to twenty different names for what is essentially the same generic drug. It also explains why the chemicals used by the brain are variously called *amines*, *biogenic amines*, *monoamines*, *neural transmitters* and so on. Each name is descriptive of a particular characteristic of these hormones, yet each name essentially means the same thing: a chemical produced by the central nervous system and involved in the functioning of the brain.)

Dr. Kuhn's first presentation of his paper on imipramine met with the same resistance his research had garnered all along. He claimed it had *psychic* as opposed to *physical* energizing properties. It didn't speed up metabolism as the amphetamine class of drugs did; instead, it worked on the chemical process of the brain itself, not on the mood or the thought process. Essentially, the tricyclic group of drugs works like MSG, a food chemical which doesn't change flavor but nonetheless enhances it. The tricyclics *enhance* the amount of certain chemicals in the brain by either increasing their production or preventing the brain cells from absorbing them. Remember, these chemicals are the "wire" by which the cell's electrical charges travel to the cerebral cortex.

The electrical charges emitted by the brain cells are in medical terminology known as *neural impulses*. The chemicals which convey these impulses to their destination are called *neural transmitters*. Tricyclics affect the neural transmitters.

Anything that has to do with the brain usually has the prefix *neur* in front of it—a brain surgeon is a *neurologist*, a university may have a *neuropsychiatric* building. (This is a good thing to remember when talking to a doctor. It's one of those little clues that tell you what is being discussed even if you don't know what's being said: Usually, if you know scientific prefixes and suffixes, you can figure out what some obscure term means, rather than having to feel like a dummy asking. For example, the prefix *hem* has to do with blood. Also, when you're talking to medical people, you can get them to take you more seriously if you can talk their language.)

Generically (which means the drug itself before the brand name is added), most of these drugs end in *ine*. This isn't an accurate way to classify tricyclics, though, since some MAO inhibitors also end in those letters. Some of the tricyclic brand names you're likely to run across are Tofranil, Aventyl, Elavil, Pertofane, and Triavil. Some tricyclics are combined with other drugs to ease side effects or provide some other action in addition to stimulating the neural transmitters.

Side Effects of MAO Inhibitors and Tricyclics

Aside from the side effects peculiar to MAO inhibitors, which have already been detailed, both that class of drugs and the tricyclics have certain other side effects in common. These reactions are not dangerous, but they are uncomfortable. It's a good idea to keep quiet about them when someone you know is taking these drugs. Let the doctor do the warning. A warning from you in addition may play into the depressive's obsession with health. Since the illness promotes a tendency toward hypochondria, the patient may believe the symptoms exist when they don't, or may anticipate them to such a degree that ordinary discomfort becomes unbearable. If there is a complaint about one of these reactions, then by all means tell the person that it's a side effect, will disappear in a while, is a normal reaction which could be expected, and *is not dangerous*. That last is especially important.

The possible minor effects are slight constipation, some difficulty with the eyes not tearing as readily, and dryness of the mouth. Also the use of marijuana with anti-depressants will produce varying degrees of drowsiness, with very vivid, colorful dreams. The mouth dryness seems to be an extremely common complaint. If it causes chapping of the lips, get some theatrical gloss rather than regular commercial sticks to prevent chapping. The theatrical gloss can be rubbed in so it isn't shiny, and it seems to do a better job of protecting the lips when they are dry. It also doesn't feel as coating as chapsticks do, and it keeps the lips more supple.

The major side effect is an intense torpor that may often turn the patient into a zombie for about two weeks. This passes as soon as the central nervous system adjusts to the medication. The feeling of this torpor is very similar to the feeling you would get if you had taken a sleeping pill, then for some reason had to get up and function. You would feel as if you were wading through molasses.

If it's at all possible, the depressed person should take some time off from work when beginning a course of anti-depressants. During my depression episode I continued to drive the car and go to work. When I began taking medication, I still drove and worked, and I'm lucky I survived either one. Once, while waiting for a light, I fell asleep. Other times I would be so groggy that I would have to pull over to the side of the road. It got so that when the sleepy feelings came over me while I was driving, I would begin to shout simple math sums as loud as I could—"one and one are two, six and six are twelve," and so on. It kept me alert enough to drive. One day, while driving down a crowded street, I was shouting out sums to stay awake—and realized that people were staring. I had stopped for a light and forgotten that my window was open. I leaned out the car window and yelled, "It's okay . . . I'm just trying to keep my eyes open." The incident haunted me for days, and it wasn't until much later, when I left England, that I realized how funny it was.

Walking around with a heavy, drugged feeling is no fun. You can't think, it's hard to move, and all you want to do is sleep. Often the drowsiness will be so bad that the person will lay his or her head down at work and just doze off. Some people literally turn into vegetables during this period. So it's wise to remember that this effect can have serious consequences, both to safety and to job security. A boss can put up with an employee's staying home for a week with the "flu," but it's less palatable if that same employee keeps dozing off throughout the day. If this is happening to your relative, have the person stay home and call in sick. Losing a job at this point in the illness can have too devastating an effect to add to the risk of it happening.

Lithium

The case for and against lithium salts is still being argued vigorously. It was one of the first treatments for depression to be discovered, but in those years of doubt about medication for depression, it languished on the shelf until the general theory of chemotherapy became acceptable.

First of all, it is a natural substance. It's an element, so it can't be synthesized in the laboratory. When it's combined with other chemicals such as phosphates, chlorides, or carbonates, it becomes a "salt." In the very early nineteenth century it was used as a treatment for gout and kidney stones, and if you collect old bottles, you'll see it listed as one of the main ingredients in the old cure-alls.

An Australian doctor, John Cade, discovered during an experiment that lithium mellowed the extreme moods of the manic-depressive. At the time, lithium had been abused in other aspects of medicine and so was considered a dangerous drug. Cade's reports on his work were read by a doctor in Denmark, Mogens Schou, who began using it on his patients. Within a short time, lithium was being used all over Europe, though America was still too cautious to experiment with the substance.

In 1970 permission was granted for doctors to use lithium in a limited way, and the real work in this country began. Lithium today is used mainly to control the violent mood swings of the manic-depressive. Many manic-depressives who have spent most of their lives in mental hospitals have dramatically become healthy and sane once they began a course of lithium. In fact, some doctors theorize that the depressions cured by lithium are really cases of manic-depressive illnesses in which the manic side is either too low to be noticed or the depression cycle is so long that the manic cycle never appears.

Lithium doesn't cure *all* depressive episodes and certainly can't be regarded as a cure-all. But it does something which no other drug known today does—it prevents a reoccurrence of depression. The impact of that discovery is still too new to have the important effects it will have in the future. Many people with endogenous depression live with the fear that having recovered from one attack, they may have another. And this fear is well founded. Statistics vary, since few doctors have the chance to follow a patient for his or her whole life, but estimates are that from a third to about half of those who experience an attack of clinical depression will have a recurring episode at another time in their lives—sometimes many recurrences. There's also evidence that the later in life the first attack occurs, the more likely it is to be repeated, and the longer the second episode is likely to be. In fact, before anti-depressants, it was not uncommon for a person to have a first attack after the age of 30, be symptom-free for ten or more years, then have another depressive episode, followed by another a few years later, then another within an even shorter period of time until the symptom-free time periods are so limited that the person had to be hospitalized.

If lithium salts prove to be an efficient method of preventing recurring attacks of depression, it will be the first preventative medicine for this illness. So far, it looks as though that's exactly what it may be. This means that an illness which is a neglected epidemic, which strikes at least 80 percent of the population, can be controlled by maintenance, just as diabetes is controlled by daily doses of insulin. There will be no shame or stigma attached to having depression. It seems that when a disease is preventable, it loses many of its social taboos.

The Possible Beneficial Side Effect of Anti-Depressants

There's a theory held by some doctors that the major anti-depressants, MAO inhibitors and the tricyclics—and lithium to a lesser degree—have an effect which, if it can be isolated, may prove to be an even better form of depression prevention. The theory is that when the central nervous system goes haywire, it forms a habit pattern of that imbalance. The imbalance then continues and creates chronic depressions. When one of the drugs acting on the central nervous system corrects that imbalance, it creates another habit pattern, a correct one. The central nervous system then begins to function normally and a condition which may have existed in some small degree for an entire lifetime is removed. It's a fact that not only do many people with a severe depressive episode completely recover—they are much better afterwards then they ever were before.

I can vouch for that theory. Before my depression I was unable to get the response I wanted in my life or from others. I felt that everyone knew a secret that I didn't know, a secret that was as elementary as breathing. These feelings of being an outsider had existed since childhood. When I recovered from depression, they were gone. Suddenly I was able to touch a potential I had only barely suspected existed. After a lifetime of crawling, I stood up and even flew. Before, the longest I had ever held a job was three months. After that, I knew I could not only hold a job, but choose work I wanted and *get* it. While the six months of psychiatric therapy I received twice a week in England were extremely helpful, the sessions certainly weren't sufficient to have created the enormous change. I believe that the anti-depressants taken that year corrected a chemical imbalance that had existed most of my life—and after that, everything was easy.

Another dissertation: My doctor in London was a private

physician named Dr. Hopkins. I can't remember his first name. His offices were on Haverstock Hill, across the street from a church. I never finished paying Dr. Hopkins. And yet, this man did more for me than any other human being in terms of helping me become the person I was capable of being. I lost track of Dr. Hopkins after returning to America. I wrote several letters, but never got an answer. At the time he was treating me, he never mentioned money and he never let me take refuge in self-pity. He was wonderful. (This isn't transference, because transference isn't needed after all these years; anyhow, even during treatment I never fell in love with him.) Once while I was taking a bath and reading a book he had lent me, I dropped it in the water. Even then he didn't get angry. During the treatment, I had some financial difficulties and moaned, "I don't think I'll ever be able to pay you." Hopkins knew I wanted to be a writer, and knew I was getting interested enough in this illness to begin doing research on it. He said, "Don't worry about the money. If you write that book you're talking about, and if you learn enough about depression to help others who have it, that's payment enough." If any of you know where Dr. Hopkins is, let him know that I've started repaying my debt to him. But also, I would like to pay him the money!

Other Drugs

While MAO inhibitors, tricyclics, and lithium are the main forms of chemotherapy for depression, other drugs are used either separately or combined in pill form with the anti-depressants to relieve various symptoms. These are usually stimulants or tranquilizers. For those with a retardation symptom, an amphetamine may be prescribed to improve function. When an agitated depression is noted, a tranquilizer which is *not* a central nervous system depressant may be used.

It's important to leave the drug prescribing to the doctor and not allow any experimentation. The most important reason is that some tranquilizers and stimulants don't combine well with certain anti-depressants. Remember, these drugs are working on an extremely delicate chemical system which controls the very life functions of the organism. If you feel, for example, that the depressive isn't getting the results from one doctor, don't rush off to another. In one tragic case, a woman whose depressed husband was taking an MAO inhibitor felt that the drug wasn't having enough of an effect, so she managed to get another prescription from another doctor, this one for a tricyclic. One day she switched her husband's medication, with *his* knowledge and permission—but not his doctor's. About a week later, her husband began convulsing. By the time an ambulance arrived, the convulsions had stopped—and so had her husband's life. You cannot switch from an MAO inhibitor to a tricyclic until the first drug has entirely left the system. Otherwise, the central nervous system may short-circuit and kill the person as it did in this case.

While experimenting with stimulants and tranquilizers isn't quite as dangerous, it's still risky. For example, an agitated patient who takes librium, a central nervous system depressant, may worsen the degree of depression and undo the good of the medication being prescribed. In fact, whenever someone who lives in or spends time in your home is taking medication for depression, it's a good idea to get rid of all the uppers and downers, including sleeping pills. It's too easy to take one, either by mistake or on purpose. If you must have them around, put them in a place where they can't be easily found.

6.

Chemical Causes
of Depression

The body works as a whole unit. When something happens to one part, the effect is never isolated. Everyone has experienced an injury to one part of the body which causes something to happen to another part—the stubbed toe which causes a headache, or an event picked up by one of the sensory organs which causes the hands to tremble. This is why a troubled mind can cause a physical, or psychosomatic, illness. And the reverse is also true. A physical impairment may cause a mental reaction.

You already know that the brain works by using chemicals to produce electricity, and the electricity "runs" the brain. The hormones that are used to do this are specific to the brain. (*Hormones* are chemical substances that are secreted by glands. More about these later.) But because every part of the body is interrelated, a hormonal imbalance from other organs can cause depression. So can certain illnesses. However, an illness usually has such a dramatic effect that we realize something is wrong and go to a doctor to find out what it is—and to get treatment. If it's a disease, such as jaundice, which is likely to produce mental changes, the doctor may warn us to be aware of that fact. But organic chemical imbalances are less dramatic and we can exist for years without knowing that the body isn't functioning properly.

To have a really thorough knowledge of depression, you would have to know a great deal about the workings of the human body—the endocrine system, the mineral and salt balance in the body, and many other things which you probably don't feel like getting involved in. So rather than giving a detailed explanation of human physiology, here are some of the organic imbalances which are known to produce depressive syndromes. Unfortunately, since depression may merely be the most evident symptom of some underlying illness, a person may go for treatment of just that symptom and find no relief. That's because the central nervous system isn't the source of the problem, so drugs which act on it have little or no effect.

If you notice signs of depression in yourself or someone else, it's good to be aware of the other factors which may be producing it beside the central nervous system. You won't be able to make an accurate diagnosis without fairly extensive medical knowledge, but you can get some idea of what else may be wrong. You can then mention your suspicion to the doctor to be checked out. Many therapists will continue to treat depression for quite some time before realizing that there's an organic or mineral deficiency or imbalance which is actually the root of the problem. Your knowledge of these imbalances may prevent that wasted time and speed up the return to normal feelings.

The Endocrine System

The endocrine system of the body is made up of glands which produce hormones. They include the thyroid, the pituitary, parathyroids, thalamus, hypothalamus, the adrenal glands, and the pancreas. Every one of them is necessary to life. The endocrine glands are also called *ductless* glands because they don't pass their secretions through tubes, or ducts. The body chemicals they secrete not only have their own functions, they also also control the metabolism of other elements in the body. An imbalance of these chemicals causes illness. One of the symptoms of endocrine illness is depression. That's why any depression that doesn't respond readily to anti-depressants should be checked further to see if it is caused by an endocrine gland. Fortunately, these depressions don't have the same clinical symptoms as endogenous depression; usually, there are no major sleep disturbances and the typical loss of all appetites does not happen to the same degree.

One of the main reasons that these glands go haywire is because of stress. When we're under stress, all of these glands are stimulated to some degree. But continued stimulation causes them to exhaust themselves, and a chronic deficiency may result. In fact, any time you or someone you know is under heavy, continuing stress, make sure two therapeutic precautions are followed: a good diet rich in vitamins B and C with the addition of vitamin supplements, and an annual checkup which measures the hormonal balance of the body. You already know that imbalances of the hormones used in brain function have the greatest effect on the emotions, with secondary physical effects. The reverse is true in endocrine imbalances. The physical symptoms are the most obvious (*if you know what to look for*), which is why knowing what to look for is so important.

Anything that interferes with the hormones may cause radical changes in emotions. It's easy to understand why the physical symptoms can sometimes be overlooked and the emotional symptoms treated. Someone may not think that a slight darkening of the skin or an increased sensitivity to cold are worth bothering about. Yet these are symptoms of specific endocrine disorders. Feeling "down" all the time is something most people notice far more than they would notice an increase in the amount of urine passed. That's why a doctor may continue to treat for depression instead of looking to the endocrine system for the problem.

The symptoms described here for each glandular disturbance aren't meant to be used for self-diagnosis or amateur-physician party chatter. But some of them *are* obvious enough so that you can suggest a professional checkup. I once did a short radio report on how to recognize thyroid disturbances, and got about forty letters from listeners who had the symptoms, went to a doctor, and were found to need medication. The letters were heartfelt *thank you*'s from people whose entire lives were changed once the medication put that gland back in order.

The Thyroid

Sometimes I wish I could be in charge of the world for just one week. All I would do during that time is make it mandatory that everyone over the age of puberty have a thyroid scan. Undetected thyroid problems are the cause of more misery than anyone would believe—and also the cause of more depressions than doctors accurately diagnose.

A Los Angeles specialist, Dr. Boris Catz, says that at least 20 percent of the population have thyroid disturbances serious enough to affect feelings and behavior. In fact, Catz says, a surprising number of patients in mental hospitals will show malfunctioning thyroids when tested.

The thyroid is one of the most important, if not *the* most important, gland in the body. To state it very simply, the thyroid regulates energy. But it does a lot more than that. Every cell of the body contains thyroxine, the chemical produced by this gland. You know that oxygen is essential to human life. The thyroid regulates the metabolization of oxygen in the body, which means that thyroxine controls how efficiently the cell will use oxygen, as well as (to a degree), how much oxygen it gets.

There are several things which set this important gland apart from the others. For one, it's the most easily manipulated gland of the body. It lies across the windpipe, just under the place where the lower jaw meets the neck. The shape is roughly like the letter H. You can feel your own thyroid by pressing gently on either side of your windpipe, just above the swelling caused by the Adam's apple. Because it's so close to the surface, doctors can tell something about the condition of the gland from feeling it. If there's an underfunction, the gland will be enlarged or swollen. This condition is called *goiter*.

The most common cause of goiter is the lack of iodine, a vital substance in thyroid function, used in thyroxine. This is why goiter is more common in the Midwestern areas of the United States, where iodine-containing foods such as seafood aren't as big a part of the diet. The importance of iodine in the diet is so well understood that most salt is now iodized; the tiny amount of iodine in commercial salt is usually enough to prevent iodine deficiency goiter. The thyroid could actually be called an iodine *trap*, since it will grab this nutrient from any part of the body it can. If you were to receive an injection of iodine, most of it would travel to the thyroid gland within a few minutes, and this mechanism is used in testing thyroid function. The patient is given a radioactive iodine pill to swallow the night before the test, with orders to eat no seafood or other food containing iodine. The next day, a type of Geiger counter scans the gland and makes a printout of the amount of iodine detected. The picture may be very light if not enough thyroxine is being produced, or very dark if too much is coming from the gland.

For some reason, thyroid symptoms are more common in North America than in any other country. Imbalances happen most often after the age of 30. They are also much more common in women than in men. Any serious stress, especially a continuous one, may cause exhaustion of the thyroid and result in *hypothyroidism*, which is an underproduction of thyroxine. An overproduction is call *hyperthyroidism*. (In fact, any time you see the word *hypo*, you know it means under; similarly, *hyper* means over. As an example of how you can translate meanings from knowing prefixes, suffixes, and root words, a *hypodermic* is composed of the word for "under" and the word which means "skin," *derma*. So hypodermic means "under the skin.")

Hypothyroidism An underactive thyroid seems to be far more common than an overactive one. It causes predictable effects, most of which stem from the fact that lack of thyroxine lowers the entire metabolism (metabolism can be compared to the miles-per-hour or speed at which your body functions). The nails don't grow as quickly. Cuts and bruises take longer to heal. Everything slows down.

With hypothyroidism, there's an overall feeling of tiredness and lack of energy. The person needs a lot more sleep than normal. Blood pressure is usually low. Also the organism can't produce heat as efficiently, so there's an increased sensitivity to cold. People with hypothyroid function feel chilled even when others are warm. Their skin becomes dry—it takes energy to produce the moisture and oils which keep skin soft and lubricated. Dry skin, along with hands and feet that always feel cold, may be a sign of aging, but can also be signs of an underactive thyroid.

In addition to dry skin, there is a dryness of the mucous membranes. This dryness may cause the nose to bleed slightly. In women, it can cause the vagina to secrete less moisture so that sex may be uncomfortable. It also can cause lips to crack and chap.

One easily recognized sign is hair loss. Low thyroid function causes the hair to become dry and to split, but worse, it also causes it to drop off at the roots. Hair thinning may not be just incipient baldness. So if the hair changes condition and if you start noticing a hairbrush matted with hair after a morning brushing, look for other symptoms of an underactive thyroid, especially if you notice that skin abrasions start taking longer to heal.

There will also be a weight gain in a person with hypothyroidism. The whole metabolism is slowed so it can't burn calories as efficiently as it normally does. You can suspect an underactive thyroid in anyone who eats very little and still puts on weight.

Another major symptom is memory loss. In fact, that's probably the first and most pervasive emotional symptom, even before depressive symptoms set in. Someone who used to pride him/herself on a good memory may find it impossible to remember a phone number long enough to dial it without glancing at the number halfway through. I know a man who got so angry, he ripped his phone out of the wall; he had called information to get a number, didn't write it down, and forgot it before he could finish dialing. He called information again, got the number and didn't write it down—and the same thing happened. The third time, he wrote the number down after the operator gave it to him. But by the time she had hung up, he couldn't remember the last digit she had given. He was so frustrated that he yanked the wire until it came out.

There are two other symptoms which aren't taken very seriously by most doctors because they are unorthodox. Yet both of them are gaining wider medical acceptance. One is an increased desire—you could even call it a craving—for starches. Someone who normally stays away from potatoes, pasta, or rice may feel such a hunger for them that a starch will be eaten at every dinner. In a way, this is an intelligent instinct at work. People who shun starches usually do so because they're using will power to keep thin. But starches are energy givers, much more substantial ones than sugars. And much better for you. The craving for starches may just be the organism's way of using its instinct to provide energy (which may also make one fatter without endangering health, however).

I have to thank Dr. Boris Catz, the Beverly Hills specialist who told me about the second symptom. It appears when there is a genetic tendency toward thyroid disease. Normally, the little finger is shorter than the ring finger next to it, but the tip still reaches above the top joint wrinkle of the ring finger. When the tip of the little finger is shorter than the line of the next finger's first joint, it's a sign of genetic thyroid malfunction—meaning you got it from your parents. This characteristic doesn't seem to occur in people who aren't prone to thyroid imbalance. The short little finger is even more significant if it's crooked or humped in the middle, right at the knuckle.

(A funny dissertation: When I did a radio report on thyroid, I included the little finger sign. The report was played twice during the hours when people were driving to work. I got a phone call from the public relations department of the Los Angeles police department, asking me not to describe visual symptoms again. A couple of traffic cops had reported that motorists were pulling over to the side of the road after the report came on and had explained to the officers that they were looking at their fingers to see if their thyroids were okay. I still don't know if the caller was pulling my leg.)

As a final check for an underactive thyroid, take an oral temperature reading. A low thyroid may cause it to be a point or two lower than the normal 98.6.

Hyperthyroidism The symptoms of an overactive gland are exactly the opposite of those for an underactive one. The differences are amazingly clear. Skin is moist, and there may be excessive perspiration. The metabolic rate is speeded up. The person may be active to the point of mania. The eyeballs protrude a little. If the hyperactivity is severe, eyes may stick out so far that it disfigures the face. The person loses weight. If you know anyone who puts food away as though it were going out of style, yet stays thin, don't envy him or her. The reason may be an overactive thyroid.

For these people, sleep is restless and light and they don't need much of it. Blood pressure rises. There may be tachycardia, which is a fast, pounding heartbeat. They are constantly on the go, super-energetic. They may even run a fever of a couple of points, as much as one or two degrees.

Hyperthyroid people are hyper on every level. They move fast, are impatient, and find it hard to sit still. One good thing about this illness is that it can make the mind exceptionally alert.

Treatment of Thyroid Imbalances   Thyroid imbalances are easy to correct in most cases. For hypothyroidism, a thyroid extract (made from animals) or a synthetic substitute is given in a dosage indicated by the degree of deficiency. When this thyroid medication is taken, it causes the gland to shrivel and disappear. The person is then totally dependent on the artificial stuff. This may sound frightening, but when medication is stopped, the gland once again grows back. Often a doctor will have a patient stop medication to see if the gland comes back with normal function, as is sometimes the case.

For hyperthyroid, a suppressant may be given, but if the overproduction is severe, the gland may be removed. The person is then dependent on thyroid medication for the rest of his or her life.

The Pituitary

If the thyroid is the master gland, the pituitary is the overseer. The hormone it produces acts as a regulator of every endocrine gland in the body. Most glandular diseases are caused by too little or too much hormone production. The source of the imbalance can be the gland itself, but it can also be the fault of the pituitary (though this doesn't happen as frequently as direct glandular malfunctions). If a glandular malfunction is caused by the pituitary, it is called a *secondary* malfunction. Because this gland produces several different hormones, a pituitary imbalance will have more effect than any other gland which goes haywire.

Like the thyroid, the pituitary stimulates metabolism in all the cells. If you believe in mysticism, you might be interested to know that in some cultures, particularly India, this gland is considered to be the location of the soul and also the "third eye" which sees on a spiritual level. That belief may come from the fact that the pituitary is buried in the brain.

The pituitary does a lot of things besides stimulate the other endocrine glands. It helps regulate the volume of water in the body. It helps balance the electrolyte metabolism, which is (simplified) the interaction of salt and potassium—a vital life function. The electrolytes of the body are so important that an imbalance causes shock. And as you probably know, severe shock—the kind that comes in reaction to an injury—can cause sudden death.

If the operation of the pituitary is interrupted in certain ways, that can cause diabetes (the form called *diabetes insipidus*). One of the symptoms of this disease is the passing of large amounts of urine.

A malfunction of the pituitary gland in childhood seriously affects growth. Too little and the child may be a dwarf; there will be no growth. Too much and there's an opposite effect: the child may be a giant, standing over six feet before the age of puberty. Although pituitary output can be corrected, the effects of abnormal growth in childhood can't, so any youngster who is abnormally tall or short for his or her age should be taken to a specialist as soon as the abnormality is noticed. (This doesn't mean a growth difference of one or two inches. Children grow at different rates. Your pediatrician can tell you what can be considered abnormal.)

The pituitary is stimulated under stress and works with the adrenal glands to produce more adrenalin. If the stress is a slow, gradual one, the extra adrenalin will come directly from adrenal stimulation. If the stress is sudden or severe, the *pituitary* will stimulate the adrenalin. As part of this stress reaction, of course, there is a rise in blood pressure. One of the pituitary hormones causes an elevation in blood pressure, so hypertension which doesn't readily respond to medication may be caused by the pituitary.

While other glandular disturbances may cause more dramatic changes in body function and behavior, imbalances from *this* gland can have far more dangerous effects. For example, if the malfunction is caused by a tumor in the pituitary, it's urgent to have it diagnosed right away. Because of the gland's location in the brain, a tumor there will press on the optic nerve. If there's enough pressure, it may cause blindness.

Hypopituitarism Unlike thyroid problems, which have clearly defined symptoms, the underactive pituitary has a number of *syndromes*. That means that the symptoms, instead of being diagnosed one by one, come in combination and are diagnosed all together, as one unit. In addition, a malfunctioning pituitary may cause what are probably the most horrible effects of any other glandular disturbance. In a disease called *Simmond's syndrome*, the facial features swell and the victim becomes senile. (Don't worry too much about this one; it's rare. Also, the mental dullness which is a symptom is not accompanied by the sleep disturbances of depression.)

The symptoms of an imbalanced pituitary are similar to thyroid symptoms in many ways. While thyroid illness is common, though, pituitary illness is fairly rare, and its syndromes are even less common. An underactive gland will cause a lower output of hormones in all the other glands. It will also cause an accumulation of fatty tissue. This isn't the same as overweight. The appearance is more pudgy, since the fat doesn't settle in the same places as in a normal weight gain. It's more evenly distributed. There will be varying degrees of depression.

An underactive pituitary will also cause an underactive thyroid, so there may be hypothyroid symptoms. But in addition, there will be a shrinkage of the sexual organs. A woman's breasts may become slightly smaller. A man's testicles will shrink a little. Women may stop menstruating, or the flow may be scanty.

The hair may become very fine and limp. The mind slows—creativity and intelligence drop. Along with these symptoms, there is constant drowsiness and an overall mental stupor.

One *important* thing: If you suspect some sort of pituitary disturbance in a depressed person, *don't mention it to the person*! The chance that a pituitary disturbance is the cause of depressive symptoms is so slight that it matches the odds of winning the Irish sweepstakes. It's very rare—many doctors have never seen it—and it's so hard to diagnose without specific tests that few physicians would even try to do so. It's sensible to suspect an underactive thyroid in a depression which doesn't respond to medication. An underactive pituitary's being the primary cause of depression is far less common. Nevertheless, the condition *does* exist and it's good to be aware of it.

Hyperpituitarism Hyperpituitarism is extremely rare. An overactive pituitary will cause dramatic growth. In one clinical case, a boy who weighed 9 pounds at birth weighed 62 pounds less than two years later. At the age of nine, he was over six feet in height and weighed 178 pounds! This overactivity can be reversed (though the growth will remain), but if it isn't caught in time, the overproduction may interfere with the action of insulin in the body, causing death from the symptoms of diabetes.

The main symptom of hyperpituitarism in adult life is a marked enlargement of the hands, feet, and facial bones. The eyes become deeply set in their sockets, and there may be increased sexual desire. Since the pituitary affects the thyroid, this imbalance also produces symptoms of hyperthyroidism.

The Parathyroids
These are small glands perched on, sometimes actually in, the thyroid. They look like little globules of fat. These glands regulate the metabolism of calcium, phosphorus, and production of bone. You probably know that calcium and phosphorus are needed for strong bones. Calcium is also a natural tranquilizer, and a deficiency will cause nervousness and jitters.

Hypoparathyroidism Hypoparathyroidism is rare except when the parathyroids are accidently removed during thyroid or other throat surgery or if there is a tumor in these glands. Hypoparathyroid creates symptoms of muscular weakness, fatigue, and lassitude. Blood calcium drops, and the lack of calcium causes muscular spasms and twitches. Pressure on a muscle, even a slight pressure such as a grip on the upper arm, may cause that muscle to go into a rigid spasm. This malfunction would tend to produce anxiety symptoms rather than depressive ones, though clinically, anxiety can sometimes be a disguise for a serious depression.

Hyperparathyroidism This imbalance is rare and usually caused by a tumor or growth in these glands. Sometimes kidney malfunction may be at fault. Its earliest main symptom is muscular weakness. There may be an increased clumsiness, and a disturbance in motor control. Remember, calcium is not only bone material, it's also the mineral used by the nervous system to pass signals along through the nerves. Our nerves allow us to move, and if they are impaired in any way, there's a matching loss of muscular control. The kidneys are very involved with the excretion and reabsorption of calcium and phosphorus, so you can see how the functions of the parathyroids and the kidneys are connected.

With hyperparathyroidism, the bones lose calcium. They become weak, but not brittle. Instead, they bend without breaking. Fibrous material can then fill in the places where the calcium should be; since the bone is malleable and soft, this fibrous material "sets" the soft bone, often in deformed shapes. So hyperparathyroid, left untreated, can result in gross bone deformation.

Thalamus and Hypothalamus

These two glands, like the pituitary, are buried deep in the brain. They are directly involved in brain function. The thalamus relays signals to the cerebral cortex. It's the hypothalamus which is important in regard to depression, though; this is the gland most responsible for our moods. The hypothalamus and the cerebral cortex have a feedback signal system (remember, the cerebral cortex is the "translator" which puts all the electrical charges of the brain cells together to make a usable thought or action). Certain kinds of extreme or dramtic stimuli to the cerebral cortex also stimulate the hypothalamus, creating an emotional "on guard" response which travels back to the cerebral cortex. The emotional response is the fight-flight reaction, the same reaction which causes the adrenal glands to produce adrenalin (see Chapter 4).

Under emotional stress, and to a degree, physical stress, the hypothalamus stimulates the adrenals to start acting. Eventually, if the stimulation continues, it may cause high blood pressure. It can also cause depression.

When the hypothalamus reacts, it pushes the autonomic (or sympathetic) nervous system into action. This is the involuntary part of the nervous system, which controls such things as heartbeat, breathing, blood pressure, and other organs such as the heart, liver, and kidneys. There will be an increase in some of the biogenic amines used by the brain as well as an increase in the functions of the sympathetic nervous system.

The hypothalamus exerts a control on the pituitary gland because it functions as a message carrier: it passes orders from the brain to the pituitary, and in a lesser degree, to all the other glands. As you've probably guessed from the interlocking functions of all the endocrine glands, there's a complicated checks and balances system between the brain, the organs, and the endocrine glands. The pituitary monitors the hormones of the other endocrine glands; but the hypothalamus, under the direction of the cerebral cortex, monitors the pituitary. (There are no absolute kings in organ or glandular function. The system can be compared to a parliamentary form of government: some cabinet members are more important than others, some have greater effect than others, but outside of an actual *halt* by one of the essential members, the system operates so that every part has some effect on every other. In that way, the operation as a whole is kept on its toes, and under ordinary circumstances, although some members might stray a little off the proper path, there are safeguards to help prevent anything from getting too out of line.)

The cerebral cortex controls the hypothalamus. The relationship between the two is a bit touchy, since sometimes one or the other will overstep its responsibilities and exert an undesired effect on other parts of the body. This is where the checks and balances help out. The pituitary, while working under the stimulation of the hypothalamus, also has enough autonomy to prevent damage from a random hypothalamic signal. One area of fascinating study is proving that many of the instinctive drives, such as the sex urge, hunger, sleep, and pleasure may be controlled and activated by the hypothalamus. Laboratory animals have had electrodes implanted in the hypothalamus, and a switch made available for the animals to use to stimulate that gland in order to produce pleasure. The animals will manipulate the switch to the exclusion of all else; they will do it constantly, refusing to eat or sleep until they die . . . happy.

The hypothalamus also works hand in hand with the adrenals and the pituitary as a unit. When a depression is primarily caused by a disturbance in the pituitary, the hypothalamus will be affected too. But a disturbance in the pituitary will cause a depressive syndrome without necessarily creating the same sleep disturbances, loss of appetites, and the vegetative state produced by depression. A hypothalamus imbalance, though, will create the *precise* clinical signs of depression that occur when the biogenic amines are out of whack. I'm not going to go into too much detail here. You are already familiar with the symptoms of depression, and further description of the causes of a malfunction in the hypothalamus would involve a description of complicated chemical chains which are hard to write about and even harder to read. A doctor can identify whether this gland is causing depression by checking certain hormonal secretions in the blood or urine. If anti-depressants don't seem to be working, make sure the person with depression has a thorough medical checkup, with tests for vitamin deficiencies, excess adrenalin, and other endocrine disturbances. In fact it's a good idea to have those tests made whenever there's a suspicion of depression. Why waste weeks of therapy and medication which may not apply to the primary cause?

The Adrenals

The adrenals are two little glands perched on top of the kidneys. If the thyroid and pituitary are workhorses, plugging along day by day, the adrenals can be called the prima donnas—always there, but occasionally making a dramatic entrance, sweeping in with startling effects and overshadowing every other gland. They are our defenses against stress. If the adrenals were removed, we wouldn't be able to survive the slightest trauma; even tiny stresses would cause death. Tests on animals demonstrate the importance of adrenal activity. Rats which have had their adrenals removed have died from merely bumping into a wall or from being gently picked up when they aren't used to it.

You could almost say that the adrenal glands allow us to accept and adapt to change. Change is life . . . everything that is alive changes. Yet human beings have a love–hate relationship with change. When we get used to something, it's disorienting to have to rethink it and adapt to it in a new form. Change is traumatic. It creates stress. In a very objective way, every traumatic event can be described as a condition of change. In neighborhoods where crime and violence are a way of life, carrying a gun to guard oneself against attack is accepted. The person who has never experienced that type of life style will be under far more stress in a violent incident than the person who lives with violence as a fact of life. Instant adaptability to change is the key to survival. Suppose you wake up in the middle of the night and your house is on fire. You can fight the change from a safe to a dangerous house by reacting with fear and panic, refusing to accept the fact that you have a different reality to deal with than the one you knew. Or you can accept the change instantly (*my house is on fire*) and deal with the priorities set by the change (*assessing the best escape route; deciding whether you will stop to rescue people, animals, or things; getting out of the fire*).

Adrenalin gives us the extra energy and mental alertness needed to deal with emergency changes. However, because we are reasoning beings, we often use those extras in a nonsurvival way. Our reason may conflict with our animal instincts and cause nonsurvival behavior. Here's an example of adrenalin's being used with reason in a stress which requires instant adaptability: A woman was watching her husband work on their car. He was under the car when the jack slipped and the wheel came down on his upper abdomen. The woman realized that his chest was being crushed and that he would probably die before she could get help. She lifted the front end of the car and shifted it away from her unconscious husband, then called an ambulance. The adrenalin allowed her to lift a weight of nearly a ton and a half and move it away so her husband could survive. We've all heard of instances where someone performed a feat of strength or endurance far beyond normal capacity in a stressful situation. Adrenalin used with cooperation from the mind makes this possible.

We've all heard, too, of people who reacted with confusion to a life-threatening change, with tragedy as the result. I recently saw such a tragedy. A young woman was hit by a train because she didn't adapt instantly to the priorities of a life-threatening change. Her car had stalled on a railroad crossing late at night. The nearest cross street was practically deserted. The car, a Volkswagen, would have been easy to push off the tracks in neutral gear, though it might have taken several attempts. The woman tried once, gave up, and ran to get help, leaving her dog in the car. She was running down the road, trying to get motorists to stop, when she heard the train coming. She ran back to get her dog out of the car. By the time she got the door open, the train was into the crossing. It hit her and threw her aside, breaking her shoulderbone, her legs, and an arm. The dog was killed. The adrenalin gave her running speed—a witness said he never saw anyone run as fast as the young woman ran back to her car—but the extra mental alertness didn't result in mind and body working together. The woman later told police that she didn't think a train would come so soon because the crossing was dark and it was late at night. She had flares in her car. They were never used, though a few of them placed on the tracks would have been visible enough to cause the train to stop. An instant adaptation would have allowed her to deal with the priorities of the stressful change: set the flares, get the dog and everything else of value out of the car, *then* try again to push it off the tracks or get help. The adrenal glands give us the material we need for action, but they don't tell us how to act.

Fortunately, we don't have to deal with life-threatening changes very often. But the daily stresses—a boss who suddenly takes a dislike to us, a shortage of money—need adaptation. Whereas the instant adaptation necessary in a dangerous situation may be the factor which decides whether we live or die, the adaptation to general stresses which are part of everyday life will decide if we will be happy or depressed, sick or well.

It's fairly accurate to say that the adrenal glands determine whether we stay healthy or become sick—and more than any other part of the body, these glands determine whether we *feel* well or sick. They are among our most important defenses against infections and illness. You've already read how important the pituitary gland is, since it controls the other endocrine glands. There is a bond between the pituitary and adrenal glands which is stronger than any other of the body's glandular bonds. They work very closely with each other, and what affects one will affect the other, to a greater degree than is the case with all the other endocrine glands. Therefore, the overall results of an imbalance in either one will be more dramatic and more immediately felt than with any other glandular disturbance. In fact, under stress, the adrenals, the pituitary, and the thyroid together produce a hormone combination which boosts the stress response of the entire body.

Adrenalin

While the adrenals produce several hormones, the best known and probably most important one is adrenalin. It makes you feel excited and afraid all at once. If you've ever been in a near accident, you know that afterwards your heart is pounding and you're out of breath. That's because of the adrenalin which started rushing through your system as soon as you reacted to a dangerous or stressful situation. Occasionally adrenalin will create excitement without the feeling of fear. This is usually the case in a mob situation, where reason has been put aside. People who have participated in lynch mobs describe the feeling as one of excitement, a "rushing" feeling marked by confidence and a complete disregard for consequences. Soldiers in battle are sometimes swept up into a war lust; they feel only the adrenalin and none of the fear. These soldiers are often capable of amazing death-defying feats, and some of them have performed incredible acts of heroism even though they were mortally wounded. The adrenalin kept them going even though their wounds would have ordinarily caused instant death.

When the rush of adrenalin hits your body, a natural survival system goes into effect. Your blood vessels get smaller. The constriction makes your heart beat faster, which pumps more blood to your brain and muscles. But blood draws away from the surface areas, the skin and its epidermis. This means that you'll bleed less if you're wounded. There's a decrease in blood clotting time, too, so that if you are cut, you won't lose as much blood. At the same time, your white blood count goes up, so that your body can fight off infections faster. It's an extremely efficient survival system.

While all this is happening, the entire metabolism is speeding up. There's an increase of oxygen to the body cells, caused by a rise in the red blood cell count; the oxygen makes you burn your stored sugar faster, creating more energy. The thyroid is stimulated into releasing more thyroxine if the stress is a general, long-term one, since thyroxine acts as an amplifier for adrenalin.

If there is too much adrenalin in the system, the person will overreact to stress. Too little, and there will be lethargy and inability to cope with stress. Both conditions may stem from stress itself. And both conditions will cause depression.

Addison's Disease

Addison's disease is a chronic condition caused by an *under-function* of the adrenal glands. Usually, the pituitary will also be affected enough so that the condition doesn't go untreated: there are too many signs that something is wrong. Addision's disease causes extreme weakness and fatigue. The heart slows down and blood pressure is low. The stomach becomes sensitive; it's easily upset and spicy foods will cause indigestion.

In advanced cases, the skin changes color too. It becomes

dingy, sometimes turning a dark gray or brown. The adrenals have nothing to do with pigmentation in the body, but the pituitary does, and of course any imbalance of the adrenals affects the pituitary as well. Although the early symptoms of Addison's disease resemble *hypothyroidism*, the dusky tinge to the skin is a giveaway to the real cause.

Appetite goes and there's a corresponding weight loss. Blood pressure drops, and there may be spells of dizziness and vertigo. The body hair becomes thin, and occasionally the hair on the head also thins out. Warts and moles may darken, and there may be an increase in the growth of new warts and moles. The electrolyte balance, which is the reaction of sodium and potassium in the body, becomes disturbed. This electrolyte balance is so essential to life that even a minor disturbance can cause systemic shock. There may be serious disturbances in the body's ability to handle sugar, and hypoglycemia, or low blood sugar, may develop. Sometimes there may even be hypoglycemic shock; in severe cases it can be serious enough to cause death.

Addison's disease causes such severe symptoms that the person with this illness almost always goes to a doctor before the disease gets serious. Therefore, since it's caught in time, it's very rare for a case to result in death.

Cushing's Syndrome

This illness is the biochemical opposite of Addison's disease, and has the opposite symptoms, except for the skin pigmentation and the muscular weakness which also exist in this syndrome. Instead of a weight loss, there is a weight gain. But the weight is strange. It doesn't make the arms and legs any fatter; yet the face, neck, and body become fat to the point of obesity. The fat is painful. A person with Cushing's syndrome will hurt every time he or she moves. The abdomen may have dark streaks on it, similar to the striations of pregnancy. There will be an increase in body hair: legs and arms will become positively fuzzy, and pubic hair will become thicker, as will the hair on the head. There will be a rise in blood pressure, sometimes leading to a case of hypertension. The sexual glands may shrink a little, and sexual function slows down. Women may stop menstruating. Men will often become impotent. Instead of the hypoglycemia associated with Addison's disease, the opposite illness, diabetes (yes, diabetes is the opposite of hypoglycemia) may result.

The darkening of the skin in Cushing's syndrome isn't as pronounced a symptom as it is in Addison's disease. But Cushing's has one very obvious symptom which is easy to diagnose: the face becomes round and pudgy and turns a deep, dark red. It's the type of face associated with the English dock worker. The red, burly shape and color are so obvious and marked a change that this illness is also rarely left untreated.

Cushing's syndrome used to be a very rare disease. But since artificial hormones were discovered, it's become almost a common illness. The artificial hormones, whether they come from natural sources or not, need careful supervision by a doctor. Steroid (hormone) therapy is used for a number of conditions, from acne to menopause. The hormones ACTH and cortisone, steroids produced in the adrenal system, can cause either Cushing's syndrome or some of its symptoms if not used properly. (By properly, I mean in the right amounts and under the right conditions. One young woman, just 18 years old, had an extremely bad case of acne. She was given cortisone to clear her skin so that plastic surgery could be done. After giving her a prescription, the doctor went on a six-week vacation. He had warned Judy to expect "a few changes," mostly in her tendency toward aggression, which can be one of the side effects of cortisone therapy. Within two weeks, Judy started growing hair on her face. By the time the doctor returned, Judy had a thick beard and mustache and was deep into a serious depression. She had thought the facial hair was one of the changes the doctor had warned her about and never realized that it had gone past the point of a minor side effect. Yes, her face cleared up, but the acne came back as soon as she stopped taking the cortisone. And she had three months of hell getting over her depression.)

Luckily, the newest hormone or steroid therapies take these dangers into consideration, and doctors who keep up with new research know what to look for and how to administer these "miracle" drugs. But there are still some doctors who feel that what they learned in medical school is all they ever have to know, so in these cases the patient has to know enough about the side effects to be able to realize when something is wrong.

Acute Adrenal Insufficiency

This is also a condition which used to be rare until the artificial hormones became widely used. While it occasionally does

Ambassador

beneficial.

Our accommodations include:

- Hospitality Room
- Large Suites
- Complete Kitchens
- Sauna Room
- Indoor and Outdoor Hot Therapy Pools
- Heated Swimming Pool
- Color Television in Every Suite
- Crystal-Clear Mineral Water
- Poolside Lounges, Tables
- Gas Bar-B-Que
- Off-Street Guest Parking
- Just 6 Miles Off Interstate 10
- Airport Transportation
- 10 Minutes to Palm Springs
- Near Restaurants, Golf and Tennis

12921 TAMAR DRIVE AT HACIENDA
DESERT HOT SPRINGS, CALIFORNIA 92240
TELEPHONE (714) 329-6441

happen without steroid therapy, the supplementary hormones are now the chief cause of this life-threatening condition. Since this is an emergency state, it doesn't have very much to do with depression in its clinical sense, but just to complete the adrenal picture, here are some symptoms: pain in the abdomen, headache, weakness, possible nausea, vomiting, and diarrhea. There is confusion and restlessness followed by a circulatory collapse and coma. The symptoms are similar to those of shock.

Adrenogenital Syndrome This illness creates one of the deepest adrenal-caused depressions because the entire hormonal balance is disturbed. The illness can be described as a steady process of *masculinization* which affects both genders equally. A boy will begin growing body and pubic hair. His penis and testicles will develop until they resemble those of an adult. He may enter puberty early, and his voice will deepen. There may be an increase in aggressiveness and muscles will develop so that even a young child will present a midget adult male appearance.

In girls, there is the same masculinizing effect. The clitoris will enlarge, and facial and body hair begins to grow. Breasts may shrink and periods will stop. The voice will deepen and take on a masculine tone. There may be a heavy weight gain.

These symptoms are the same for young girls and adult women. In adult men, there is no sexual change unless it is an increase in sexual aggressiveness. Rarely, the condition may have a feminizing effect on a man and he will undergo the opposite symptoms.

Degrees of Adrenal Imbalance In all the illnesses described, we've been talking about major imbalances of the adrenal glands. Yet the intimate link between *depression* and the function of these important glands does not depend on degree. Even a slight over or underproduction will cause a wide mood swing, and since the adrenals react to any stress, mental or physical, we are frequently out of adrenal balance for varying periods of time. Luckily, the test for adrenalin production is easy and far less expensive than other endocrine gland hormone tests. Adrenalin is carried in the bloodstream, so a simple blood test will show whether too much or too little exists at any given time. If the test results show an imbalance severe enough to require further investigation, the more complicated adrenal function tests can be performed.

There's a strange correlation between suicide and the adrenal hormones which may make this test a lifesaver *if given at the proper time*. Scientists have noticed that an onset of a depressive syndrome is marked by an increase in the steroids (or chemicals) of the adrenal cortex, a part of the adrenal glands. The increased activity of the adrenals show in the urine, where more of these hormones are excreted than usual. Patients who were recovering from depression showed *decreasing* levels of adrenal steroids in their urine. But patients who went through a depressive crisis, who attempted suicide, or who succeeded in killing themselves, showed a dramatic *rise* in adrenal output. In patients who had shown no signs of suicidal behavior before, suicide attempts were precipitated by a rise in adrenal activity. *Those patients whose suicide attempts were successful showed the highest rise in adrenal hormone output.*

This connection has been tested too many times for the results to be dismissed as coincidental. There's also another connection. Medicine has a term for the depressed person's literally "flipping out" and having to be hospitalized. It's called *psychotic disorganization*. There is some belief that this is the mind's way of escaping from the pain of depression—a divorce from a reality too subjectively horrible to face. It doesn't happen much in endogenous depressions, but it's not uncommon in other forms of depression. During this leave-taking from reality, tests show these patients to have very large increases in steroid output.

Right now, medical experts are debating cause and effect. Does the increase in steroids cause the mood change that leads to suicide? Or does the increased stress of the mood call forth the steroids, and is the suicide a result of the mood? The increase is not due just to the contemplation of the *act* of suicide, since autopsy tests show the steroid increase has been consistent over a period of time.

In time, the evidence will probably show that the suicides are the result of the increased adrenal activity. Depression has now been largely accepted as a biochemical disease. Certainly we know that the hormones affect our feelings, especially the adrenal hormones. Cushing's and Addison's illnesses *always* cause serious depressions. And in endogenous depression, there is almost always an overabundance of adrenalin in the system. It's a feedback situation. Our stress makes us produce more adrenalin. A chronic excess of adrenalin makes us feel depressed. The depression creates more stress, more stress means more adrenalin. Soon the system stops working responsibly (that is, in response to stress). Of the suicides who showed heavy increases of adrenal activity, most were seeing their doctors, some were on their way to recovery. Few showed any setback, change in mood, or increase in depression. Few gave hints that they were thinking of suicide. But the adrenal hormones had increased—and the result was a successful suicide. Wouldn't it be a lifesaving idea for every therapist treating a depressive to give a urine test every visit? Thus, when steroid levels went up, the doctor could take extra care not to "lose" the patient.

The connection between adrenal output and depression is an established medical fact. Yet many of the doctors who treat depression attempt to learn about a patient through words only. These doctors never even try to learn how a patient's glands are functioning. This oversight is almost criminal, since an entirely different type of medication is necessary if there is a glandular disturbance. It's an established fact that Cushing's syndrome, for example, *always* causes depression. *Always!* And yet Cushing's doesn't have to be severe enough to cause the beefy face and obesity typical of this disease. In a mild case of Cushing's, how long would a doctor go on talking to a patient, treating verbally for depression and using an anti-depressant which has no effect, before deciding to look inside the patient for the cause of the illness?

The Pancreas

The pancreas is considered an endocrine gland even though it has a duct, or tube, which is used to release its chemicals. The pancreas is located in the intestinal canal, right near the stomach. It produces the most powerful of the digestive juices, and it also makes insulin. You can see the connection between diabetes and the function of the pancreas. Essentially, diabetes is a condition caused when the body can't store sugar. The sugar has no place to go, so it accumulates in the blood. This interferes with carbohydrate metabolism. The activity of the pancreas is directly involved with the hormonal output of the adrenals, the thyroid, and the pituitary, and so these hormones have a relationship with diabetes. Diabetes is a common disease; there are nearly four million diabetics in the United States (it is also on the increase).

A lack of insulin, which is what causes diabetes, causes a

minor depression, but it's not accompanied by the major disturbances which mark clinical endogenous depressions. The only
illness of this gland which produces serious depression is cancer
of the pancreas. Since an imbalance of the chemicals produced by
the pancreas do not have as significant an effect on the mood as
the other endocrine glands, there's no reason to go into any deeper explanation.

The symptoms described in this chapter are of course the
more extreme ones of serious endocrine disturbances. But any
imbalance in the endocrine glands, no matter how slight, can
have a chain reaction effect and *will* cause varying degrees of
depression. If a doctor is treating someone you spend a lot of time
with, you're in the best position to gauge the efficiency of the
treatment. A doctor must, by reason of the limited time of a visit,
make broad judgments when dealing with an emotional state;
that's why labels are so important in psychiatry. The patient is too
close to the problem to have real objectivity. But you, the observer, can make the most valid judgment about lessening of
symptoms over a period of, say, six weeks. If there's not much
improvement during that time, you might suggest some endocrine tests. And now, knowing the symptoms of these glandular
disturbances, you might be aware of the evidence of various endocrine disorders in people close to you, and in yourself. (Again,
remember that parlor diagnosis is out of order here. Even a
trained doctor will only *suspect* glandular malfunction until tests
are taken, since the symptoms of glandular disorders are similar
to those of many other illnesses.)

In order to gauge what is happening inside you, you have to
to be very aware of your body. You have to know exactly how it
feels when everything is working at maximum efficiency. In other
words, you have to memorize how it feels to be healthy. And you
have to be so aware of your body, and of this feeling, that when it
changes even the slightest, you will be aware of the change.
When your car develops a knock or miss or begins to handle
differently, you notice it. Should you expect any less perception
where your well-being is concerned?

7.

Living
With a Depressed Person

If you live with or spend a lot of time with a depressed person, you have to protect two people, the depressive and yourself. Depression affects both of you. You're dealing with someone who is vulnerable, unable to cope with the normal give and take of a relationship, and in serious mental pain. That situation requires a lot of giving on your part. But you are going to feel angry, hostile, and irritated—and guilty for feeling that way. Your resentment may make you do things you'll regret, and the regret will make you even more angry and hostile. While you are suffering all this emotional turbulence, the depressive will be feeling he or she has no right to burden you, that you would be better off if he or she wasn't around and, if the situation is serious enough, that maybe it would be better for everyone if that bottle of sleeping pills or gun or razor blade were used to end the misery.

The least of the tragic consequences of serious depression may be that you too end up with the illness. Your relationship may crumble, or the two of you may live together with a double case of depression, sliding deeper and deeper into that dark night of the soul which squashes all human promise.

Doctors aren't quite sure why the majority of people who live with an untreated depressive for a good length of time will also end up with depression. One reason may be the stress of dealing with the illness. Being around a depressive is exhausting. It requires patience, tact, diplomacy, and the giving of constant reassurance. You must often direct the other person's life. And lots of times you also have to pick up on responsibilities the depressed person may be too immobilized to take care of. It would tire out a saint.

Exhaustion due to such constant stress practically guarantees that you will come down with depression yourself. We've already established the connection between stress and depression. Here you are, trying to help someone else in a situation analogous to nursing a child when you are eating nothing yourself. As you are draining your energy to help your loved one, nothing is coming back in to replace that energy.

There's also a relatively new theory to explain the infectious nature of depression. It's still too new and radical to have gained widespread medical acceptance, but a number of authorities are admitting that the explanation fits the facts. (This, of course, doesn't mean much. We're still ignorant of how the brain really functions; we know only the barest outline. The trouble with finding out more about depression is that one can come up with five different theories, and all of them fit the facts. If you've ever read any of the medieval medical books, you'll be familiar with some of the farfetched and primitive explanations for illness. Sometimes the theories were on the right track, but the terminology and technology needed to make sense of them didn't exist yet. As an example, there was no knowledge of germs or bacteria in those days, and hygiene was nonexistent. People had the idea that "humours" in the blood caused disease, or "humours" in the air. Humours were like drafts: you couldn't see them but they could do you in. How were these primitive medical people to know that bacteria, not humours were actually at fault? The theory was that you could prevent the spread of plague by isolating those who had it. In those days they would lock up plague victims inside their houses and post a guard at the door who would stay until everyone was dead or had recovered from this disease. That was based on the knowledge that plague spread from one person to another. They knew it was contagious, but they didn't know why. Nor did they realize that you could lock up every plague victim in the world, but one hopping flea could spread the sickness throughout the city. It never occurred to these medieval experts that perhaps plague didn't spread by human-to-human contact alone. In fact, except for the pneumatic form of plague, it isn't really contagious! Because these people had the right *theory* without the right facts, plague killed over one-third the population of Europe between the thirteenth and sixteenth centuries. Essentially, we are as much in the dark about depression as the medieval doctors were about physical illnesses. Our theories work—we can use electric shock, anti-depressants, or verbal therapies to cure symptoms—but time must prove whether they work because they are based on the right facts. While *melancholia*, as depression used to be called, has been known for more than three thousand years, the first real break in understanding and curing the illness came less than 30 years ago. We're still waiting to learn enough about the brain to know what actually causes the biogenic amines to malfunction.)

The new theory, which is gaining some credence from medical scientists, is the *depressive field* theory. It's based on the belief that an "energy field" surrounds each human being (and for that matter, all living things). In humans, this energy field is electrical in origin and is generated by the electrical impulses from brain and nerve cells. Electricity has strange effects on humans. For example, electricity applied to the brain will cure symptoms of depression. Heavy electrical shocks will cause a memory loss or disorient someone so that the person can make no sense of words or communication.

According to the depressive field theory, the electrical impulses generating the energy field around a depressive are different from those of ordinary energy fields. The depressive's energy field has a greater effect on people who spend time within its range. Supposedly, people are more vulnerable to the depressive field than any other. There's no way now of measuring whether this theory is accurate, but it's a fact that people "catch" a bad mood more easily than a good one. Perhaps we humans are naturally pessimistic, or perhaps our culture, with its "if-it-feels-good-it-must-be-sinful" attitude, makes us more open to depression than to joy. Whatever the explanation, if you live with or spend time with a depressive, it will bring you down too. So . . . protection.

Your Natural Feelings

Protecting yourself while protecting the depressive against what *you* may do in reaction to your feelings is a hard job. But it becomes a lot easier when you realize that the well-being of two people depends on it. That doesn't mean you should suppress your feelings. Quite the opposite—most of the trouble caused by anger and hostility comes from suppressed feelings. When a person tries to be giving and helpful, burying all negative feelings, these feelings will pop out in subconscious ways to damage and hurt.

We've already discussed the symptoms of depression, but what hasn't been mentioned is how it feels—how it feels to the person with the illness, and how you will feel watching someone you love and depend on going through those symptoms. (It doesn't necessarily have to be someone you love and depend on. Many live-in relationships, married or not, have lost the love and dependency and become a relationship of tolerance. When depression occurs in this kind of relationship, the nondepressive doesn't feel the same degree of fear, but there's a lot more anger and irritation.) Here are several things to remember:

- You are not evil for feeling this way.
- Resentment at having to give so much to an adult acting like a helpless baby doesn't make you bad.
- The fact that someone else has an illness which causes him or her pain doesn't lessen your pain from having to cope with the illness.
- You probably won't get the sympathy you deserve in the situation because people who don't know about the illness won't realize what you're going through, and it's only natural that you react to this with resentment.
- You will flare up and do things you feel sorry about, but you must have some release. You don't have to expect yourself to be a saint.
- You didn't cause the other person to become ill. Your feelings are normal and right, and you do not need to feel guilty about them.

Many books that discuss feelings, move blithely along talking about letting yourself go or expressing your feelings, while a reader is saying, 'yes, but in my specific case . . .' The difficulty of taking advice about making yourself feel good is that the writer, who doesn't know you personally, doesn't see the difficulty of the problems in *your* specific case. You can come up with dozens of different reasons why this or that approach won't work. Yet sometimes it helps to know that your problems or feelings aren't specific to you alone. The feelings of loved ones in a case of depression have been charted thoroughly enough so that they can almost be predicted. It might make you feel better to know you are not alone, just as the knowledge that others are in the same situation is one of the biggest helps to the depressive.

In a close relationship with a depressive, the first thing you will probably notice is that he or she seems to be irritable much of the time. That isn't the first symptom to manifest itself: the first symptom is *anahedia*, or lack of joy, but very few people notice that another person isn't enjoying him/herself or feeling much pleasure, especially since it's very subtle at the beginning. Irritation, though, is noticeable because it is *directed*. It's easier to notice an expressed emotion, especially when we are on the receiving end of it. The usual situation is that the partner notices the irritation, excuses it on one ground or another, then finally brings it up in discussion. (A note on terminology here: I'm going to refer to the person dealing with the depressive as the *partner*. First, because if you are that person, you *are* a partner with a common goal—recovery. Second, because it doesn't matter whether you are helping a mate, a parent or child, a relative or friend or co-worker—the basic technique and your basic feelings will be pretty much the same no matter who the depressed person is. And third, because it's terribly awkward to keep searching around for a descriptive adjective and that gets in the way of writing clearly about a complicated subject.)

If the partner decides to discuss the irritability with the depressive, the partner is dealing from a (let us suppose) rational basis, bringing up a change in personality which is disturbing the relationship. The depressive will rarely see any change, because he or she will usually not be aware of acting irritable. The depressive *will* be aware of feeling irritated more often than usual, and will bring up the reasons why. In most cases, the two will then begin arguing about whether the reasons for the irritation are valid and neither will notice that (A) that was not the point of the discussion, and (B) nothing is being resolved. The situation will rest for the moment.

Shortly after, the depressive will usually begin to withdraw, turning down social activities and beginning a series of delusional beliefs, though at first these are so subtle that they don't seem delusional. Ralph's behavior is an example of this. As an advertising executive, he made a good salary and he and his family used it to live quite well. They were paying off several major purchases—car, home, and mountain cabin—but they weren't in financial difficulty. Ralph started complaining, though. He said the family was spending too much money and cutbacks had to be made. It sounded reasonable. What family adult hasn't looked at the budget and tried to call a halt to some of the spending?

Within a short time, Ralph was complaining that too much was being spent on entertainment and he ended the family tradition of going to the movies on Sunday. He stopped delivery of the paper, saying it cost too much money. When his wife bought new school clothing for the children, he blew up. His conversation started dwelling on the family's financial insecurity. His wife tried showing him that they were in good financial shape, but Ralph wasn't having any of her reasoning. Money became such a sore subject in the family that even a chance remark could set off a tirade. He began questioning his wife about her pantyhose. How many pairs did she buy this month? Couldn't she make them last longer? Couldn't the ripped ones be salvaged somehow?

It took Ralph's wife a long while to see that something was wrong. When something begins in a reasonable manner, it's hard to judge when it passes the point of reason. That's why it takes so long for many alcoholics to recognize their condition. The before-dinner drink which turns into a before-and-after dinner drink, which turns into the lunch drink and the between-meal drink, then the several drinks, then the secret drinks—the point at which it slips from social drinking into alcoholism is subtle and vague. In Ralph's case, his other symptoms were obvious enough so that his wife got him to seek treatment, eventually.

The withdrawal phase usually causes slight puzzlement in the partner, but as yet there is not much negative feeling. The partner may notice that the depressive falls asleep after dinner, dozing off without meaning to and staying groggy much of the evening.

Then, in quick succession, come the other symptoms. The depressive feels helpless and loses all energy, doesn't want to move or do very much. He keeps talking about how inferior he is, how unworthy and sinful. These remarks may be subtle also: "Do you really want me to carry this down the stairs? You know what a klutz I am." Or, "You'd better do this, I don't think I can handle it." Or, "You drive, you're a better driver than I am." Or, "I don't think I should go to church. I'm such a sinner that church couldn't do much for me anyhow."

Personal hygiene deteriorates and the early morning awakenings may start here. At first, the partner tries to cheer the depressive, coaxing him or her out of the blue mood. That's all the partner usually thinks it is at this point—a blue mood which seems to be lasting a long while. There will be concern at this time, and if the relationship is a close one, loving concern. When the coaxing and concern don't work, the partner will feel a little annoyed, believing that the depressive could snap out of this funk if he or she really tried.

As the situation continues, the partner begins to get definitely irritated. There may come the suspicion that the depressive is doing it on purpose, trying to make the partner angry or to exact payment for some fancied wrong. The partner feels like a target. Little arguments begin. On the partner's side, the arguments may open with the words, "I'm getting sick and tired. . . ." As the weeks pass, the partner may suggest that the depressive "see" someone. The depressive will usually refuse. Tension builds. Now the partner begins to feel angry, and the anger is shortly accompanied by feelings of active hostility. The former feelings of pity and compassion for the depressive evaporate and are replaced by sarcasm. Or, if the partner is the long-suffering type, there may be a tired resignation with suppressed anger, tight lips that say nothing lest they reveal a building resentment. Finally, the partner removes as much contact as possible, no longer trying to communicate about the problem and leaving the depressive alone.

Of course, this sequence doesn't happen if the partner knows about depression and realizes what is happening. But no matter how much knowledge there is, the partner—*you*—will be bound to feel frustrated by the situation. How could you not be? Your sexual desirability is ignored, the depressive no longer wants to prepare food or eat it, intelligence lessens until the depressive seems unable to think normally. The intelligence part is important. We get used to the intelligence level of someone we are close to. We adjust to it without even thinking. You'll see this if you take an objective look at your speech patterns. Everyone talks to people in different ways. You have friends with whom you may use certain words you wouldn't dream of using to others. They may be slang words that some people wouldn't understand or large words that people with lesser vocabularies may be unfamiliar with. We all temper our speech to fit the understanding of others. When a person's intelligence lowers, he or she is not able to communicate in the same way. A fantastic punster, for example, may not have the same level of wit that allows a quick-thought play on words. The puns may not be up to standard. Doctors who specialize in depression will almost always hear the same complaints from mates: "I can't seem to talk to him any more . . . he doesn't understand things lately." The depressive will need more time to assimilate a thought, to react to it either in action or verbally. Getting used to a changed reaction time is also frustrating.

The little frustrations are the worst because they are the least obvious. And there are many of them in depression. The partner must adjust to a familiar person who suddenly begins staying in the bathroom a long time, for example. Or one who promises to do something, but, uncharacteristically, just doesn't do it. Or a person whose conversation changes to consist only of negatives and complaints about how no one likes him, no one wants him, he is unlikeable, and so on. Many of these changes are trivial, but they add up. So does the parnter's exasperation.

The feelings of frustration, exasperation, anger, and hostility aren't *wrong* feelings. Not only are they normal, but there is something deeper than normality to these emotions, something which makes them healthy as apart from normal. (*Normal* really means *constant*, it doesn't mean *right*. So a badge of normalcy doesn't mean merit. It's normal to find the body of a murder victim on a dark street in big cities every so often. It's normal for banks to expect to be robbed and for industries to build things in such a way that they will break down so that customers will keep coming back. It's normal because these things happen and they do not come as surprises. But that doesn't make them good. In an important way, the negative feelings in reaction to a depressive are good, because they are like survival mechanisms.)

Frustration is a goad to action. Anger needs release. When you are frustrated and angry with another person, you will usually do something about it. When faced with a depressive, if you know what you're dealing with, you will get some kind of professional help for the person. The more frustrated you are, the harder you'll try to get that help. Since one of the symptoms of depression is a reluctance to see a doctor, you'll *have* to work hard to get him or her to go to a specialist. So your frustration gives you the force you need to do what you have to do. When you're angry with someone, it's usually because the person has done or is doing something you don't like. Anger is used to express your dislike of the action, but it's also a way of stopping the person from doing it. With the anger, you are actually attempting (on some level) to change or prevent something; if you thought there was no hope of changing or preventing the situation, you would either resign yourself to it or accept it. Thus, your anger at the depressed person will, *if used properly*, provide the force to make treatment desirable, to help the person get back to health quicker.

If Used Properly . . .

How can you *use* your negative emotions about the depressive instead of letting emotions merely make you feel like hell? Well, you're going to go through periods of feeling like hell no matter what happens, but you don't have to let that drag you down. Regardless of what anyone tells you, living with a depressive or spending a lot of time with one is not going to be a glorious experience. It's going to be painful for both of you. But there's a key to minimizing your own negative feelings, and it's one that can also be used by the depressive as a way of keeping hope alive. It's this:

Be mad at the illness, not the person.

Memorize this rule. It should stand as a barrier protecting both you and the depressive every second of the day and night. As long as you can keep it in mind, your anger will have a proper perspective and you won't be eaten up by it. And when you turn your anger toward the illness, it will make you that much more determined to get rid of it, to fight *it* rather than the depressive.

It's very hard to explain how depression feels to someone who has never had it. Of course everyone has gone through periods of feeling down. But clinical depression is a lot different. Have you ever been in a situation where you felt so unconfident, so unsure of yourself that every moment was agony? All people have experienced a time of feeling fragile, of castigating themselves for being a fool or doing something stupid, of knowing that they've blown it beyond repair. The pain and regret are like torture. Now triple or quadruple those feelings, and imagine how it would be to feel that way every moment of the day. Depression causes a total loss of self-esteem. There's no confidence at all. Without confidence, ability goes.

During part of my depression, I became convinced I couldn't drive a car. Why? Because I had lost all confidence in my driving. Never mind the fact that I had been driving for ten years, that I held a driver's license in three different countries. The moment I started to pull out onto the road, I became convinced I would miss a stop sign, run a light, or pull out into another lane and bash into someone else.

One of the terrors of driving in Europe, for someone who is unfamiliar with it, is the roundabout. The roundabout is in the center of an intersection. It's a circular piece of road, and it allows you to go around until you get to the street you want. There are no real lanes; all the drivers do the best they can. Surprisingly, there are very few accidents. I had done very well on the roundabouts of England. But one day, in the middle of one, I became convinced that I couldn't dodge the cars cutting in and swerving left and right in front of me. I was afraid to move over to get off the roundabout. There were five streets leading off of it, and I wasn't even sure which one I wanted. I circled around about four times, then decided to risk an exit. But as I moved over to it, instead of going with the flow of traffic, I looked at all the cars speeding around and lost my courage. I was so positive that I couldn't do it that I shut my eyes and crashed into another car which was also getting off the roundabout. After that, I was convinced I couldn't drive. So I didn't. Yet the ability hadn't changed. I believed I couldn't do it . . . and that became true.

The depressive believes he or she can't really do anything. That only reinforces the lack of self-esteem. This is why patience during depression is so important. A depressive interprets others' impatience as a reinforcement of the inability to do anything right, or even do it at all.

Earlier I said that we get used to another person's intelligence and automatically relate to him or her on that level. But we also get used to our own intelligence. We come to rely on it. You have a report to write, but you take time to watch a television show. Why? You trust your intelligence. You know how long it will take you to write the report. You have shopping to do, but you leave it until the last minute. You know that your mind will work to take you there, to pick out what you need at the best price, and you rely on the speed with which you can trust your mind to coordinate all the necessary actions. You rely on your mind as you do on your strength—you always have a good idea of how much effort you need to expend to get something accomplished, and you don't panic over the prospect.

The depressive does. The depressive can no longer rely on his or her mind. Intelligence usually drops by fifteen points. That's a meaningless statistic, but it can make the difference between a person of normal capacity and retardation. Not being able to solve problems as quickly or easily as usual is pretty hard to handle. And problems aren't necessarily troubles. Problem solving is one of the major functions of everyday life. You're in a rush and the elevator is slow—should you take the stairs? You've forgotten to make a phone call—should you make it now or wait until tomorrow? Easy problems to solve, normally. In depression they're hard. Not only because the mind isn't as sharp as it usually is, but because indecision is a major symptom of the disease. Simple problems such as deciding what to have for lunch or what television program to watch become agonizing to the depressive. The three qualities—intelligence, problem solving, and decision making—are so closely connected that you could say they are three aspects of the same thing.

The drop in intelligence, difficulty in solving problems, and indecision are also the three qualities that most interfere with performance. In severe cases they immobilize the person. That leads to another emotion: guilt. At first it may be only slight guilt at being unable to perform as well as usual; then it turns to a feeling of guilt at putting everyone through all this trouble. This "trouble" is of course magnified in the depressive's mind. The guilt may become delusional. If a friend or family member falls ill, the depressive may feel responsible for it. If anything goes wrong, the depressive may take the blame. Let someone prove logically that the depressive can't possibly be at fault. He or she may then turn it into mysticism, claiming to be a jinx, unlucky for everyone.

These things all cause pain, but even without them, there would still be enormous pain. It hurts to be blue. When you're down, you're in pain. The depressive is down all the time.

With this kind of pain, it's hard to turn outward enough to cope with it on a realistic level. The depressive is overwhelmed by it. He or she can see nothing else because the pain is so great. This can cause a vicious cycle: the pain causes a turning inward and others react to that by expressing irritation, which convinces the depressive that all the feelings of inferiority and guilt are valid, which causes more pain, which causes further withdrawal, which causes more irritation in others, and so on.

Now . . . how do you handle all this?

Let's start out with a pretreatment case. You're just beginning to suspect that something is wrong and maybe you're already wondering if it could be depression. Your friend (you wouldn't be caring for the depressive unless you cared about him or her, so "friend" is an apt term) admits that something is wrong but doesn't want to seek help for a variety of reasons. Among the usual excuses are: "No doctor can do anything for me" . . . "I don't want to go; they'll find out I'm crazy" (usually unspoken) . . . "There's no sense wasting the money" . . . "This will pass; it's nothing a doctor can treat" . . . "I don't need to see a doctor" . . . "Things will be okay as soon as . . ." (completed by some circumstance which may change in the future) . . . "I don't mind seeing a doctor, but let's wait a while, next week maybe" . . . "I don't trust Doctor so-and-so, I want to find a better one," and so on.

You may be lulled by the logic of the depressive and let valuable time slip by without getting treatment. Maybe the symptoms are still vague, or perhaps it's a mild case and the symptoms are too slight to alarm you. Perhaps you have even found reasons to show that they aren't symptoms but valid responses to a current situation. You wait for the depression to pass.

Time goes by. The illness may get worse or the symptoms may become chronic and stay the same. In any event, it doesn't get better. The depressive still makes no move to see a doctor. You bring it up frequently, but nothing is done.

Okay. At this point you should talk to the physician who is familiar with your friend. If you aren't living with the person, talk to relatives or close friends about seeing a doctor. Discuss the symptoms. You have to take into consideration here that the physician or the person's relatives may not know very much about depression and may dismiss your concerns. Don't let that stop you. Call your local suicide prevention league or center (or whatever it calls itself in your town) and ask for an appointment with one of the psychiatrists. If you live in a small town and there is no suicide prevention organization whatsoever there, call the nearest university and ask to speak to the psychiatry department. Talk to one of the professors who is *also in practice*. A professor without a practice may be knowledgeable, but that knowledge will be more theoretical than practical—it will not have been put to enough use so that it has the proof of experience, and therefore, you can't place as much trust in it.

You'll have the best chance of contacting the right person for your needs if you begin by asking for someone with a *background* in depression. Notice the word *background*. If you ask for someone with *experience* in treating depression, the operator will think you are calling for yourself and trying to get a free consultation. That's exactly what you are trying to do, but you've got to get to the doctor through the operator, and the operator often will have a standard series of gambits to discourage members of the public from trying to get over-the-phone consultation. Using the word *background* implies that you are searching for advice rather than personal treatment. If the operator asks what you wish to talk to the doctor about, say you're doing some research on depression and need to speak with someone who is familiar with the condition. Your priority here is to get through to someone you can talk to, so you have to outwit the bureaucratic minds which may be *under* that someone. Besides, you *are* doing research.

Tell the doctor you finally reach that you are concerned about your friend and would like to discuss some of the behaviors which seem symptomatic. *Behaviors* is a scientific word, but you're not getting technical enough to make the doctor feel you're invading private medical territory. If the therapist says no opinion can be given over the phone, refuses to meet with you, or says that the depressive has to be seen in person before a diagnosis can be made, stress the fact that you are merely trying to determine whether treatment is necessary, since there's a reluctance on your friend's part to seek help. If the doctor still isn't cooperating, ask for the name of the best specialist in depression that the doctor knows. This is a psychological ploy, a slightly underhanded way of saying, "If you won't cooperate with me, I'll find someone else." If that doesn't work and you also can't find a specialist, call your local hospitals and ask to speak with the medical director. Ask for the name of a good specialist in depression. Unless you click right away with a contact, get several recommendations and talk to them all. You can use the doctor's reaction as a screening device. If there is no sympathy for your concern, there will probably also be an absence of the compassion necessary to work well with a depressive.

Of course, if you can persuade your friend to go for help without all this checking around and consultation, everything will be a lot easier. Sometimes you can persuade just by making the person aware of the fact that the illness has a name and is treatable.

Don't just pick a psychiatrist out of the phone book. Talk to the doctor, find out what his or her views on depression are and how treatment is usually handled. If the therapist believes in ECT (electro-convulsive therapy), you have to realize that it may be used and decide if that's acceptable to you and your friend. However, once you've decided on a doctor and have satsified yourself that the choice is a good one, don't interfere unless you strenuously object to something. Keep a close eye on the course of treatment, and by all means keep in touch with the doctor by phone, but let the doctor be the doctor.

Supposing that you can't get your friend to seek treatment? You can wait for a time when he or she is vulnerable and open to suggestion, then act. And act immediately. If your friend says yes, call the therapist you have chosen right away and ask if you both can be seen in the next hour or so. Obviously, that means that you don't bring the subject up when you know the specialist isn't going to be in the office. If the doctor can't see your friend for several hours (and when requesting an immediate appointment, make sure you express the fact that it has to be *now*, that you're afraid the person will have a change of heart), then don't sit around the house waiting. The depressive *may* decide not to go. Get the person out of the house, even if you have to drive aimlessly around. Be ready to go from the house to the doctor's office, making sure you don't have to return to the house for any reason. Don't bring up the coming appointment unless the depressive wants to talk about it. Be relaxed and matter of fact. Above all, don't reconvince your friend. Don't say something like, "You'll feel better now that you've made this decision," or "You should have done this a long time ago." These are judgmental statements, and may cause your friend to refute your judgment with the doubts which caused resistance to getting help in the first place. If the person wants to talk about it, listen to the comments and be reassuring. Convey the fact that depression is an illness, it can be cured, and no harm will come from a visit to a specialist. Very often there may be a fear that the appointment is just a plot to get the doctor to sign commitment papers. Remember, most depressives have the fear that they may be going crazy. Don't laugh at this fear. When one's mind suddenly shifts to another state of being and seems out of control, it *feels* like insanity. You have to be reassuring and calm. Tell your friend he or she is not insane, and that if commitment were really on your mind, you wouldn't have had to go to all this trouble to do it. Express your love and concern and say that you realize the pain of the condition, and because you care, you want to help the pain to go away.

Medication—the First Weeks
Once the doctor has evaluated the degree of depression, anti-depressants will usually be prescribed. These have some side effects, especially during the first ten days or so. Some people may be turned into dullards or even zombies. Some people are never affected, but let me tell you how it feels, so you can relate to what is happening without anxiety or impatience, and so you can reassure your friend when there is concern about the situation.

The most precise comparison is one which you may not have

ever experienced. It's the feeling of groggy exhaustion when you try to get out of bed with a dangerously high fever. There's a sense of unreality. You can't think, you can't move. All you want to do is sleep and be alone. It can also be compared to that groggy, dazed feeling that comes just before a sleeping pill starts to work. Mentally, you feel as though a fog has descended on your mind, numbing it, creating a drowsiness that's like a haze. You have to concentrate even to make sense of what someone is saying. Physically, it feels like moving through molasses. Everything is an effort. There's not much coordination, and exacting work like embroidery or fine carpentry is difficult if not impossible. There seems to be a weight over mental and physical action, pressing the patient down into a soft nest of sleepiness. This is the side effect at its extreme, but even in lesser degrees it creates an intense desire for sleep.

The feeling sounds terrible, but it can actually be comfortable if it's accepted without fighting it or feeling fear. It gets uncomfortable if the depressive has to struggle out of the foggy haze to perform in any alert capacity. The best thing you can do is encourage your friend to sleep. Make your friend comfortable, tuck the covers in, and don't wake him or her up for meals or anything else. The depressive may not feel like eating during this period. You don't have to force big meals, but basic nutritional needs must be satisfied. Have some food available which can be prepared quickly. When you see the person is up, tell him or her to come in and eat, the meal is ready. If it is refused, *you* refuse to accept the refusal. Don't argue about it, just act as if the idea of refusal is nonsense—you've got the food prepared and it has to be eaten.

During this adjustment to the medication, you may have to give reassurance regarding some delusions such as (a common one) "the medication is actually a poison," or "the confusion caused by the pills will never end."

There may be other symptoms, such as blurred vision and dryness of the mouth. The vision problem is best helped by avoidance. Have the person lie in a dim room, perhaps with a damp cloth over the eyes. For mouth dryness, have a supply of Life Savers on hand. Sucking them will relieve it.

While this adjustment period continues, you may feel somewhat annoyed at this great hulking person walking around in pajamas and acting like a vegetable. Remember that you wouldn't feel so annoyed if the person had a broken leg or serious case of bronchitis. The *illness* is causing all this trouble, and it is the *illness* and not the depressive that is the source of your anger. It's only because the major symptoms affect behavior that you even feel annoyed. But this two weeks or less of dazedness is the first step toward ending the whole problem.

Steve Guddy's case can be used as an example of what can happen if you don't handle the adjustment problem right. His wife, Martha, agreed to begin taking anti-depressants after the family's physician diagnosed the illness. But Steve didn't realize what those first two weeks felt like to Martha. He was already suppressing his irritation toward an illness that had made her unable to prepare his food and clean the house, and with the medication she was unable to do even the few chores she had been doing. He began complaining that Martha was turning into a vegetable, which, of course, was exactly what Martha felt like. She thought the pills were doing her more harm than good, even though her system was almost used to them and the effects were beginning to ease off. So, even though she had gone through the adjustment period, Martha stopped taking the medication. When Steve realized what had happened, he begged Martha to start the medication again. But once burned, twice shy—Steve's reaction had been so negative that Martha was afraid to take them any more. Her symptoms lasted for eight months—period of hell for her and Steve—when they could have begun ending in less than eight weeks.

You may also have the problem of *patient* reluctance to deal with. Your friend may dislike the side effects so much that he or she wants to stop taking the medication even though you've been positive and encouraging about the treatment. I once knew a man who had suffered from chronic depression for twenty years without knowing that there was a name for his condition. When he found out what the disease was, he was very open to taking medication for it. But after a week and a half he started complaining that he felt like a vegetable. He stopped taking the pills. He still has depression.

You're going to have to watch for signs of reluctance, and when they come up, you'll have to keep assuring your friend that this is a temporary stage. Suggest that he or she probably didn't like the taste of wine or beer at first. Most new things require a period of adjustment. And it won't hurt to make sure the medication is actually being taken. If the pills are causing mental dulling, it's easy to forget to take them. So ask. Or give them yourself. At the very least, keep an eye on the container to see that the pills are being used. One caution, though: don't check in an obvious fashion. You'll create suspicion and distrust, which is exactly the opposite of the environment the depressive needs.

Another caution: there are many types of drugs which can be harmful in combination with anti-depressants. You should inform the doctor of any medication your friend may be taking. And you should keep any prescription drugs which may be lying around in a safe place. (Since drugs deteriorate with time, this may be the perfect occasion to clear out the medicine chest and get rid of that old bottle of sleeping pills or codeine or diet drugs or whatever that you've been saving "just in case.")

After the Adjustment

Once that initial drowsiness wears off (and in some lucky people it never happens at all), your friend will be looking for quick relief from the symptoms. You might be too. *It's not going to happen that way*. The anti-depressants are correcting a long-term chemical imbalance and they don't do it overnight or even over a few weeks. There will be a minimum of two weeks before any improvement at all will be felt. During this time the patient may become discouraged. You've got to provide a lot of support during this period and so does everyone else involved. If your friend seems very upset at not being better already and your encouragement doesn't seem to be working, have the patient call the doctor for some heartening words. This is a waiting period. The medication will begin to work gradually, and by the end of the first month its benefits will be noticeable. You have to keep hope alive. This may mean repeating the same words of encouragement over and over again until you're bored with them. Keep doing it anyhow. Your continued support will make this waiting period bearable.

During this time you also have to take care of your friend in other ways. Alcohol is a central nervous system depressant and doesn't mix with most anti-depressants. The combination may cause intense sleepiness so that your friend may just crash, falling off to sleep in embarrassing places. Alcohol can also cause dangerous changes in blood pressure. People who are used to wine with dinner or the occasional social drink may find stopping undesirable or may not know how to turn down a drink. The typical weight loss in depression doesn't allow the excuse that he or she can't drink because of a diet. And the person may be reluctant to refer to the medication. However, a *special* diet can be used as a good excuse for turning down a drink. Don't make the mistake of having your friend stay away from social gatherings where liquor may be offered. One of the symptoms of depression is a desire for isolation, and so you should be encouraging your friend to get out into the world again. Also you can substitute juice for wine at dinner. There's no sense in creating a feeling of deprivation by drinking wine frequently in front of someone who can't have it temporarily.

Another off-limits substance may be caffeine. You should check with the doctor about this. Caffeine is a stimulant, and most stimulants can't be used with anti-depressants. If your friend is a real coffee lover, decaffinated brands may provide the solution. But if the person is used to drinking coffee, there may be a time when he or she just has a cup and forgets to specify decaffinated only. If possible, get the person to drink juice in place of coffee. An added benefit will be the extra nutritional value of fruit juices. But go for pure fruit juice and stay away from those sugary juice "drinks." They contain only about 30 percent real juice and lots of white sugar. If the doctor has decided against caffeine, remember that coffee isn't the only place it's found. It's in tea, cocoa, and some aspirin compounds; so if you have any of these in your medicine cabinet, throw them out and buy pure aspirin.

Spend some time talking to the doctor about the medication. Find out what can't be combined with it and in what unexpected places these forbidden substances may be found. Memorize the forbidden list. It will save you a lot of trouble later. If you see that your friend forgets and takes that drink or cup of coffee in social situations, it may be a good idea to go without the medication for about six hours before the gathering. But check with the doctor before taking any such action to stop the pills.

The Improvement Stage
Once the right medication is found and the adjustment period is over, there will be a gradual relief from the symptoms of depression. This doesn't mean that anyone should count on a

straight diagnosis, two-week adjustment period, and oh-boy-everything's-all-right-again sequence. The right medication may take months to find. Remember, it takes real expertise to decide which factor is actually causing the depression. The medication has to be matched to the specific chemical cause, and that may require several tries. The doctor may start out with a tricyclic type of drug and if the results aren't good, switch to an MAO inhibitor. There may be combinations of drugs; for example tranquilizers or sleeping pills may be taken with anti-depressants in certain cases. Lithium may be tried in combination with other medications. You can't count on the first prescription being the best one possible. So you may have to *wait* for the right drug to be found, *wait* for the adjustment period, then *wait* for the medication to start taking effect.

The effects will be gradual, and you may not notice them at first. Your friend may become more responsive, but still not respond as thoroughly as before the illness. The sleep disturbances may stop for a day or two, begin again, stop for a few days, and gradually dwindle away.

This will be a very hard period for *you*. You have watched someone close to you deteriorate, you have found a doctor to diagnose the illness, you have gone through the adjustment period and the medication changes . . . and you're probably thinking it's high time this business came to an end. You may even suppress these thoughts so that you don't feel your frustration. You may transfer your feelings to other causes. Your job has got you down, or you're "coming down with something." You feel jittery, a bit anxious and restless. You may start to feel a little uneasy, a feeling almost like fear, but without having a source you can focus on.

This is the time you have to take care of *yourself*. That doesn't mean just getting enough rest and eating a proper diet. You have to reward yourself for all you are doing, since it's a pretty sure bet that no one else (except perhaps the doctor) is aware of the pressure and burden on *you*. This is also the time when you can easily exhaust yourself into a depression even though your friend is being treated and is on the way to recovery.

I can't tell you how to make yourself feel good because I don't know you and have no idea what will please you. But I can give you methods of pleasing yourself with those things that *do* make you feel good. You have to give yourself pleasure. So the first thing to do when you feel hemmed in by the world is to make a pleasure list.

Write down everything you can think of which would make you feel good. It may be browsing in a do-it-yourself shop or taking a weekend trip to the mountains. You may feel good about buying a new outfit or getting some accessory for the car. Then again, hiring someone to come in and clean the house may be the best thing you can do for yourself. Write down whatever you think will be an enjoyable treat.

Now . . . cross off all the impossible things. If you can't get away for the weekend because you have no one to watch the children, cross it off. Don't cross it off for *should* reasons, just *can't* reasons. Let me explain what the difference is between *shoulds* and *can'ts*. A should statement is based on guilt. You'd *like* to take off for the mountains, but you can't because you shouldn't. And you shouldn't because . . . name any reason you like. The fact is that those are excuses, not reasons. Should you leave your depressed friend? If the answer is no, who says so? *Can* you leave for the weekend? *Yes*. Of course you will have to get someone to take over for you and watch the depressive, but you *can* go. Separate the absolute *not possibles* from the guilt-ridden *shoulds* on the list. Practice letting go of the shoulds. (There's one difference here: if you or the doctor is worried about suicide, then you *can't* leave the person and a weekend trip gets taken off the *should* list.) Should you buy a new outfit? Maybe money is tight and you shouldn't. But *can* you? Yes. It's probably worth the expense if it will take away that nervous feeling.

Your pleasures don't have to be goals. It may not be possible to make yourself feel good by spending money, taking a trip, or doing something you've always wanted to do. Give some thought to small pleasures—a four-hour tub soak with a new novel, a luxury food you love but rarely have, a drive to a wooded area where you can take a long walk and be alone and think. Whatever you decide, you now have the idea. Give yourself a feeling of being pampered. Reward yourself. It will go a long way toward overcoming exhaustion.

One thing you must learn to do is relax. You're in a tense situation, one in which you are trying to carry another person along toward health while keeping everything going and handling your own responsibilities plus the responsibilities of the depressive. You can't do this if you allow the burden to get to you. It will, unless you create moments of peace for your mind.

One of the great methods of mental relaxation is meditation. Unfortunately, meditation has become so associated with movements or religions that many people ignore its benefits. Others may practice meditation only as a source of spiritual enlightenment and ignore its basically practical advantages. Investigate various methods of relaxation through meditation. They will help quiet your mind while you are waiting for your friend to recover. More, they will provide a depressive with a way of coping with anxiety and tensions. Both of you can use these methods for greater peace of mind.

You, the Pill Giver

Along with all the other things you have to deal with, you may have to make sure that medication is taken in the right amount and at the right time. We've already discussed the fact that you must keep an eye on the pill bottle to see that it's being used. If you feel that the depressive is forgetting or not taking the medication when he's supposed to, don't nag or start questioning. Put the bottle in a conspicuous place, a place where you would naturally be able to reach it, and begin saying, "It's time for your pill. I'll get it." This job may be a little harder if the person goes to work and has to take medication during work hours. But there are two things which you should do: First, check with the doctor to make sure exactly what time the medication should be taken. If the bottle says "three times a day," ask the doctor how many hours apart each pill should be taken and whether medication should begin before or after food is taken. Since the medication in effect is a substitute for a malfunctioning chemical (by balancing production rather than replacing it), it must be in the system during all waking hours. Once you know the hour separation for each pill, you can then adjust the schedule if necessary. Suppose the pill sequence is every four hours and the last one is to be taken at 10:00 P.M., but the depressive goes to bed at 9:00. You can start the sequence earlier in the morning so that each medication time is moved up an hour. In an illness marked by sleep disturbances, it would be silly to wake a patient to give a pill.

Now we come to the most common syndrome of recovery.

Your friend is better. He or she sleeps all night, is beginning to laugh again, looks forward to tomorrow with gusto. You *both* feel good. The dark times are over. So you both decide to stop the medication.

A week or two goes by. Your friend feels a little tired and asks if it would be possible to stay home that night. You don't mind. The next night your friend is quiet and goes to bed early. And that morning you are awakened by the sound of quiet crying. It's back again. The depression has started all over again. How could it happen, just when things were going so well?

It's hard to remember, if recovery seems to be an accomplished fact, that the symptoms of the illness are not the illness itself. The medication relieves the symptoms and maintains the chemical balance in the system. *It does not cure the disease*. So much heartache is caused by people stopping anti-depressant therapy too soon that I can't warn you strongly enough not to stop medication or let the depressive stop taking it . . . and he will want to.

Just as an indication of depression is the reluctance to seek treatment, an indication of recovery is a reluctance to continue medication. Don't let that happen. A relapse is almost guaranteed if medication is stopped too soon.

If your friend gives you an argument about continuing to take the pills, don't argue back. You can point out that deciding that anti-depressants aren't necessary now is like a diabetic saying that because he feels so good he doesn't have to take insulin any more. It's the medication that's curing the symptoms. If your friend doesn't believe that, don't fight about it. Just calmly and matter of factly be there with a pill when it's time for one. Make sure the doctor knows about the reluctance to continue medication. This is such a common syndrome that most therapists and physicians are prepared for it.

There's one other thing you have to keep in mind. It may just be possible that the depressive is having a bad reaction to a certain drug. Side effects usually show up at the beginning of treatment, but occasionally they take months to appear. Nancy, a 31-year-old depressive from New York, is an example. Nancy had been taking Stellazine for three months without any bad effects at all. One day she began feeling nervous and restless. She had to keep moving her fingers and legs and couldn't sit still. Soon the movements had spread to her whole body, which was twitching in little jerks. This wasn't involuntary. She could control the movements. But she only felt "human" when jiggling; she felt an unbearable pressure without the movements. A neighbor had been helping Nancy through her depression. Nancy called the woman and said she wanted to stop the Stellazine, it was making her nervous. The neighbor said to keep taking it. The next day, Nancy began yawning to relive a feeling of pressure in her jaw. The yawns grew wider and wider until they actually hurt. Then Nancy found that with each yawn, she was jerking her head down and to the side. She thought she was doing it herself—until she tried to stop. The movements became involuntary. Now they were painful spasms. She called her doctor in a frenzy, hardly able to speak because of the distortion of her mouth. The doctor recognized what was happening and sent the neighbor to the nearest drugstore for a prescription of strong antihistamine. After three months, Nancy had become allergic to Stellazine.

Watch for drug reactions in your friend. They may not be as obvious as Nancy's reactions. If, for example, mental lethargy doesn't begin to ease off within ten days after beginning a new medication, or if the depressive is having nightmares or stomach cramps, or becomes unusually aggressive or hostile, tell the doctor and ask if the medication could be at fault.

8.

The Minor Depressions

You may be living with a depressive without knowing it. You may even *be* one without realizing what's been wrong with you all these years. The minor depressions, the ones so mild that they don't produce symptoms strong enough to notice, can be the most destructive. Moderate and severe cases of depression are obvious. Everyone knows something is wrong, and eventually, someone will usually find out what it is. In the mild cases, a person may go through an entire lifetime without discovering that he or she has a curable illness which has prevented a fully productive and enjoyable life.

There is a very famous writer living in Hollywood who has had depression for about twenty years without doing something about it. The man sells his work for good money. But for all his fame, he hasn't been able to produce much over the last decade, and he lives like a hermit, unable to keep friends or maintain relationships. His personal life is in chaos and few publishers will sign him to a contract because he can't meet deadlines.

I met the man some years ago through his wife, who was on the verge of leaving him. She was his third wife and had called me after a television show I did on depression. On the phone, she said, "I think my husband has something like the thing you were talking about. Could someone have it and still not have the symptoms you discussed?"

I told her yes, but it would only seem to be symptomless. Actually, the symptoms would be there in such a mild degree that they would not be noticed as symptoms.

We agreed to meet, and she told me what James (not his real name) was like. Although he had acclaim from the entire world, they were broke. He seemed purposely to do things which would professionally destroy him. He would accept an assignment to write a script, article, or story, then not begin work until the day it was due. When bill collectors called, he wouldn't be content with just telling them he couldn't pay at the moment—he would regale them with tales of the contract he was just about to sign or the big check he expected next week. He refused to put things away. Clothing, tools, papers—whatever he touched lay scattered around. Worse, he refused to allow his wife to put his things away. He would tell her that *he* wanted to do it and that he would, as soon as he got around to it. The couple's home was always dark. James had bought heavy drapes and had a double lining put in them. He insisted that the drapes be closed at all times, saying that the sun would fade the rug. The lights were on even at noon to keep the house from total darkness inside.

As the years went on, James grew more vague in conversation and had an even harder time establishing relationships. He had a routine—a set of compliments which were mistaken as warmth during a first meeting—but it soon became recognizable as a shallow system of gaining response from others. James never communicated what he really felt. He would find justification for what he did by attributing it to emotions and attitudes that he said he "Hadn't known he was feeling at the time." But these excuses wore thin after a while.

He would sleep at odd hours throughout the day, staggering to a couch or bed and flopping down to fall asleep instantly. In sleep, his posture was rigid. He would lie on his back, arms pressed close to his side and fingers clenched into fists. His wife, Janet, said, "He sleeps as if he were a West Point cadet lying at attention." He refused to let Janet handle the finances or personal correspondence, yet didn't take care of it himself and refused to hire an accountant or secretary. Janet was ready to climb walls. James was so negative that he objected to anything she suggested. If she wanted to go out, he would say he had to work. Then he would sit watching television. If she wanted to put new curtains up in the kitchen, he would have several reasons why it wasn't a good idea. As a result, nothing ever got done.

He was very good at mindless, repetitive tasks, such as doing dishes. It would take him four or five hours to do a sink full of dishes. It took him an inordinately long time to do *anything* he attempted. Very few of the projects he started ever got finished. The house was littered with half-built bookcases, broken dishes James meant to fix, and bits of hardware he had bought for new projects. People thought James was a bit lazy and at times somewhat eccentric, but no one seriously thought there was anything wrong with him—he functioned. Minimally, true, but he was able to work and interact with others.

What finally brought Janet to me was the episode of the pipe cleaners. James smoked a pipe, and didn't want Janet to throw out his used pipe cleaners. He said they would be useful for something someday, so the dirty brown used cleaners lay in little stacks on tables and shelves. One day, Janet could stand it no more and she threw them all out. James didn't seem to notice. But later, she had to go into James's desk draw for a stamp, and she had difficulty opening the drawer. It was stuffed with dirty pipe cleaners. The next day, Janet saw the show and called me.

I came to their home for dinner. James was jovial throughout the evening. If I didn't know about masked depression, I would have thought Janet was making the whole thing up. But as I talked to James, he grew evasive about depression. Then he grew very expansive about how he was able to cure depression in others. Without expressing doubt about his statement, I suggested that his cures could come from the fact that he was personally familiar with the illness. He agreed . . . saying that *Janet* was often depressed!

Finally, after two months of begging, threatening, and ultimatums from Janet, James agreed to go to a doctor. The therapist talked to them both. On the way home, James said to Janet, "I think he thinks *you're* the sick one." When Janet told the doctor about this, he said that this kind of transference is common, and that James would probably want to blame Janet for most of his problems while in therapy. The therapist decided to give James a few weeks of blaming others before beginning to dig into James's psyche. At that point, he was going to try to get James to accept the fact that his life situation was being produced and directed by him.

James had been in therapy one month—two weeks of blaming Janet and others for everything and two weeks of being asked to examine the inside of his own head—when he decided to stop seeing the doctor. He told Janet, 'I'm well now." And he certainly seemed to be. He was writing again. He had started a story, the first one in three years. He seemed to be a lot more open and communicative with Janet. She was lulled by his quick "recovery," and decided that treatment was no longer necessary, especially when James told her that the time he was spending in therapy could be spent writing and earning money now that he was well. They stopped therapy. Within a few weeks, James was back to his old patterns. Janet left him shortly afterwards. His illness has worsened over the years. James is now living a half-life, buried alive in a depression he refuses to believe he has. The medication the doctor gave him never got used. This man, a famous writer, will never give the world the benefit of all his gifts nor experience the joy of what he could achieve. If his depression were a little more incapacitating he would be a lot better off. At least then he would have to admit that something was wrong.

The case of James is a little more extreme than most. But the half-lives lived through minor depressions can be real hell for those who have them or who must live with them.

How can you recognize these mild cases of the illness? It's difficult, because many of the signs look like ordinary personality quirks. There's a passive attitude. But passivity can be a part of the personality. There's a lack of energy, an inertia that keeps the person from rising to the top of his or her ability. But not everyone is a go-getter. Diagnosing minor depressions is more a question of judgment than of recognizing symptoms. Many minor depressions will last for a few months and then disappear. But some are chronic and last a lifetime. Some will also come on in cycles. This kind of depressive can have a mild episode every autumn or at the beginning of every summer. It will be easily dismissed with some remark like, "Oh, the holiday season is always a bad time for me," or "I just always seem to get lethargic during the warm months." One deceiving factor is that when necessary, the depressive with a mild case can put on a short-lived burst of energy which seems to overcome the illness. But this respite soon passes.

The major symptom of a minor depression—in fact, the only overall symptom common to every case—is a lack of psychic energy. Any extra effort is too much trouble. Like James, the person will usually function enough to at least get by. Other people will dismiss the depressive's behavior as plain laziness or lack of mental ability. One side effect of every kind of depression is a tendency toward hypochondria. In a serious depression, the victim will be convinced that he or she has a serious disease for which there is no cure, that a cancer is eating away inside, or that the stomach is rotting from some unknown cause. In a minor depression, the victim may go to doctor after doctor complaining of fatigue and lack of energy. Doctors may prescribe pep pills or tranquilizers. The drugs may make the person feel a little better, but there will be no recovery.

Minor depressions are also contagious, far more so than serious ones. Existing in a depressing situation for a long period of time can make depression a habit pattern in the brain. For example, in the media business in Los Angeles, everyone knows which shops have "morale" problems. One station, a network affiliate, has had consistent morale problems for the last ten years. Even though the goal of every reporter is to work for a network-owned station, this particular one is never overwhelmed by applications. The problem first started with a top-level management person who was very rough on the workers. His attitude continued until it became customary to treat the employees with little regard for their feelings. An atmosphere of insecurity and oppression was created. This naturally depressed the workers, whether they were producers for local shows or reporters for the news. The depression has become a habit. The company has been trying to change the situation for several years, with no results. It doesn't realize the problem isn't morale, but depression. One staff producer told me, "It brings you down just to walk into the place. The very walls seem to radiate clouds of gloom. After a day at work, you feel so drained that you can't shake the feeling off." While depression is a chemical illness, it is most always triggered by a series of stresses or events.

If you were suffering from a mild case of it yourself, you would feel tired all the time. You might put the lack of energy down to all the work you've been doing, or all the problems you're dealing with. One of the most common observable effects is a messy home. This doesn't mean a place that's slightly disorganized. I'm talking about a real mess—piles of clothing, a dirty kitchen and bathroom, filthy floors, stacks of old papers and letters. The home is a good reflection of the state of mind. That bachelor living alone may not know how to keep a place clean, but he or she will at least attempt to keep things neat. The person living in a cluttered, sloppy house or apartment may be showing the only obvious sign of depression. The problem is worse for people who function in what appears to be a normal way, showing up for work on time, doing their job, going to parties and social functions. This person usually *remains* an undetected depressive, and may waste an entire lifetime without being able to use his or her full talents.

Perhaps the most pathetic cases affected by this disease are young people who leave home and find that they can't seem to make their wonderful plans for their freedom come true. The depression may have existed while they were living with parents, or it may come afterwards during the stress of having to take responsibility for their survival. You see so many of these people—going to singles bars, sitting in the corner at parties with an unhappy, tense expression on their faces. Some of them become frantically active, jumping from one social activity to another, always with an expectant smile. But if you look at their faces long enough, you will see in an off-guard moment that the mask slips, the face turns blank, and the eyes show the distress. Many of them turn to drugs or promiscuity. Depression in the late teens and early twenties is so prevalent that it is an epidemic. And it is people this age who have neither the money, the desire, or time to go to a therapist for help. In fact, few of them realize that their feelings of unhappiness may be caused by depression and that it can be cured. To anyone who knows the statistics of suicide among untreated depressives—even those with minor cases—and who realizes that the largest cause of death among those 17 to 25 is suicide, the neglect of this situation is shocking.

On the next pages you will find a chart which can be used to diagnose a *minor* depression. It's not a cut-and-dried check list.

Since minor depressions vary so much with each individual, no single test or chart can give a diagnosis. But this chart will give an indication that all is not well in the feeling good department. If you compare it to the chart in Chapter Three, you will see that there is a basic difference in these questions. The first chart measured observable symptoms typical of moderate and serious depressions, as well as feelings and self-perceptions. This test measures behavior and goal orientation, the two factors affected most in mild depressions. You will notice that each question is to be answered in degree—*never, rarely, sometimes, often* and *always*. A straight yes or no answer is of little use, since there are few straight symptoms in mild cases of the illness. It can be compared to having a sore throat and fever, which is an indication of many viral diseases. Only when the symptoms get more specific can a diagnosis be made. Similarly, with specific symptoms such as sleep disturbance or a total loss of appetite, any lay person can tell that depression is at fault; when symptoms are less specific, there has to be a wider latitude in looking for the cause.

Give this chart to friends you think may be suffering from mild depressions. Take it yourself, especially if you have been living with a depressed person. Fill in the answers carefully. It may be more accurate if you take it twice, say at the beginning of the week and the end. Put your first set of answers away and don't look at them until you have completed another set of answers. Then compare the two. You may be surprised to learn that a particular behavior or attitude remains fairly constant, yet you never knew it was part of your personality.

Count all your answers in each category. There are 34 questions. Obviously, a majority of *never* and *rarely* answers indicates depression. If more than 7 are *never*, the depression is far more severe than a mild case. A majority of *rarely* answers interspersed with more than 5 *never* answers also indicates a more than mild degree of depression. The average mild case of depression will have at least 4 *never* answers, 7 *rarely*'s, and the majority of the rest will be in the *sometime* category. There will be few *often* or *always* answers.

A nondepressed person will have a majority of answers in the *often* column, with fewer than 10 checked off in the *sometimes* category, and fewer than 4 in the *rarely* section. There may be 1 or 2 answers in the *never* column and 2 or 3 in the *always* section.

	Never	Rarely	Sometimes	Often	Always
I feel good about who I am					
When I meet people, they like me					
I sleep well					
I'm usually quite alert until it's time to go to bed					
I sleep until it's time to get up					
If I miss a meal I get hungry					
I enjoy the company of friends					
People see what I'm like without misunderstandings					
I can make friends					
Sex interests me					
I find it fairly easy to keep my home organized					
I make plans about what I want to accomplish					
I carry my plans out					
I finish things I start					
I feel I should have some good things in life					

	Never	Rarely	Sometimes	Often	Always
I know how to take care of myself					
I enjoy a good meal					
My clothing is clean					
My feelings throughout the day stay pretty much the same					
My health is good					
It is normal to feel sad some of the time, and my sad feelings are normal					
I am worth loving					
If I feel depressed I know it will lift.					
I feel like an adult should feel.					
I make decisions easily.					
I stick to my decisions.					
I get on well with others.					
There are things I want to do in life.					
I know what I want in most cases.					
I occasionally buy something to treat myself.					

	Never	Rarely	Sometimes	Often	Always
I know what I'm doing in most situations.					
If I'm not happy with what I'm doing for a living, I know that I will someday be able to do what makes me happier.					
I have enough energy to do what I want to do.					
Sometimes I go out of my way to get something I want or to do something for others.					

If a majority of answers fall into the *always* category, that's actually a sign that something is wrong. No one *always* enjoys the company of friends or sleeps until it's time to get up or always makes decisions easily. However, people with masked depression may try so hard to convince themselves that they *are* happy, *are* keeping everything together, *are* taking care of all responsibilities, and *are* liked that they won't admit to any negative feelings. If you fit this description, please don't tear your set of answers up and throw them away. Use the information you have gained to get rid of a chemical-caused illness that has kept you from enjoying your life and using it to make your world a happier one.

The Depressive Environment
Depressed people seem to show a similar set of environmental arrangements in their homes. They like it dark, and may keep the drapes drawn all day. They will allow dirty dishes to accumulate in the kitchen, use the same dirty towels and sheets for weeks and even months. They may refuse to leave their homes or apartments.

In serious cases, the person won't attempt to find excuses for sitting in a chair day after day or not getting out of bed until late afternoon. The person with a mild depression *does* function, but the symptoms will be rationalized as justified anxieties. There may be a fear of being spied upon or seen by someone passing by, so naturally the drapes will stay closed to prevent prying eyes. In the minor case, the person will leave the home to go shopping or to work or social functions, but will often be nervous and anxious. The most common excuse for the anxiety is the fear of burglars. The mild depressive may even go so far as to rush home to "take a look," certain that burglars are even now loading the stereo and typewriter onto a pickup truck and taking off with it. There may be a call to a neighbor with a request to run over and check on the place. This fear of burglars may exist even when there's nothing really worth stealing. One doctor told me of a 19-year-old patient who had just left home and who lived in an apartment where the only things that belonged to him were his clothes. Even those weren't the kind to create envy in anyone—jeans, T-shirts and an extra pair of tennis shoes. He didn't even have a magazine in the place. Yet every time he left the apartment, he was obsessed by the fear that a burglar was about to rip him off. He started therapy at the suggestion of his clergyman, and the therapist stopped the fear cold by asking, "So what if someone rips you off . . . what will they get?" The boy had to face the fact that his anxiety wasn't really about burglars at all.

When you live with a depressive, it's a little easier to change what may have become a depressive environment. If the depressive is a friend who lives apart from you, the job will be harder.

The first thing—the first two things, in fact—are to put the house in order and let some light in. This is important. I said before that the state of the home reflects the state of the head. You are going to try changing the state of the head, and there will be a cause and effect connection between the illness and the environment. Dim rooms create a hiding environment. The depressive is hiding from the world and from his or her illness. You want to create a sunnier atmosphere. Your friend may have let the house get into such a state of chaos that there's no way to put everything away and no place for all the books, papers, and objects lying around. So before letting light in, get the place in some semblance of order. Stack the books and papers in neat piles rather than letting them stay scattered all over the room. You may run into some reluctance here. Your friend will tell you that he knows where everything is or that the things are spread out this way for a special reason. Don't argue or try to reason about the cleanup. Lie. Say that you're not changing anything or throwing anything away, just putting it in order. The biggest fear may be that you will throw something away. Regardless of how dismayed you may be at an irrational desire to keep old newspapers or pieces of string or whatever, don't show it. If the person makes a specific desire known—"Don't throw away those playing cards even though some are missing; I got those when I went to Florida"— then don't throw the cards away. Put them somewhere—"Okay, but see, I'm putting them in the drawer here." Tell the person where you are putting things. But those items which can be of no possible useful or sentimental value such as crumpled bits of paper or empty matchbook covers can be tossed out. However, *don't* let your friend see you throwing anything away. You don't have to be sneaky about it, just discreet. Start by throwing some real junk away—emptying wastebaskets or ash trays—into an opaque garbage bag. Ask about anything you're not sure about in a very positive way: "You don't want these old magazines, do you?" Sometimes you will get an objection to throwing away something you know the person can't possibly want, such as old envelopes or wrappers. In that case, if there's a massive amount of useless stuff, sneak some of it into the garbage bag and leave enough around so that the disappearance won't be missed. Even when you are done clearing out, there will still be a lot of things left for which there is no room. Get some boxes and pack these items in, telling your friend that you're putting things in boxes "for now." Stick the boxes in the cellar or in a closet. Get them out of sight so that the place *looks* neat and orderly. Then let the light in.

Letting the light in may mean opening drapes or painting walls. The house or apartment may be one of those dark places where sun doesn't come in. Then you have to brighten things up by other means. Buy some light fabric and use it as a throw over a dark couch. Get a light-colored throw rug. Wash the walls or paint them. But remember that the depressive can't be put through too many changes, especially where the home is concerned. Don't try forcing your friend to move and don't change the place so radically that it doesn't seem like home anymore. All you are trying to do is create order, not change.

In many ways, the neatening and lightening task is a lot easier if the person is someone you live with. However, in some cases, you may also face a stubborn resistance to the change. If this happens, you may have to enlist the aid of a friend who will suggest "fixing the place up a little." In minor depressions, one room will usually take on the bulk of the mess. Most often it will be the room the person spends the most time in, especially if it's a working room. For a housewife, it may be the kitchen. An executive may create the most chaos in a den or office.

You must realize that by attacking the mess in this room, you are striking at some deep cave of protection. True, the cave is like a hidey hole where a sick animal has crawled for shelter; nonetheless, it's the only shelter the depressive has. So you must move gently and avoid giving even the implication that you are ousting the *person* with the junk. Use all your perception here. The change will be frightening and annoying to the depressive, but look beyond that fear of losing a possession. While heavy depressions are marked by apathy, the slightly clinically depressed may hold on to one or more possessions with an attachment that borders on compulsion. (Remember James and the pipe cleaners). If there seems to be conflict about any particular object or series of objects, leave them alone. You may also try a rather sneaky technique. You can move some things out of sight, wait to see if they are missed, then after a period of time get rid of them if they are in the junk category. But make sure the junk categorization is an objective one and not made by you from a personal judgment that may not be held by the depressive when he or she recovers. It's better to have a little more mess than to create a further feeling of deprivation in the depressive.

If throwing out junk or even getting it out of sight is an impossibility because of the resistance, then don't push it further. Instead, concentrate on putting it in order, arranging things in some system and eliminating at least the look of chaos. Many of the symptoms of minor depressions are relived somewhat when there is more organization in the environment. You may have to start a system of "a place for everything and everything in its place," just to get the person started on a system of keeping things organized. Once the person is taking medication or undergoing professional therapy, this organization of the environment becomes even more important. As the condition improves, there must be an improvement at home.

In many cases, the whole attempt to clean up and to keep things in order is too exhausting. Don't feel bad about it, but don't give up either. Sometimes the best thing you can do for yourself is to hire someone on a regular basis, one day or one afternoon a week, to come in and get things in shape. If you live in a small town where domestic help is not as available or inexpensive as in larger cities, hire a high school or college student to do the work. Many of them will be glad for a few extra dollars a week.

Therapy Versus Therapists

There are all kinds of nonmedical therapies available today, from groups where everyone just talks to each other to encounters where people yell the vilest of insults at their parents. Most of these groups interact in a way which can be compared to a sexual experience. There is a bit of foreplay while the rules are explained and everyone breaks the ice by smiling at each other. Then intercourse begins, the action for which all have come, whether it's talking, touching, soaking in water, yelling, acting out fantasies, hitting, or whatever. Then comes the climax, the release of some inner wall and a collapse of defenses. This may be marked by tears, a feeling of overwhelming love for the others in the group and for the world at large, a building of self-esteem, or all three. They can be very nice experiences and even very intense emotional ones, cleansing the emotional system, as it were. Unfortunately, the results seldom last, especially in cases of depression. As long as the support system is present (which is only as long as the group is together and static in its mood), the warm feelings will remain. But as in any group, the cycle shifts even if it remains in the same place with the same members. The triggering release factor dissolves or becomes ineffective with repetition and no longer works. The basis on which the lessening of depressive symptoms rests goes away and the symptoms return, sometimes stronger than ever because of the loss of that good group feeling. So when you come down to it, nonmedical therapy may be great as an *addition* to professional medical help for depression, but it will not take its place.

Occasionally you may find yourself involved with a form of nonmedical therapy headed by a respectable doctor. Again, the same rules apply. Punching a pillow or lying in a dark tank or hooking up to a machine which helps you control your energy is an *aid* not a replacement for old-fashioned one-to-one counseling. Even counseling isn't the best type of therapy, but it's just about the only thing a depressive has going in the verbal help department unless a good friend or relative has enough grounding in the way minds work to do the job.

In major depressions, the main concern is a relief of symptoms so that the person can begin to function again. In minor cases, therapy may be the way the depressive clears up misperceptions and disorganized behavior. But wherever you are involved with a depressed person, you must watch to see that the therapist isn't really imposing a personal view of reality on the patient. For example, a woman whose depressive syndrome is focusing on the restrictions of her life as a housewife will not be helped by a doctor who sees his job as trying to convince her that she will be normal when she feels better about being a housewife. A man who is naturally passive and gentle will gain no benefit from a therapist whose idea of normal is aggression in a man. One of the most unfortunate aspects of psychiatry is that it is in the hands of people who use judgment, and all judgment requires subjectivity. Some therapists have a definition of *normal* into which they try to mold all patients. These kinds of doctors don't realize that the definition may not be *normal* for the person involved.

9.

A Therapeutic Life Style

You are now aware of the two most ruthless aspects of depression: first, it is contagious, and second, there is no immunity. In fact, one episode makes a recurrence even more likely. That's a grim outlook. But there is a way to overcome these factors and guard against the illness. One of the overriding themes throughout this book has been self-protection. It's a basic essential to prevent your coming down with depression, or catching it from someone else. It will also help eliminate the likelihood of a recurrence if you have ever had the illness.

It's imperative that every depressive and every potential depressive learn a system of self-protection. There is no innoculation against depression. One episode may pass with a full return to normal function, then years later the illness comes again, devastating the person and instilling a lifetime fear: *How long do I have this time? Will it come back? Is this slight lack of energy the beginning of another episode? Will this blue feeling go away or am I in for another cycle?*

It's a fear that many depressives live with. Nor will the reason for that fear go away through counseling and therapy. Depression is the only physical illness in which the patient must cure him/herself no matter how good the doctor may be. It's also the only illness in which the patient *can* and *must* prevent a recurrence, and no one else can do it (though therapists and friends may suggest various methods or give moral support). The depressive, as well as the nondepressive who wants to stay nondepressed, must develop a *therapeutic life style*.

Life *style*? Yes! You need a defense which does more than allow you to guard against depression. It must give you such an awareness of self, such a knowledge of what is going on at any time in your conscious and subconscious mind, that you can recognize depressive mechanisms instantly and know what to do about them. It must allow you to be so aware of who you are (with acceptance) and of what is happening in your life (with understanding) that you never feel any part of your life is out of your control.

The major depressive mechanism is a downward cycle of nonrecognition. To give a graphic analogy, imagine that you are in a deep pool of water holding a heavy rock. The rock pulls you down, and as you look up to where you used to be you say, "I'm sinking." The thought makes you feel even worse, so that all you recognize is the fact that you are sinking lower. Soon you can't even see the surface where you began your descent. You sink lower and lower, feeling only the passage down. Like a circle, your thoughts go to "I'm going down," which makes you feel lower, which makes you sink more, which makes you feel lower, and so on and on. All the time, the problem is not the sinking . . . it is the rock. Letting go of the rock is the answer.

"Letting go" of the depression before it begins dragging you down is the key to eliminating a full depressive episode. Only a therapeutic life style will teach you to recognize when the "rock" appears. Only the recognition will allow you to drop the rock so that the episode is prevented or at least minimized.

Throughout this book we have dwelt on the biochemical reasons for depression. But certain life habits make one vulnerable to the illness and even make one depression-*prone*.

We are aware of the effect of personal habits on certain other diseases. For example, living a sedentary life style while eating a rich fatty diet may make one prone to heart disease. The life style may not *cause* heart disease, and not everyone who lives that way *gets* heart disease, but it certainly makes one vulnerable to it, or even *prone* to a heart attack. We all have bad physical habits. We smoke, drink, or eat too much. We overtire ourselves and don't get enough rest. We don't eat the right foods, don't get enough exercise, and then wonder why we come down with colds and flu or other illnesses.

Most people are aware of what constitutes a bad physical habit. But there's no national campaign against bad mental habits. And it is the collection of bad mental habits that makes one depression-prone or creates barriers to the achievement of what one wants out of life.

These bad mental habits can't be cured by therapy. There is a flaw in therapy of any form. It's external. Therapy is a growth business (no pun intended). It takes various forms—religions, doctors, self-improvement systems, cults, gurus . . . all of them external. We're urged to use faith in the name of Jesus or God as a problem solver. We're told that if only we say certain words over and over again we will achieve self-realization. There are cults of the touch—respectable, such as encounter groups, secret, such as swapping clubs—all of which guarantee to make you more of a person. You can get *it* from EST, find the right path from a guru, be your own best friend, deal with your hidden child, or scream yourself sane. Choose from dozens of fifty-dollar-an-hour psychiatrists who will listen to whatever you have to say, join hordes of do-it-yourself seekers with shelves of books on curing your emotional problems. Every single one of these approaches depends on some *outside* factor. All you have to do is follow the way. Or believe. Or let yourself go. Or accept some other person's definition of *your* perfect state of mental health.

With every form of therapy which exists today, you use the therapy to find the answer. But the goal of the therapy is to get you to hit on the *one* answer already dictated. You are given help in going down the path, but your destination is predetermined.

There's also the school of the facile solution, which is most often found in self-help books. "Take responsibility for your actions," this kind of book will say. "You can choose what you will and won't do." "Don't let anyone make you a victim, because you are in charge of your life." Very profound and very true. But to the person with a family to support who is stuck in an unrewarding, unpleasant job—to the woman trapped in a loveless marriage who has no skills with which to enter the job market and no one to watch the children if she did—there are no methods telling how to get from *here* to *there*. And while the facile solution may be inspiring, it has very little long-term effect on most people.

Why? Because these are mass-produced solutions. They work in generalities which touch a specific case in a general way. They attack a major problem, true. But they leave thousands of tiny reinforcement habits which keep the major problem in place. Compare the problem to a tent which is supported by a main pole whose shape is reinforced with many guy wires. If the guy wires, subtle and overt reinforcements of the basic structure are strong enough, and if there are enough of them, the collapse of that main pole does not destroy the structure. True, it sags, just as the major personality problem may diminish, but the basic structure is so reinforced that the main pole—the major personality problem—is easily put back in place again. And since the "main pole" of most people's problems has been built over the years until it is an ingrained habit, it's very hard to knock down. Especially when the guy wires sturdily reinforce the basic structure.

In the nonindividualistic approach to mental health, the main pole is the thing both patient and therapist (or therapy) try to knock down. The method of doing this is to equate that main pole, the obvious source of the patient's problems, with the distance the patient stands from the preconceived idea of the perfect healthy state. But that perfect state of mental health is someone else's perfect definition. And the definition changes from therapy to therapy, as well as from time to time. Twenty years ago, a woman who felt tied down and frustrated by the role of housewife would have reached a state of mental health when she lost her feeling of confinement and adjusted to being a housewife. The woman who needed help channeling her aggressiveness into a successful business career would most likely have been regarded as having the problem of *being* aggressive or *wanting* a career. Likewise, the man with a lack of aggressiveness or distaste for the world of business would have been counseled in such a way as to return him to the typical male stereotype. Those stereotypes for men and women were regarded as states of mental health. The well-adjusted woman didn't wheel and deal and the well-adjusted man didn't stay home and do dishes. Though most forms of therapy today take individual personality needs more into account, we still use external definitions to gauge mental health.

In order to become healthy emotionally, each *individual* must realize under which mental state he or she functions best, and what type of behavior allows life to be lived in harmony, happiness, and peace of mind. There is only one area where an outside definition of health overrides the importance of an individual's definition. That is in the areas which make civilization possible, the basic absolutes which permit a society to function. The ability to abide by the social contract is an essential factor in emotional health: we all agree not to murder each other, not to become overly aggressive with each other, not to steal from each other. Those who violate these precepts are criminals. We have begun to realize the emotional health factor in crime. We still punish violators of the social contract by taking away their mobility and right to make social choices, and we will continue to do so. But we are beginning to look upon criminal acts as symptoms of emotional illness which must be cured by a personality change; we're realizing we rarely cure criminals by hoping the fear of punishment will stop them from committing that breach of social contract again.

The social contract allows us to live in some sort of order. And we would all be in much better mental shape if it were a set of clearly understood and necessary rules obeyed for the benefit of all. But we have confused ourselves and mired our thinking with rituals and taboos which in themselves are extremely unhealthy. For example, we are taught in childhood not to lie. We then discover the person who tells only the truth is eccentric and usually a social outcast, that lies and half-truths are the oil that permits society to conduct business and pleasure without friction. We are conditioned when young to be kind to others. When we grow up we learn that we have to fight to get ahead and that one must limit kindness in order not to be taken advantage of. The problems resulting from our systems of split belief naturally create emotional difficulty. It's a sign of mental health to be able to *cope* with that difficulty!

Under the social rituals and taboos which have surrounded the social contract, we must act in signals and symbols to convey subliminal meanings. You meet someone, you like him or her. The relationship proceeds in a systematic fashion: you are careful not to transmit certain kinds of enthusiasm or reveal certain things about yourself. Your feelings are tempered if the person is of the same gender. They are tempered if the person is the opposite gender and has a spouse. While eating in a restaurant you may find that there is meat on your T-bone or chicken leg which you can't cut off with a knife. Even though you want the meat, you don't pick it up with your fingers—though you would do it at home. Or you're sitting on a bus, or in a luncheonette and a stranger sits next to you. You ignore him, he ignores you. You each pretend the other doesn't exist.

Some of these rituals and taboos are necessary. Others have come down through tradition and have nothing to do with reality. Men do not wear certain colors. Women do not sit with their legs in certain positions. We refrain from using particular sounds to describe various bodily organs and functions, yet other sounds to describe these same functions are perfectly all right. We have different sets of behaviors which become automatic—one for home, one for work, one for social gatherings.

Yet a social custom which exists for *any* reason other than to maintain an orderly society or to create an easier understanding and communication between members of that society is a personally oppressive and limiting custom. In an ideal society, it would be adopted only as a matter of personal choice, not social pressure.

I must be truthful and say that that "ideal society" smacks very much of the school of the facile solution which I decried before. Because no matter how silly you may think the social custom of not picking up your food in your fingers may be, and no matter how much you may want the rest of the meat on your T-bone, you probably won't pick it up and eat it with your fingers.

Missing out on that little bit of steak isn't really going to make you very unhappy. But depression-prone behavior begins when one creates an emotional dis-ease, (as in un-ease) by personally oppressing oneself. What are you missing out on in life because of habit, custom, or social pressure? And how much of that missing out is due to necessity, versus how much is due to your not having really questioned whether you *can* do something without social ostracism?

As we mature, we give up various things in order to prevent

friction. Some of them, like getting that last bit of meat on the T-bone or going kite flying instead of to work on a warm spring day, do not interfere with our feelings in a damaging way. Some things bypassed are "laters": "I'll take time for my child later; right now I have to pay attention to my career," or "I'll pay attention to the exercise and diet parts of my health later; right now I just don't have time," or "I'll take time for my personal enjoyment later; right now I'm busy."

But as we devote our attention to things only because of the end result promised from that attention, we give up the present for the future. And since the future is out of reach, always, we lose contact with the present. We turn into a mechanism, responding to a desired goal which can be reached by certain immediate steps; we put personal gratification and fulfillment of the *present* self aside. And by losing contact with ourselves in the here and now, trading it for a planned script of the future, we eventually lose awareness of the self. Any time we are unaware of ourselves, of what is going on inside our heads, we lose control over part of the self and of our life. Eventually, if there's too much loss of contact, we begin to feel helpless.

Helplessness and Depression

There is something all depressives have in common besides the loss of self-esteem. It's a feeling of helplessness. The feeling often precedes the depressive episode. The person feels his life is out of his power to control, that he has no mastery over what happens to him. The feeling may take the form of stress, as a result of too much to do, too little time. We're all familiar with the minor depressed feelings which come when we look at a mountain of work waiting, whether it's a house to be cleaned or a pile of papers to be processed. We feel helpless to get it all done, and that's depressing. Feelings of helplessness always accompany depression, but it's hard to tell, in clinical cases, which is cause and which is effect. The biochemical view is that a long-term feeling of helplessness creates the same toxic changes as stress. But it's also possible that depression creates the chemical changes which cause the feelings of loss of power over one's life.

Experiments with rats and other lab animals have demonstrated the effects of induced helplessness. In one experiment, cats were given electric shocks from which they couldn't escape.

After a while, the cats stopped trying to escape the shocks. They became passive and apathetic. Many stopped eating. The cats became lethargic and were no longer able to complete mazes which they had once found easy. Their intelligence, measured in reaction response, dropped drastically. They lost weight. In other words, they showed all the signs we associate with depression. Dogs and rats which were placed in mazes where there was no way out would try to escape at first. They would become frantic, rushing from one end of the maze to the other. It finally dawned on them that they were helpless to escape. And they would fall into the same passive, depressed state.

On the surface, none of this would seem to relate to human research. After all, we are *reasoning* animals. But other experiments done with chemicals were performed on both lab animals and human volunteers. One series of experiements used a drug which depleted the biogenic amine *norepinephrine* in the central nervous system. Monkeys injected with this chemical withdrew from social contact (monkeys are very social animals) and lay in one corner of their cages, ignoring the other monkeys. They refused to eat and wouldn't respond to petting. They showed all the signs of depression. Even monkeys that had been high up in the monkey group pecking order had so lost their self-esteem that they acted subservient to monkeys that had been much lower on the group social ladder. Rats injected with the same chemical showed the same passive, helpless behavior. In one test, the rats were injected and then given electric shocks which could have been avoided just by walking away. But they accepted the shock as though they were helpless to escape it, even though all they had to do was move out of range.

In one famous series of tests, human subjects were injected with a chemical which disturbs the biogenic amine balance in the brain. Within a *few minutes*, these people experienced a full-scale depression! They became suicidal, felt helpless and insecure. They lost every positive feeling about themselves and felt overwhelmed by self-hatred. One group of people on whom this experiment was performed were convicts known for cocky, aggressive behavior. The fact that one small injection could reduce these men to helpless apathy, could create a profound depression which lasted as long as the effects of the chemical did, is a bit horrifying. It seems to indicate that humans are affected more by chemical responses than by the reasoning power of the mind. But the experiments also showed something else. In the short time before the depressive feelings hit, all the human subjects described one dramatic change in emotion. They *all* said the first feeling after the injection was one of helplessness. They felt ineffective and powerless. They described their existence as "miserable" and said they felt helpless to change it.

One of the things doctors hear most often when treating a depressive is *I can't*. The depressive feels helpless to change his situation, his feelings, or any other part of his life. The pessimistic attitude of *What's the use, nothing will get any better*, which is so common in depression, is also another way of saying, *What's the use of trying, nothing I can do will change anything*.

Controlling One's Life

One of the biggest factors in recovery from depression is regaining a feeling of control and mastery over one's life and environment. But this feeling of control is important for more than recovery. It must *continue* to prevent a recurrence.

Since my major depressive episode, I have experienced the beginnings of a recurrence twice. One was when my son, Andros, was still an infant. The chores of the life style I had chosen—a self-sufficient, do-it-yourself environment—were too overwhelming. I had let too much slide and it seemed I would never catch up. The garden was full of weeds and the new crop hadn't been planted. The clothing for the coming winter for which I had bought fabric was still unmade; the quilt wasn't even cut into pattern pieces. The canning of the food I had planned to "put by" hadn't been done; boxes of wholesale fruit and vegetables had rotted because I hadn't gotten around to them. Bundles of laundry were waiting to be ironed. They had been waiting for months. Half a dozen unfinished projects littered the house. I began sinking, dragged down by the weight of all that had to be done. Luckily, I saw the signs in time and stopped the cycle. I made a list of what had the highest priority, discarded the idea of canning that summer, started no more projects, and forgot about making winter clothing that year. Even though doing that hurt my image of myself as super earth mother, I realized the image and reality needed a bit more connection if there was to be peace of mind. I stopped expecting so much of myself and started feeling in control again. And strangely enough, taking the weight off allowed me to catch up and begin doing all those things—the garden, canning, sewing—and getting everything done without stress.

The next time depression came close again was when my career blossomed almost overnight. It was the time of the Whole Earth movement. I was suddenly "hot." There was more radio and television work than I could handle. The Johnny Carson show called—would I be on? Before I knew it, I was writing a monthly column for a magazine, doing a weekly talk show on one radio station, working two days a week on another, plus the five days a week for the news station I had been working for, plus a regular weekly five-minute segment on a television station, and various guestings on other shows. In addition, I was writing and recording a syndicated radio show which involved extra research for subjects that would be interesting on a national rather than local level.

I was able to keep it all together for about five months. Then came county fair time. I had 41 entries which had to be finished over a period of three weeks. (Even writing about this period in my life gives me the shudders. I remember that feeling of pressure, hoping that the big earthquake everyone was talking about then would come along and get me out of all this.)

About halfway through the major effort for the fair I found myself unable even to think of doing another lick of work. Yes, I could have forced it. But the very idea was so overwhelming that I stopped and took a sensible look at what was happening. I loved each individual thing I was doing. But put together it was all such a burden that I was hating the conglomerate whole. So, much as I hated giving up any of these wonderful opportunities and projects I loved, I quite every job but the television segment and the news station, stopped all the efforts for the fair, and swore that never again would I let my work burden wipe me out. And this included work in the home or in my career. I recognized that this particular behavior was *my* style of depressive-prone action, and I would have to guard against it. To this day, I have never again felt that buzzy-headed, hollow-stomached feeling of panic and helplessness which is the first signal of a depressive episode for me.

For any depressive, being in control of one's life is like health insurance. Each person must discover which things give that feeling of being in charge. In my case, I use a system of self-sufficiency to give me that feeling. I may buy food, but I like to grow some of it. I may hire someone to fix my car, but I know I can do it myself if need be. These are the kinds of things which make me feel good. As long as I feel competent, as long as I feel I am learning, I feel that I am in charge of my life. You may use another system for gaining a feeling of mastery over your life. But each person working on depression *prevention*, whether a former depressive or not, must work out a series of actions which will reinforce that control, which will give a feeling of personal power to effect change where change is wanted. And if you are living or associating with a depressive, *you* must see that he or she becomes aware of what behaviors will create those feelings of control.

To a large degree, setting up such a system requires changing certain personality patterns which have become ingrained over a lifetime and which have created an opening for a situation of helplessness to creep in. In my case, I had no idea of my limitations. Many depressives have unrealistic goals all their lives, expecting too much of themselves, aiming for heights which will drain all energy *before* they are reached. Some lucky people may achieve those goals, but they are few. Most people will eventually realize that the self-expectations will never be quite met. A case of depression follows soon after. The hormonal changes in men reaching their late thirties and early forties account for many serious cases of depression in this age group. But a large number of these men are already depression-prone because they are at the age when they realize they *are* what they're going to be when they grow up. And if reality is too far away from their image, depression is a natural result.

Thus, one key to depression prevention, as well as to cure, is self-awareness. This doesn't have anything to do with the spiritual or human potential movements which are so popular right now. Self-awareness just means, purely and simply, knowing yourself—being able to see an overall pattern and identifying the self within that pattern. And to do that, you must identify all the actions that fit that pattern. Once you have examined and become aware of your patterns, you can start arranging or rearranging them in better order. With self-knowledge, you can eliminate the actions which come from unconscious motives and desires. The woman who always chooses a man who treats her badly, the man who always chooses a woman who hurts him—these people don't end up with those partners by accident. Nor does the person who can't keep friends, hold jobs, or ever quite achieve any planned goal end up with those results by accident. These people are acting out patterns because they are looking for something. When they find out what it is, they can take steps to find it in less destructive ways. It's the same with any action which prevents one from getting the result wanted from the world.

I regard mental health (which means far more than just being "well-adjusted"—one can adjust so beautifully to an unhealthy situation that the idea never dawns that perhaps it's not too healthy to stick around that situation in the first place) as a state of mental comfort. Satisfaction and happiness are prime signs of mental health. A whole school of therapy could be based on the simple saying: *if you're not happy, something's wrong*. No one can shift the blame for unhappiness to someone else in this definition of mental health, because it certainly isn't healthy to continue allowing another person to make you unhappy.

You've already read that the generalized approach in defining what's emotionally right for everyone is a large reason for the ineffectiveness of various therapies. But that's not the main reason therapy has such a dismal efficiency rate: solutions which last a lifetime take almost a lifetime to achieve. The main reason psychiatry and other therapeutic aids fail so often is that they attack the major problem first.

Look at Joe, a perfect case in point. He can't seem to control his actions. He finds himself saying things he's sorry for later, things which antagonize his co-workers and friends. He finds himself spending money he doesn't have, buying things he regrets later. And the reason he "finds" himself doing these things is because there's never any awareness before or during his actions that they are taking place. Joe has to have everything at once and finds it hard to keep up the effort of long-range plans. He's impatient. He doesn't have time for anything he can't get immediately or accomplish in a very short time. He goes to see a psychiatrist about these behaviors because he feels like a failure and isn't getting the responses he wants from the world.

The psychiatrist and Joe talk about these problems. They discuss Joe's past. They talk about Joe's problems at work. Joe is gradually able to see how the negative situations arise, but it takes years. Even then, he's only slightly better at resolving things. He feels better about himself, but that's because he's adjusted more to who he is, rather than because he has made basic changes in the actions which were causing his unhappiness in the first place.

Why didn't therapy clear up Joe's problems in a short time? Because the doctor tried to help Joe change a major part of his personality without doing much to change the thousands of reinforcements which make that personality factor a part of Joe's *style*. (Remember the "guy wires"?)

We think of the personality as a unit of separate habits. A person's mannerisms and responses *are* the personality. A full description of any individual would take a long time: he or she likes or doesn't like to gossip, is talkative or quiet, is energetic or lethargic, is sloppy, neat, dresses well, doesn't care about clothing, is nice, is sarcastic, is good with money, is bad with money, and so on. It's a fragmented view of the individual. We're geared to look at the self as a combination of hundreds of details; that's why we need help to see overall patterns.

I call these personality patterns "styles." Joe's style, for example, is impatient and impulsive. That's why he finds it hard to establish long-range plans. It's why he spends more money than he should and why he says things he regrets later.

In therapy, Joe will be asked just to work on solving the *problems*. He'll be helped to find causes for the problems—but not to examine the overall *style* of personality except where it relates to an obvious problem. For example, Joe will be asked to examine why he bought an expensive tape recorder on an impulse when he knew the mortgage payment was due. And maybe this technique will work—maybe Joe won't buy an expensive toy when he has a bill to pay elsewhere—but it's more likely that he will do something similar many more times before that kind of action stops, because Joe has gotten very little reinforcement in breaking the pattern sequence which causes him to impulsively buy things he can't afford.

Both Joe and his therapist will spend much time working on the areas where Joe's personality *style* has its most obvious negative effects. In time, he may resolve many of those areas. But it will take a lot of time and money. Even then, there are no guarantees.

A personality style permeates every part of an individual's life. While Joe works on his obvious problems, he's probably totally ignoring those parts of the impulsive, impatient style which *aren't* "problems." Neither Joe nor his therapist will regard the way Joe drives as having anything to do with his problems unless the driving itself causes trouble. But driving is like a bottle garden. It's a closed environment, a world in miniature. Every part of one's approach to life can be seen by the approach to driving.

Joe has never observed that he always pulls into the pedestrian crosswalk when stopping his car for a red light. He's so impatient at having to wait, so anxious to get going again, that he doesn't control the urge to move his car as far forward as possible. Joe is only vaguely aware of the nasty looks pedestrians give him as they walk around his car. He doesn't really think about stopping *behind* the crosswalk because he's unconscious of where his car has stopped while waiting for the light to change. If the definition of an impulsive action is one performed without much rational thought, then this aspect of Joe's driving is a symptom of his overall problem: impulsive impatience.

In therapy, Joe will work on controlling his impulse to spend money, as well as on his impatient manners with others. These are major symptoms of Joe's style. They require constant and intensive effort to control. But Joe brings his problems to that effort! He impatiently tries to control his impatience. He is impulsive in trying to control his impulsiveness, and impatient with his lack of results. He doesn't have much luck fighting his major symptoms.

It seems that few therapists recognize the irony of trying to solve a problem while being handicapped by the problem itself. It limits our efforts. If timidity is a problem, one will be timid in trying to change it. If aggressiveness is a problem, one will try to fight it aggressively. If there's a difficulty in being consistent, there will be inconsistency in the attempts to change. These tendencies double the effort of getting rid of negative personality patterns.

Suppose Joe *does* make headway in changing his impulsive, impatient pattern. The *style* which creates the problem will still be reinforced every time he stops for a traffic light.

Stopping for a traffic light is a triviality. It's such a minor thing that no real effort is required to become aware of stopping *behind* the crosswalk.

Suppose the therapist (or suppose Joe, on his own) looked at every one of his actions from the viewpoint of a personality style. Suppose, instead of the major, all-out effort needed to work on personality *problems*, Joe worked instead on the problem-causing *style*. The therapist would then be able to help Joe rid himself of hundreds of minor reinforcements of that style. One by one, Joe could become aware of each one and eliminate it.

It's easy to become aware of these reinforcements. For example, if Joe establishes a habit of stopping behind the crosswalk, he's gained control over one element of the style which is giving him such trouble. And every time he successfully stops behind the crosswalk, he reinforces that control. Furthermore, each bit of gained control gives added strength to work on the next, perhaps more difficult, area of the personality style

If Joe—or anyone wanting to change something about themselves—worked on changing a *style* rather than solving problems, the "cure" would come about much faster, with far greater efficiency. Easy things would be tackled first—minor patterns which reinforce an overall personality style. Each result will give a feeling of accomplishment (a feeling which is necessary to keep on with any effort.)

It's easy to see why all the forms of therapy, which use the approach of working toward a predetermined solution, are woefully short on results. They all begin with a person's weakest point, going after the area which neds the *most* work. Suppose a person with a broken leg goes to the hospital. A doctor straightens the leg and puts a cast on it. Now the bone is held firmly in place; so the patient gets up and starts to dance. But there's nothing to reinforce that external cast, even though it has given *some* improvement. Yes, the leg is stronger. But it still isn't strong enough to stand on. It collapses. The pain continues.

When a bone is broken (or when a personality is flawed by a problem) it isn't cured just because the "break" has been set. Millions of cells must grow and provide a link between the two fractured ends. In the same way, a person wishing to alter negative aspects of his or her personality must alter thousands of minor reinforcing actions to change an overall pattern. Each new cell of a healing bone grows on a base of other new cells—but the healing began in the smallest way, one cell at a time.

The person trying to eradicate emotional and personality problems must begin in the smallest possible way—with those things that are easy to handle because they aren't really problems. Working from the bottom *up* the climb is much easier.

This is especially important for depressives. A depressive episode shakes up the personality, acting like an earthquake. There's no better time to make sure that when everything settles down again, it does so in a way guaranteed to eliminate the patterns which may have made the person depression-prone in the first place. Every depressive who has gone more than ten years without a recurrence also describes a major personality change which occurred during the episode. Many of these people say they felt as though they were reborn, that after their depression they were able to touch a potential which had been hidden all their lives. This sounds good from a clinical standpoint, but I have better and more scientific proof than that, since this is the tenth year since my own depressive episode. I believe the lack of recurrence and the ability to achieve goals—something I could never do before my depression—stem entirely from my eliminating depression-prone behavior. Too many other depressives have the same belief for me to think that my case is only coincidence.

During depression, a person's ego is in its most fragile possible state. It certainly isn't the time to achieve fantastic results from therapy. The intelligence is lessened, perspective and perception are distorted, the person is weakened in all respects. Tackling major problems is too much effort. But even during a depression, a person can gain enough self-awareness to create necessary personality changes. The only way, though, is to start with the easy things.

Making Changes

Suppose you want to change a major behavior in your life, or you are helping someone through depression and want to help him or her eliminate a type of depression-prone behavior. It may be that something started is never finished, or never finished as well as expected. It may be a lack of confidence necessary to make a success out of life. It may be shyness, aggression, sloppiness. There are a host of personality problems which keep us humans from being happy with ourselves.

The first step is identifying the problem. That sounds easy, but it isn't. We are none of us very good self-observers, and we may identify something which *we* assess as a problem, while missing the real trouble entirely. Or we may project our own biases onto the person we are helping. Identifying the factor that is really causing mental and emotional disquiet requires hours of quiet objective thought.

Forget *causes*. You may be the personality you are because your mother and father committed unpardonable sins upon you. You may have adopted certain traits because your subconscious told you that was the best way to survive. But the continuation of those behaviors is no longer necessary. *Any factor of the past which no longer exists but is still responsible for actions you take today is a part of your life which is out of your control. It is nothing less than slavery to the past.* The past is dead and gone. It has only the effect you allow it to have. It is important to realize how much effect it *does* have, and to let your losses go. If your parents didn't love you the way you wanted them to, it's unfortunate and sad. But you will never again be a little child and they will never make it up to you. And, *your parents do not have to love you for you to be a* whole *person—* substitute any other word for parents. If you made the wrong choice, if you made a mistake, no matter what the past has made of your history, you must let it go. The only place you have to make it different is right now, in the present.

That does not mean to forget the *lessons* of the past. The woman whose child was hit by a car will always be extra careful about telling her children not to play in the street. But if she refuses to allow the children anywhere *near* a street, the past is dictating too much of her present perception.

It's surprising how many of our problems are really just dictates from our past experiences. Eventually, they become habits and the original reason for the behavior is forgotten. One good example is a fear of spiders, a phobia shared by many people. It's an easy fear to work through, if you feel like trying an experiment. Start out by thinking where the fear comes from. Is it the way they crawl, the web, an association? What *exactly* is so frightening about spiders?

Once the source of the fear is located, you'll probably find it's more revulsion than fear. Revulsion is easier to control than fear. That is, if you're afraid of spiders you'll probably never actually like them, but you can get rid of the panic created by the very word or image "spider." This is using an intellectual approach to an emotional situation, a form of self-imposed mind control.

Jennie, a former co-worker of mine, used to regale friends with stories of her spider phobia. Once one crawled across the page of a book she was reading. She slammed the book shut on it, threw the book into a chest, slammed the lid on the chest, and refused to sleep in the room with the chest until a friend removed it *from the house*, then took out the book and threw it away!

I had known that Jennie was prone to mild depressions, and one day we got into a discussion about her fear of spiders. Like most depressives, she carried several compulsive, unexamined fears. She had never examined her fear of spiders. Jennie had a ready explanation of the *reason* for her fear: a childhood incident where a spider frightened her. But she had never asked herself why she was still carrying the fear from that childhood incident into her adult life.

Jennie had quite accurately assessed the major problem in her life. She had no feeling of control, she felt that everything that happened to her was brought about by forces that she had nothing to do with and that were unrelated to her efforts. I asked her if she wanted to try an experiment which might allow her to change aspects of herself that she was unhappy with. When she said yes, we began working on changing her *style* to give her more control over her life.

Jennie had a pattern of confusing reasons with causes. She knew the *reason* for her spider phobia, but had never understood that the *cause* was only the fact that she had never examined that reason in light of her present-day knowledge and experience. While tackling a deep-seated fear like her fear of spiders isn't really a *little* thing, it's the one we began with. We went for a picnic in a field, something Jennie had never done because she was so afraid that a spider might "get on" her. And sure enough, a tiny white field spider did crawl over the edge of our picnic cloth. It took a lot of effort for Jennie to *control* her urge to run away screaming. But she sat there, asking herself out loud, "Why am I afraid of this tiny thing . . . it can't hurt me!" Of course, that didn't get rid of her fear. But it allowed her to examine it from a more objective point, and to take enough control of the situation to decide whether she *chose* to be hysterically afraid of spiders. The idea of *choice* was something new. And choice, being able to *choose* a course of action, is the essential ingredient in having control over one's life.

Jennie has never overcome her disgust for arachnids. But she has now reached the point where she will refuse to panic when she sees one in her home. Instead, she will put a glass over it, slide a piece of paper under the glass, and carry this improvised trap out the door, letting the spider go. It is one measure of the control she has gained.

Once there was some achievement over the spider panic, Jennie began examining the other factors of her life over which she felt she had no power. In some cases, the feeling was an accurate assessment. Her job was one where she could not hope for promotion. This situation wasn't consistent with her goal of a much higher salary and position. She had never examined this in a realistic fashion. If she wanted a better job and yet was holding one in which she had risen as high as possible, she had to either give up her desire or get a better job. Yet the security of the job was too pleasant to leave. She was afraid of taking a risk and losing that security. That fear—*and* the desire for security—was so strong that Jennie had never examined the fact that she must make a choice in order to get what she wanted. Since her job was a part of her life which she didn't have the courage to tackle, and since it was the source of many depressive cycles, she worked on getting rid of other, minor powerless reinforcements first.

Jennie wasn't really timid, but she had a horror of "scenes." If a waiter didn't bring the right order, she would never dream of sending it back. A course in assertiveness training helped her deal with this pattern. In driving, she would wait for a long stretch of open traffic before moving into another lane, even though her turn signals were flashing. She often missed her freeway exist and had to either drive in the slow lane all the way to and from her destination, or go past her ramp and double back. At ramp entrances, she would sometimes come to a full stop and wait for a secure opening instead of flowing with traffic.

After the spider problem showed some signs of being resolved, Jennie began working on lane changing. It took a few weeks to break this habit, but soon she was making lane changes in crowded traffic with perfect calm (and safety). Then came the sending back of food orders. One by one, Jennie dealt with these minor reinforcements of her overall pattern of letting unexamined fears take her control away. It took a lot of examination to recognize things at first, but after a short time she was able to pick out those aspects of her life which contained the unexamined-fear-out-of-control-pattern without any effort. I had thought it would take at least a year before Jennie would be able to start looking for another job, but less than six months after the "experiment" began, Jennie got a better offer and took it. "It's frightening," she told me. "I'm jumping ahead of myself with courage I don't have yet—but I'm choosing to take control and take the risk."

Making changes in this fashion is a lot easier than working through problems in conventional therapy, especially during depressions. Start by putting down on paper what you think your overall personality style may be. This should not be a personality test. You may be lovable, kind, intelligent, and witty, but that has nothing to do with whatever factor is causing you unhappiness. The factor may be a combination of several things: Do you always feel someone is trying to take advantage of you? And are you angry about it? There may be a combination of paranoia and anger. Remember, you also want to avoid the self-destructive urge to hurt yourself, should you have one (or have one toward the person you may be trying to help).

You probably won't be able to assess the style in one or two short tries. It needs a lot of self-observation (or friend-observation). If you drive, examine what you do. What is your reaction when another driver cuts in front of you? Are you hostile? Do you beep your horn, the motorist's way of shouting? Do you feel a sense of grim satisfaction, knowing that someone who drives that way will sooner or later have a nasty accident? Do you roll up the windows and turn up the radio, walling yourself off from whatever is happening outside your own little car world?

Look at how you run your gas tank. Do you let it go all the way down, then fill it all the way up again in an orderly, systematic fashion; or do you let it surprise you with how low it gets, occasionally running out of gas? Do you fill it in routine sums, always five dollars' worth; or do you just say "Fill 'er up"? Are you a miser type who hates to give out even when you know it's necessary, so that you always fill up in small sums, knowing that you'll just have to go back to the station that much sooner? Compare your gas tank system to the system by which you keep your bank account. Is there a similarity?

The environment also reflects the state of mind. Is your home comfortable and lived-in? Is it kept compulsively neat, so that

appearance counts more than substance? Is it sloppy and disorganized, without order, always seeming beyond your control to
keep neat? Is the surface tidy, but with chaos reigning behind
the scenes in drawers and closets?

Compare and look for patterns. Does your love life match the
way you run your home? Does the way you handle your business
have anything in common with the way you pay your bills or
keep promises? How do people treat you? Do you always end up
setting the trend, or on the outside wondering where it's at? Do
you have a pattern of one close friend and many acquaintances;
do you easily admit people to the level of "close friend," or do
you keep everyone at a distance?

After a few weeks of examination, you'll not only know a lot
more about yourself, you'll know where the patterns are. There is
one thing to keep in mind. All of us share certain basic feelings,
mostly insecurities, which we all hide with varying degrees of
success. All of us are afraid that we have secret murky parts
which would disgust anyone who learned about them. All of us
worry about being smelly, being laughed at, making a fool of
ourselves. We all go through periods of thinking that no one
really likes us or that we are basically unlovable. These things are
normal, meaning *held-in-common*, parts of the human psyche.
They are most often unwarranted feelings. In trying to isolate
your style, keep the judgmental factor out as much as possible.
You aren't judging yourself, just observing.

Start with one small part of the pattern first. It may be something as simple as the fact that it takes a long time after one roll of
toilet paper is gone before you reload the holder. Or it may be that
you never have the right change for the bus because you never
remember to get it in time. Tackle something that doesn't take
much concentration or will power. As you conquer easy-to-break
habits and begin working on habits slightly more difficult, the will-
power and concentration necessary to erase them will develop by
itself. At first you may have to write reminders for yourself. After
a while, the process will develop a momentum of its own, and
you will have established a pattern of keeping aware of whatever
reinforcement habit you're trying to break.

The process can be broken down into a system: you become
aware of a small part of the overall pattern you want to change;
you work on becoming aware of doing that small part; once

you're aware of doing it, you then work on using that awareness to *stop* doing it. Self-awareness (or control) works like a muscle. The more it's exercised, the more strength is developed. Soon there will be such development of awareness that nothing can sneak up on you—certainly not a depressive episode. And, as has been stressed throughout this book, a depressive episode will be far lighter, or even totally prevented, if it can be recognized and dealt with in time.

Since depression *is* biochemical in origin (though the chemicals are almost certainly a reaction to stress or some other emotional disturbance), you can't hope to totally eliminate the problem just by recognizing your personality style and restructuring it. But you *can* eliminate depression-prone behavior, and in doing so eliminate almost all the triggers which may start the descent into depression.

The Depressive and Time

Most depressives have a problem with time. It may be that they feel it passing without any accomplishment. It may be that they feel there isn't enough of it. (That feeling is by far the most common; many studies show that depressives are *doers* who aren't *doing* either what they or the world expects of them.) But time problems seem bound up in the depressive psyche. It isn't strange, then, to learn that one delusion shared by most depressives is the one of being old or looking far more aged than the years of life would indicate.

There seems to be a pattern among most depressives of not being able to judge time with any efficiency. It took me a while to become aware of this in myself. I like making my own clothing, and every time I was going somewhere special, I would start to make a new outfit. But I would start to make it the same day I was to go out. It's embarrassing to remember: the times I arrived so late that the event was nearly over because I stayed to finish my new whatever; or the times I spent all day in a frenzy, finally giving up hours after I should have left for the someplace special, having to wear something else because the project was nowhere near done. One time, at a convention in New York, I still had not finished the special outfit I was making for my then-husband to wear to make the guest of honor speech. We went out and rented a machine. While the gaiety of the convention swirled around me,

I sat inside the hotel room, sewing. He was due on the podium to make his speech and I was kneeling in front of him taking up the hem on his pant legs. He kept his audience waiting 20 minutes, and still made his appearance in clothing tacked here and there because I didn't have time to finish the garment properly.

I had not yet learned the secret of time: the truth in the old cliche, "Time is money." Why is that so? Because you *spend* and *make* of each what you want in exactly the same way.

The time problem was part of my personality style. When I began to approach it with the same sense I used about money, it was resolved easily. Before, all the vows, all the embarrassments, nothing had served to change my inability to handle time. Since then I've worked out a time sheet which a number of doctors now use in treating depressives whose depression-prone behavior involves the handling of time. It's not an efficiency expert's system. No system in the world will work without a full self-awareness of how the problem begins and when it is beginning. All it is is a timetable, a statement of fact which allows no argument. If one has a sixteen-hour day, and eight of those hours are spent at work, two spent getting ready for and going to and from work, that leaves six hours. If eating takes one and household chores take another, that leaves four. There's no way to argue with it—the four hours are all that are left. If that's the schedule and if you have something to do that's going to take more than those four hours, either you have to borrow the time from something else or you're not going to get it done. Period. It's as simple as that.

Using a time sheet, you're always aware of how much time you have to spend. It allows you to choose how to spend it so that you get the results you want. It also gives you a more realistic picture of yourself.

During my many struggles to get a new outfit finished in time for the big occasion, I truly believed that I could finish a shirt or dress or pair of pants in a day. Never mind that I had never done it; somehow nothing had ever disturbed the illusion. It was only when I started keeping the time sheet that I realized it took me an hour, for example, to make a collar and attach it. No matter how I hurried, no matter how much of an emergency it was, the clock was immovable. It was going to take an hour for that collar. That meant that if I had to leave for a place in ten minutes and all that had to be done was the collar, I had to count on being 50 minutes late if I stayed to do it. For the depressive who can't get time under control, the self-knowledge of how long it takes to finish a task is essential. It prevents one of the greatest banes of depressives: the mountain of work waiting because nothing ever gets finished—or sometimes even started.

Below there is a time sheet you can use to figure out your time budget. It may not solve all the problems you (or a depressive you are helping) has with time. But it will make you aware of what you have to do to resolve those problems, and the next step is easy. Remember that the main part of eliminating depression-prone behavior is acting out behavior that *instead* makes you feel good about yourself. The only way to feel good about yourself—really good in a secure way—is to do those things that create good feelings. Unless self-liking comes from within, from having a good opinion of your *self*, it is hollow and easily destroyed. No matter how many people think you're wonderful, you'll be insecure and prone to depression unless *you* think you're wonderful too.

Time Sheet/Section One

Use only weekdays when counting hours or figuring times. If there is a one-day-a-week special activity or extra work period, divide it by five and include it in the daily figures. Try to be as accurate as possible without guessing. If necessary, time yourself with a stopwatch for a week.

_____Usual time of getting out of bed.
_____Usual bedtime.
_____Total of hours you are awake during the day.
   Write this number in the total time space in Section Two.

   Figure the section below in hours or minutes per day, whichever applies.

_____Hours spent at work (count hours from start to finish, including lunchtime. If you are a housewife, count the hours it takes to complete all daily chores *except* shopping and preparing dinner.)
_____Hours spent preparing food and cleaning up after preparation and eating. You may have to average this over several days.

_____Hours it takes to prepare appearance and clothing. Count washing and styling hair, laundry, ironing, etc. Average this out over a week.

_____Hours of "must" time—classes, meetings, regular social activities, time spent with relatives, etc. Include time spent on getting ready, driving to destination, etc.

_____Hours spent on shopping for food.

Add the total of minutes or hours in this section and fill the number in the taken time section below.

Time Sheet/Section Two

_____Total time. (This is the amount of time you have available to you. It is like capital—some must be spent in ways over which you have little choice, such as working, eating, etc. Unless you go into debt to your sleep time, it is all the time you have.

_____Taken time. This is the amount of time which must be spent whether you like it or not. It is similar to bills which must be paid.

_____Total of time left when taken time is subtracted from total time. This is what you have left over to spend as you wish. It's like money you can choose to save or spend foolishly or use to get something you have always wanted. This is the only sum over which you have choice.

Time Sheet/Section Three

In this section, you'll try to budget your available time so that you can feel you've gotten something for it. This section requires some careful thought plus some timing work with a watch. For example, if you like to read a newspaper cover to cover, it's going to take more than ten minutes, and you have to budget your time to allow for newspaper reading. If being well informed makes you feel good about yourself, then by all means regard a newspaper as essential to your well being. If taking care of correspondence is a sore point and bothers you, budget the time you need to take care of it and get rid of any internal nagging. The goal is to use your available time to level mountains and maintain the clear space where you won't be bothered by shoulds. If at any point in your life you are prevented from full enjoyment of any moment because of something else you know you should be doing, you have lost control of that moment and are acting out a depression-prone behavior.

What undone or half completed tasks are bothering me?
(Write them down in priority order, and include everything—closets or drawers you have been meaning to clean out, mending and darning, letters to be answered, that bundle of clothing to be ironed that's been sitting around for a while, the door handle that needs to be fixed, the leaky faucet, etc.)

_____

_____

_____

Make an estimate of how long it would take to do the first task to completion. For example, could you answer one letter in half an hour? How many letters wait to be answered? Is the closet an all day job or a two hour one?

_____

_____

What enjoyable activities do you do on a regular basis, such as watching a certain television program, reading a monthly magazine or daily newspaper, etc.?

_____

_____

How long do you spend on each of these activities, approximately?

_____

_____

What improvements do you want to make in yourself or your environment, such as learning another language, learning a new craft, making a new wardrobe, doing some remodeling or redecorating your home, planting a garden, etc.? Write down those projects you have always dreamed of as well as those which are definite plans "as soon as I can find time." Write them down in priority order. This will take some thinking!

_____

_____

_____

_____

Take the first item on the above list and figure out how much time it will take for you to accomplish it.

_____

Now add the total of all your time estimates.

_____

Compare this time figure to your total available time figure.
_____ Time needed to do what you want
_____ Total Time Figure

Okay. You now have a rough idea of how much time you need to do all the things you can to make yourself feel good. Don't get discouraged at seeing how much time you need and how little time you have. Work out a budget for that time, similar to a regular installment payment. Suppose you spend an hour a day on finishing a half done or unstarted project, just as an experiment. See how long it takes to get it finished and how you feel when it's done. Be disciplined about it; set a timer if you have to, but work only for that one hour (or whatever time period you set for yourself). Set a budget for the highest priority thing you *wish* to accomplish. If it's a class you have always wanted to take, start the steps needed to accomplish that desire. Find out where the course is available, figure out if you can afford it in both time and money. If it's too difficult, save that goal for later and go onto the next one on your list. But the accomplishment of a "someday" dream—actually putting a long-held desire into motion—does a lot for the self-esteem. It's often beneficial for someone in the throes of a depressive episode, since a feeling of accomplishment is even more important then. If you're helping someone through, you may have to push the person into doing something he or she has always wanted to do. You may have to deal with protestations that he or she is unworthy of having that desire fulfilled, with an unwillingness to undertake something new, or even with the reluctance to go out of the house should the goal be something that can't be done at home. Push the depressive gently, but firmly. Remember also that intelligence is lowered during this period. It will probably be harder for the person to learn something new, and you may have to help your friend.

Make a schedule and stick to it. Use available time as a guideline, but never make the mistake of filling out all that available time with plans, or devoting all of it to one project. Little segments of project time are best. Plan on, say, twenty minutes a day or an hour a day or whatever for various projects. This will keep warm the desire to *do*, rather than wearing it out by trying to get too much done or get too much of any one thing done. It will also help eliminate waste motion. If you're cleaning out a closet and have only an hour a day to work on it, you're not going to want to stop in the middle, so you'll use your budgeted time more efficiently. You'll be surprised at how much you'll get done with budgeted time when you compare it to how much you got done with random time before. As an example: With all my responsibilities, I never had the time to work on the book I always wanted to write. When I began budgeting a certain amount of available time, not only did the book begin taking shape, but the discipline necessary to write it became a part of my life. After a while, budgeting time was no longer necessary. The knowledge of how to handle time became so ingrained that I didn't even seem to need a conscious effort to accomplish everything I wanted with my time. And surprisingly, I seemed to have more time to do things than before. Again, it's a process of awareness. When you become *aware* of time—the time you have and the time it takes to do the things you normally do—then the only occasion when you overdraw your time account is when you choose to.

When you start budgeting time, there's one area of future trouble to watch for. The method is so successful that it's easy to overdo it. One doctor told me of a patient who used the time/budget method to get his life in order. He became so meticulous about keeping times that he knew to the second how long it took to get to work, put on his clothes, eat his breakfast, even have his morning bowel movement! He worked out his budget in such minute degree that he became a slave to it, becoming obsessed with ordering his life by the clock. He allowed himself a prescribed amount of time for phone calls to friends, and when that time was up he would abruptly say goodby, even if the conversation was interesting. He was well on the way to becoming a mechanical person with no spontaneity in his life before his therapist helped him to realize that he was overdoing the whole budget system. Remember that this method is similar to medicine: it's necessary and must be used regularly, but too much is even worse than none at all.

Unrealistic Goals

As you learn to gain control over your life by making your personality style more to your liking and using your time to get what you want, you'll face another problem shared by many depressives. This is the unrealistic goal. The depressions that hit so many men in their late forties coincide with the realization that they *are* what they're going to be, and they will never, never be President of the United States or a top sports figure or even a powerful executive. Many depressives expect too much of themselves and are ready for a fall; depression comes along destroying self-esteem and, with it, false hopes based on unrealistic goals. One of the traits shared by a majority of depressives is being a perfectionist. You may *want* to be the super-parent, super-worker, super-everything; but if it's just not possible to accomplish all of these *wants* at the same time, you will disappoint yourself. The depressive (and those eliminating depression-prone behavior) must work on realizing what is possible and what isn't. For example, a woman who works and also cooks for her family is going to have an almost impossible time keeping her house immaculate as well, especially if her definition of immaculate is based on the perfectionist ideal. Something's got to give. Unless she wants it to be her nerves, she should either give up the idea of the immaculate house or else hire someone to come in and do it. The man who has a high-pressure job, who is also head of his service club, and who wants to spend time with his children, will exhaust himself if he tries to be the perfect home handyman as well. Although it will probably be the hardest job of all to admit our own limitations, it's something that must be done to prevent an onset or a recurrence of depression.

As an example of the unrealistic goal, consider Sue. A woman in her early thirties, she still hoped to be a top ballet dancer. Her family encouraged her in this dream and never minded when she spent hours at classes or started special lessons with a new teacher. She would discuss her future career with friends as if Carnegie Hall were right around the corner. But Sue began to exhibit bizarre behavior which caused concern to both friends and family. She thought she had fallen in love with the husband of one of her friends, and begged the *friend* to tell her how to "win" him! She began to push her children away when they touched her or tried to climb in her lap. No one realized that

Sue was trying to maintain the illusion that she would be a ballet dancer in the face of the realistic knowledge that this would never happen, that she had passed the age for a ballet career. And while her family thought the support of this unrealistic goal showed love, they didn't realize that it was the worst thing they could have done for her.

Sue's husband finally left her, precipitating a breakdown which eventually brought her back to reality and the smashing of her unrealistic goal. But how much pain could have been spared if Sue had come to grips with her unrealistic goal before it tore her apart!

While Sue's case is an extreme one, we all have goals which are unrealistic because we either aren't capable of or just plain won't accomplish them. Since a depressive episode is no time to face self-limitations realistically, it's best to assess ourselves before a depression shows any sign of beginning. Essentially, this means making a compromise between our idealized picture of ourselves and our reality. If you are the type who wants to finish your work perfectly, but if that perfection goal keeps you from finishing at all, it may be best to lower your standards of perfection. Don't make the mistake one young girl from Pittsburgh made. She was well on her way to becoming a successful actress, having appeared in local stage and television productions over several years. Finally, her "big break" came. She was accepted by a stock theatre company in an important city in New York. After a month, during which time she had moved up from walk-ons to major supporting roles, she was fired. Why? Well, one of the jobs of each member of the company was either to paint the flats (the set backdrops) or to wash the paint off. The young lady took five hours to wash flats, a job which usually took only a half hour. Instead of using the pressure of the hose to rinse the most obvious color away, she didn't feel the job was done unless every bit of color had been removed—from corners, even from the back where no one could see. After this had happened several times— in fact, after the canvas had become so soaked that it could not be painted over properly for that night's show—she was fired. The resulting despondency kept her from trying for more work for nearly a year.

The unrealistic goal makes us put pressure on ourselves which can interfere with our perception and judgment. This is not the same thing as the normal standards most people have of achieving on an ever higher level. The unrealistic goal can be defined as the quality of expecting more of ourselves than we would of another in the same situation, of being impressed when someone else does something but dismissing it when we do the same thing ourselves, or of excusing someone else for certain shortcomings which we berate ourselves for having.

The unrealistic goal doesn't stop with our own self-expectations. Often it's assigned to others as well. If you expect your children always to be quiet, your mate always to be sensitive, that's unrealistic. It's much easier to judge the reality of our expectations in others than our expectations in ourselves. All you have to do is spend some time thinking: "How often am I disappointed in other people? How often do they let me down?" If the answer is *almost all the time*, reassess your expectations of others. If a best friend, and if every best friend through most of your life, has disappointed you over and over again, wouldn't it be nice to stop the hurt and pain of that disappointment by changing your expectations a little? If the children drive you up the wall because they never stay quite as clean as you would like, wouldn't it be better to accept the fact that they are going to get dirty and not take that trip up the wall? You don't have to let go of all your desires and expectations, just relax them a little and bring them more into line with the way things actually operate.

Patterns of Depression

The therapeutic life style involves three things. The first two we have already discussed: becoming aware of the self so thoroughly that no element of your *self* is a stranger to you; and changing your personality *style* to eliminate depression-prone behavior and instead instigate behavior that makes you feel good about yourself. The third factor is recognizing your physical and emotional *trends* as well as any cause and/or effect of those trends.

A *trend* could also be called a *tendency*. It refers to how you react to various stimuli, both emotionally and physically. For example, if you get too little sleep for a period of days, what does that do to your personality? If you have several drinks at a party, do you have a tendency to feel lethargic and dull the next day? Recognizing these trends—how you react to stress, to rainy weather, to certain foods—helps you chart a connection between the various stimuli you pass through and any depressed feelings you may experience as a result. This is the final step in becoming aware of any possible pattern between depression and those things you can control.

One of the most important parts of this awareness is any connection between your mood swings and the food you eat. Although I have included less on diet in this book than I would have liked, diet is extremely important in depression. A depressive episode can sometimes be controlled or lessened by eating the right foods. Anyone who has a history of depression or who lives under stress needs a diet that is high in protein and high in B vitamins. This includes such foods as organ meats, grains, unrefined flour breads, and in many cases special stress formula supplements. (A word to the vitamin taker: don't buy stress formulas with vitamin C in them. The B complex is expensive and C is cheap. Don't spend your money on a B complex which has been diluted with C. Buy a strong B formula and take your C separately. In addition, don't bother buying "organic" C. There is only about 10 or 12 percent of the rose hip powder in even the most organic of these health food brands; if you want to make sure you metabolize every part of the vitamin, eat an orange along with the ordinary C. Ascorbic acid (vitamin C) will work just as well whether all or part of it comes from the lab. You may buy organic B if you wish; the natural yeast, liver, and other organic extracts do seem to have more effect than a totally synthesized B complex. However, make sure you always take B *with* C, since these two vitamins are synergistic. One won't work unless there's a sufficient quantity of the other. There's more on depression, vitamins, and diet later in this chapter.)

Personality *trends* can be pre-depression sequences. Many people have what could only be called a *ritual* of depression which, if attention is paid to it, can be used to predict and forestall an episode. In cases that border on manic-depressive illness, a short period of high spirits or a feeling of calm well-being can be a clue. Several depressives have told me that they can tell a low cycle is on its way when they go through a three- to four-week period of high creativity and a feeling of "having it all together." Don't feel that this makes you a manic-depressive if you go through the same mild cycles. Many times you can use a depression ritual to your advantage, forcing yourself to act in a way that may influence a biochemical response. For example, if you know that a pre-depression ritual is to let your hair go unwashed for longer than usual, force yourself to wash it. Of course, this type of action only works in minor depressive episodes—they could more accurately be called mood cycles—but learning to have an effect on the minor cycles will also give you more control over the bigger ones.

The most efficient way to chart your personality trends is to make an actual mood chart, writing down how you feel each day and what your daily activities are. A sample of one such chart follows. It concentrates most heavily on food, and was designed to detect a pattern between depression and such things as various kinds of protein or sugars, amount of sleep, and so on. The result is a graph which shows how the mood cycle is moving. The pattern between the items on the chart and the move toward or away from depression will show if there's any connection between the mood and these controllable items. You can make up a chart of your own containing elements you feel may have more connection to your own feelings. For example, if you go on a shopping spree as a depressive episode is beginning, that should be an important factor on your chart. Be careful to separate cause and effect when making up your charts; make two, if necessary, one showing the connection between various things and depression, the other showing the *effects* of depression. A *cause*, then, would be a setback at work or going without sleep. An *effect* would be going on a buying spree or not washing your hair.

To use the following chart, check the various spaces indicating mood and foods eaten, and fill in the questions in the spaces provided. Do this every day for one month. Then spend at least an hour examining the chart to see if there is a pattern between mood and sleep, or food, stress, and energy.

You may have to keep the chart going for six weeks or more to determine whether a pattern exists. Pay attention to your body's cravings as well. If you notice that a week of stress is followed by the eating of salad every day, think about the type of salad dressing you choose. Is it very acid? There are many people who need a higher degree of acid in their body to cope with stress. This is especially true of women just before their menstrual periods, when there may be an increased desire for tart salad dressings, citrus juices, or foods made with vinegar. See if a few days without sleep increase the amount of candy you eat. Cravings are an intelligent way the body deals with its necessities, whether it needs more acid or more of a certain vitamin or mineral. If you suddenly think a banana would be the most delicious thing on earth, when you don't give a hoot about bananas any other time, that may be your body's way of signaling that it needs potassium. If red meat seems a lot more appetizing suddenly, you may just be craving more iron. Unless a craving is obviously destructive, such as one for alcohol or sugar, it is something that you should pay attention to and perhaps research. Each individual needs different amounts of the vitamin and mineral nutrients. In fact, the dispute about the so-called minimum daily requirement is the wrong angle. Health food fanatics say these requirements are too low, when what they should be arguing about is that they are too general. Saying that everyone needs a certain amount of this or that nutrient is like saying everyone should wear a size 10 shirt. You may need three or four times the B complex that another person needs, and you may need far less of another nutrient than the MDR calls for.

Date	Amount of Sleep	Mood Upon Waking	The Day Was: Stressful	Calm	My Overall Mood Was: Depressed	Normal or Varied	Good

Number of Meals	Check If You Ate Any of the Following:							Energy Level:	
	Salad	Meat	Cheese	Eggs	Candy or Dessert	Alcoholic Beverage	Cereal or Bread	Tired	Energetic

Figuring Your Own Requirements

The contradictions of medical science are amazing. Doctors discount the importance of nutrition, medical schools spend probably less time on the subject of diet and other preventative aids than they do on anything else. Yet any horse breeder or dog breeder knows the importance of feeding a prize animal a special diet so that it stays in good condition. Any farmer who raises animals for meat knows how the food eaten flavors the meat. Corn-fed cattle have a reputation for tastiness, because of the flavor the corn imparts to the muscles, which are turned into table meat. If food can make such a major taste difference, isn't it logical to believe that food also makes a difference in energy and well-being, especially when we are talking about human beings, whose chemical balance is so fine that the slightest upset can radically alter personality and mental health? Isn't it also logical to wonder why the health profession spends so much time studying ways to cure the effects of illness, and so little on helping its customers *prevent* the illnesses which require so much money to repair?

Since you can get so little help from the medical profession in figuring out what to eat to satisfy *your* body's requirements, here is a list of symptoms caused by a deficiency of various vitamins and minerals. Use these symptoms as a *rough* guide to your needs. For example, you may have minor nosebleeds and slow healing that indicate a lack of vitamin C, but these same symptoms might be the result of glandular disturbance or other illnesses. Vitamins and minerals are *nutrients*, not medicines. But proper nutrition may help prevent the need for medicines if used regularly.

Deficiency Symptom	Nutrient Required	Possible Toxicity
Rough skin Night blindness Sensitivity to light Dry skin	Vitamin A	Yes. Don't take more than 20,000 units per day.
Fatigue	Vitamin B complex	Little toxicity. Too much niacin may cause flushing tingling.

Deficiency Symptom	Nutrient Required	Possible Toxicity
Cracked skin Sores in corners of mouth Edema (swelling) Morning "sleep" in eyes Depression Itchy or sore skin Lethargy Lack of ability to concentrate Fatigue Stomach distress Irritability	Vitamin B complex	Women need more of this vitamin if they take birth control pills.
Slow healing Bleeding from gums or nose Easy bruising Red capillary bursts under skin Susceptibility to infection	Vitamin C	Like all water-soluble vitamins, C is virtually non-toxic. Too much (5,000 mgs. daily) may cause some side effects. You need more of this vitamin if you smoke.
Soft bones and teeth	Vitamin D	Get this from milk and sunshine, not pills.
Rupturing of blood cells Lack of vigor	Vitamin E	Virtually nontoxic.
Spasms in muscles Softening of bones Tension	Calcium	Excess dose may cause calcium deposits on bones.
Large thyroid gland Dry skin and hair	Iodine	Check with doctor if you have thyroid problems.
Nervousness Muscle twitches	Magnesium	Yes, in some people.
Memory loss Apathy and lethargy Poor digestion	Potassium	No.
Weakness Pale face Anemia	Iron	Yes, if too much is taken daily.
Slow healing	Zinc	Very little toxicity.

It's a good idea to get several nutrition books and study the needs of the human body. From this basic knowledge, you can work out how you feel when you eat foods containing certain nutrients. Don't get attached to catch phrases or fads. High-fiber diets, low-carbohydrate diets, high-protein diets—all of them are meaningless without a basic understanding of good nutrition. Not everyone needs the same amounts of fiber or protein, just as not everyone gains the same amount of weight eating the same kinds of foods. If you notice that you feel better than usual after several days of eating liver, sweetbreads, or brains, you'll know that the probability of the high B vitamin intake you had helps you feel better. If you've eaten beets or dark green leafy vegetables several days in a row and it makes you feel good, you'll know that you have a high iron requirement. Learn what's in food—then learn how your body reacts to various foods. That way, it becomes easy to select a diet that is right for *you* and will give you the best possible nutrition.

It's especially important for all depressives to realize the benefits of proper nutrition. Since depressives need a lot of the B complex, it's also important to know what conditions destroy that vitamin, both in food storage and preparation and in the body itself. This is information available in most nutrition books, but as a rule of thumb, remember that anything stored too long a time or subject to high heat will have very little B left by the time it's eaten. Alcohol destroys some of the B complex in the body. So does chocolate.

In Closing

If depression is properly treated and handled, it can be the best thing that ever happened to a person. A depressive must *grab* onto health, and in doing so, usually becomes more stable, more self-aware, and better connected to reality. The recovered depressive who lives a therapeutic life style will count the day of recovery from depression as a day of rebirth. Life will seem less out of control and more joyful.

We are a long way from knowing enough about the brain to know how to prevent depression entirely. It is one of mankind's oldest diseases—it is also the only illness in which recovery can put the patient in a better position than he or she has ever been before.

If you're in the middle of a depressive episode right now, or if your mate, relative, or close friend is struggling with the disease, you may feel as though you're in a dark pit which has no way out. It helps to remember that it will pass. You will recover from your depression. Very few people nowadays have a serious uncurable case, and as new drugs become available, even fewer will have to suffer a lifetime with depression. It's hard to have hope when the whole world looks black, but as someone who has been there, I can promise you that the sun will come back again. It may seem like you've been waiting for recovery forever. You may start to give up, thinking that you've gone crazy or that depression will never end. Don't give up. The struggle is worth it. There will come a time when you'll look back on this dark period and measure your growth against it. Because you *will* have grown. In the middle of a depression there never seems any hint of light. But it's there. And in time, you or your friend or loved one will stand in the light of recovery and realize that you've come through one of the worst kinds of pain the human mind can undergo—and you made it. You're standing free.

10.

Depression Prevention

The modern methods of medical science have given us some genuine miracles, both in surgical and chemical remedies. But ironically, those very advances have kept medicine from advancing as a healing science. Drugs and surgery are like a dustpan and broom—they clean up the mess *after* it's happened. They do nothing to *prevent*, and the medical field will never achieve its logical goal until it knows as much about prevention as it does about cure.

When it comes to areas which affect feelings and behavior, this syndrome is even more obvious. It's no exaggeration to say that the field of psychology has been stagnating ever since the discovery of tranquilizing drugs. That tension and anxiety can be "cured" by taking a pill has slowed any widespread work by the average therapist at helping the patient learn to prevent anxiety and tension from becoming a problem in the first place.

In the past few years, we've seen a radical change in attitude, as traditional medical practitioners saw more and more of their patients seek alternative forms of medicine that viewed the patient as a unit of mind and body. This reluctance to see the connection between mind and body has been the greatest barrier to the growth of preventative medicine. Even today there are doctors who refuse to see depression as anything other than an "emotional" disease, refuse to believe that something which causes mainly psychological symptoms could have its origin anywhere else but in the mind.

The discovery of chemicals and enzymes produced by the body which affect our feelings of pleasure or pain is one of the fastest-growing and most exciting new fields of medicine. Science is beginning to look for natural, self-originated cures, looking at ways in which the body can heal itself without drugs. In the same vein, these scientific researchers are examining the ways in which the body makes itself *sick,* either physically or emotionally. For the first time in medical history (which goes back to the earliest beginnings of human civilization), medicine is shifting from an external to an internal view. Illness was once regarded as a kind of possession by the devil or as retribution for some kind of sin. Then it was regarded as the fault of "humours," vague spirits of the air which settled into some hapless victim. In modern times, bacteria and viruses have been our external malefactors; anything which affects the mind has therefore been doubly frightening because the external factor which may have caused it is totally unknown.

Now doctors are realizing that the *internal* aspects of medicine have been ignored to the detriment of the patient, and that the body can not only cure itself in many cases, but the mind can cure the body and the body can cure the mind. It has already been accepted that the reverse is true: we know that emotional stress can do serious things to the body. The past decade has seen a lot of research into the connection between stress and ulcers, high blood pressure and heart attacks, as well as cancer, endocrine disorders, and the like. We know that physical stress can cause a mental collapse, and we're all familiar with overworked film stars who make headlines by being hospitalized for "exhaustion."

While the science of coping with stress is one of the fastest-growing fields of medicine, unfortunately there is still very little research available into ways in which depression may be prevented. Even the examination of stress is being dealt with mostly from an emotional standpoint. Patients are given emotional and intellectual ways to cope, and diet or other physical factors are given the barest attention.

Even before I finished the original edition of this book, I had begun researching ways to prevent depression. Yet I found that this was an area where there was practically no exploration by the medical field. Many areas which needed to be investigated had no body of scientific research which could have assisted me or anyone else interested in preventing depression before it happens. At the time, I found that physical use of the body was an effective anti-depressant, and began working out exercise programs which might be used in preventing depression. At the same time, a doctor in San Diego, California, announced that he was using a new therapy to help patients with depression. Instead of using verbal or chemical types of therapy, this doctor would take a group of patients jogging. He found that symptoms disappeared in the majority of patients, and in nearly all others, depression was reduced to a marked degree. But his announcement disappeared from the news wires with little effect, and his research went largely ignored by other medical practitioners.

The only effect his discovery had was that jogging, which had been sweeping the country at that time, was suddenly considered by many joggers to be the factor which in and of itself cleared or lessened the depressive symptoms. But it isn't jogging which is the active factor, because that form of exercise is no more miraculous than any other form of exercise. It's the physical use of the body which does so much for the patient, and there are a number of obvious reasons why.

Exercise as Prevention

In one experiment to demonstrate the effects of exercise on depression, I worked with a group of forty women who suffered from serious pre-menstrual symptoms. Some became so depressed that they found it hard to move for the few days before or during the early part of their menstrual cycle. I discovered that these "bad" periods weren't at all consistent. Some months would go by without a marked degree of symptoms, others would be severe. In looking for some common thread to connect these variations in each person, I found that, more often than not, the women who had the least amount of depression during any cycle had been physically active shortly before their period began— about a week or ten days before. Women who began a physical fitness program suddenly had far fewer pre-menstrual symptoms to worry about.

In another experiment, I also discovered that men who were

under serious work-related stress could get rid of it physically far quicker than they could by trying to control their reactions mentally. We all know that stressful emotions such as anger and frustration can be "worked off" by hard physical activity. Who has not heard of someone who chopped wood or cleared snow from a driveway as a way of getting rid of some negative feelings? But exercise is perhaps the greatest unacknowledged *preventative* for depression, a far better *preventative* than a cure, because once the illness has actually progressed, the depressed person just doesn't have enough energy to use his or her body effectively. Worse, once the illness has passed into a serious stage, the exercise doesn't seem to do as much good, just as vitamin C won't do much good if you wait until you've got a cold to begin taking it.

There seem to be no in-depth medical studies yet showing how exercise actually fights off depression. However, we do know some of the things that being physically active can do for the body. So far, most of this knowledge is based on the benefits of exercise to the heart, so research has concentrated on such things as the reduction in blood fats and the increased capacity of the blood to carry oxygen. But we can use our common sense as well as history to tell us a lot more.

Until the machine age, people had no choice but to be active. In earlier days life was harder and shorter, but there probably was far less depression. There is a correlation between the increasing ease of modern life and its increase in stress and depression.

People who exercise, whether by jogging, playing tennis, swimming, or in the course of their work, have increased feelings of self-esteem. Take the case of would-be actor Tony Hernandez.

Hernandez was earning a fair living as a bit player on television and in an occasional movie. He never got any really big parts, but the small parts he did get came often enough to allow him to buy his own home and drive a late-model car. When I met Tony, he was feeling very despondent because he was beginning to realize that he might never make it as a big-time actor. The thought had never occurred to him before. He had just assumed that his parts would become bigger and bigger, that he would get more important parts until he eventually became a star. Lately he had been having trouble remembering his lines and was feeling too fatigued to make his "rounds" as energetically as he had always done. There was a faint air of defeat surrounding him, an attitude which is certain death in Tony's field.

Then came a strike by Hollywood actors. Tony was out of work and didn't have enough mony saved to see him through the strike. He had to get a job.

Through a friend, he landed a job in construction. It meant that he would be outdoors most of the day, carrying heavy equipment and timber. The first few weeks were hard on him, but as his strength improved, so did his attitude. He began to radiate well-being and confidence.

"I realized how much I had changed when I found myself singing as I pounded nails into a roof on one job. I realized I hadn't felt so good in years—the last time I could remember feeling so good about myself was when I belonged to a health club."

Before his construction job, Tony's life had been fairly sedentary. He drove to and from his agent's office and the studios. He sat around waiting to go in front of the camera or memorizing his lines at home. Occasionally he would go to the beach, but aside from that, his body got very little use.

The increase in self-esteem has been well documented by people doing research into the effects of exercise, but no one has yet come up with a reason. Yet the reason should be obvious, given what we do know about the changes in a physically active body as opposed to a sedentary one.

We know that muscles build up certain toxins, among them lactic acid. In fact, to a large degree it's the buildup of lactic acid that causes the sore muscles after an unaccustomed workout. But if the body is used on a regular basis, there is no buildup of lactic acid, and a number of other toxins and waste products are efficiently carried off in the form of sweat. The body was *meant* to sweat, because this is the best way to get rid of waste products that aren't eliminated through normal elimination channels. But this is probably not the most important factor when it comes to depression. The reason exercise has such an effect on depression is because of what it does to the metabolism.

Exercise speeds up the metabolism, and when an exercise program is first begun, this speedup happens only during and immediately after the workout. But once exercise becomes a daily part of life, the whole metabolism changes. It becomes faster and more efficient, and these effects stay even after the exercising is over. The added oxygen in the bloodstream lasts as well, and this also provides extra oxygen to the brain.

In depression, the metabolism slows down, and the bloodstream becomes less oxygen-efficient. Since depression is a central nervous system illness, it's only natural that a more efficient metabolism will help make the central nervous system more efficient. We know that exercise makes the nerves better able to transmit electrical impulses. The major symptom of depression, which is a loss of accuracy of perception on all levels, is caused (as are most of the other symptoms of depression) by the faulty transmission of electrical impulses from the brain cells. If a chemical imbalance causes these impulses to reach the cerebral cortex either too late or in too distorted a way, then anything which improves the efficiency of transmission may help overcome the problems caused by an inefficient central nervous system.

Exercise may serve as a function comparable to the lubrication in a car. If a car doesn't have a regular lube job, the doors will be hard to open and close, there will be rattles and squeaks, and the operation of the car itself will be stiffer. There will be a loss of what, in the human body, could be called flexibility. The unexercised body will become stiff in the same way. Just as a car will operate without regular lubrication (we're not talking about engine oil here), the body will operate without exercise. But that operation will be more difficult, causing small operational problems which will actually shorten the life of the car as well as the human body. Physical exercise not only keeps the muscles flexible, it increases their efficiency.

Nerves are imbedded in muscle in such a way that when the muscle is exercised, the nerves get a workout as well. It's quite possible that that movement may have the same benefit for nerves that muscular movement does. We know that exercise works off muscular waste products which would otherwise make the muscles sluggish. There may be some as yet undiscovered type of waste material that builds up in or around the nerve sheath. If so, this would explain why a person who is in good (meaning exercised) physical shape also has a more efficient nervous system. The person who jogs, swims, plays handball, or rides a bike regularly has much faster and better reactions than the sedentary person. This may be due less to increased muscular tone than to the decrease in toxins which are produced by the nerves.

Some of the by-products of exercise have no medical explanation, though there are many theories. The increase in self-esteem is a major benefit. Most doctors attribute this to the fact that people feel good about themselves once they have the self-discipline to embark on a regular program which tones up the body as well as makes the body more appealing to look at. Yet it's more likely that the nerves tone up as well; and the central nervous system, which is in charge of producing the chemicals affecting our feelings of self-esteem, can function more efficiently because it has more energy to work with. Exercise also increases certain enzymes involved in the production of energy, so it's only logical that this overcomes depression's symptoms caused by a *lack* of energy. The full connection between physical exercise and the state of the mind has yet to be medically documented, but until it is, those who have depression, or who worry about being affected by it, only have to know that exercise works in order to gain its medical benefits.

If you're trying to help someone with depression, you have to remember that there will be resistance in this area, just as there is to all other beneficial factors of treating depression. The depressive not only has no energy to begin using the body, but has an active distaste for trying. People with minor depressions may begin a program with every good intention, but after a few days their discipline flags and they find it easier to make excuses than to get up and get started.

The way to overcome this is to think of exercise as a varied form of medicine. Don't stick with one "medication," meaning one form of exercise, and don't expect instant results. Jogging may be perfect for the person who likes the feel of breezes on the skin and the sight of scenery moving by. Someone else may feel slightly paranoid about being seen by others or about the way his body looks, or may feel uncomfortable outside the shelter of familiar rooms and spaces.

If you are trying to cure your own depressive symptoms with exercise, you're going to have a hard time sticking to a regular program by yourself. The depressive who has someone helping him or her, a person who will encourage exercise and, if necessary, accompany the depressive to make it easier for a regular workout to be met, has it a lot easier. Doing it by yourself means you'll be subject to all the emotional interferences that make you view your physical efforts with less than enthusiasm. What's worse, no one will be pushing you to overcome them. You should expect reluctance. Remember, depression interferes with normal self-discipline. You may start out realizing that regular jogging, swimming, raquetball, or tennis is the way to feel better, but even that knowledge won't keep you at it.

The first week or two of a self-administered exercise program usually isn't much of a problem. But then you may notice that even though you're feeling some benefits from it, your reluctance to begin each session is growing. It grows in a somewhat disguised form. You'll find that once you're actually in the process of working out, you enjoy it—sometimes enjoy it quite a lot. But the effort needed to make yourself begin becomes greater and greater. The more serious the symptoms of depression, the greater the reluctance to begin will be. To overcome this, exercise has to be given the same inescapable importance that going to work has in the mind: you don't expect to love each working day, but you know that you can't realistically expect to keep your job if you only do it when you feel like it. Another thing: don't expect to automatically feel better after a few days of exercising. The speed with which benefits become apparent varies from individual to individual. One person may feel less depressed after a few days, while another may not see any results for a month or more.

Types of Exercise
Don't automatically choose a particular form of exercise because it's the current rage. Whether you're making the choice for yourself or for someone else, find a knowledgeable doctor who can tell you the benefits of various forms of exercise by comparing them, and who can also suggest the one which will give you the results you're after. Except for tennis and raquetball, most of the faddish forms of physical exertion exercise the lower part of the body more than the upper. When using exercise for minimizing or eliminating depressive symptoms, the most efficient method will be one which works each part of the body in a rhythmic and systematic fashion.

Very few doctors know a lot about the effects of one form of exercise compared to another, though they may have read the popular literature in magazines and newspapers. But this doesn't give much technical information. However, a doctor can tell you (and should be asked to do so before an exercise program is begun) how much exertion your body can safely handle. Your best bet, in learning how to get the benefits you want, is to get in touch with a doctor who deals specifically in physical fitness programs or who works with a stress evaluation center. These centers are a new type of "feel better" treatment—half gym, half physician—used to giving customers better skills in coping with stress through programs of diet and exercise. Most large cities have them.

Aside from exercising all parts of the body, your program should offer several other goals. You want to work up a sweat, so any muscular (or nervous system) waste products will be eliminated. You want your blood to circulate faster to lower blood fats (another beneficial by-product of exercise), and you want to increase your rate of respiration so that there is additional oxygen in the bloodstream, which also makes your heart and lungs work more efficiently.

Be aware of what else will be required when choosing your program. Jogging means public exposure, which, as I mentioned before, may upset the depressive who is self-conscious (a problem which affects the majority of people with depression). Tennis is extremely strenuous, and also requires a court and a partner. Your best bet is a sport or exercise that requires little or no special equipment or environment, such as a court or swimming pool, and that also doesn't depend on the participation of another person. If you're starting something which is going to be difficult to maintain for emotional reasons, there's no sense in giving yourself (or someone else) additional possibilities for excuses, such as a friend who can't make it or a special environment being too far away or not open at the time you want to use it.

One of the most perfect exercises is bicycling, providing you don't live in extremely hilly terrain. Of course, if you do, you can get almost as much good from just *walking* the bike up and down hills! Bicycling exercises just about every muscle in the body in a very rhythmic manner, so that no part becomes overworked.

If there is a reluctance to engage in outdoor activities, dancing is another excellent form of exertion. One of the effects of depression is that the victim loses visual "touch" with his or her body. The distortion in perception causes the body to be seen as hideous or deformed, fat, or otherwise imperfect. A large area of self-esteem is personal perception of the body, and sometimes this can be recovered, when depression has caused it to be lost, just by dancing in front of a mirror. Get one of those light-weight mirrors that can be put away when not in use, and establish a nightly dancing ritual. Put a favorite record on, turn the lights very low, and practice moving the body in stretching positions to the music. While these positions can't really be called dancing, they should be done to the music and done without speed, in a smooth and assertive fashion. As an example of the type of positions which are most effective, start the music with the following routine: stand up as straight as possible with the arms hanging down loosely, fingers straight. Slowly lift one arm up, reaching as high as you can. Now lift the other arm. Feel your back muscles moving as you do this, and don't be surprised to hear crickles and cracks as muscles and tendons stretch. Now stand on your toes, reaching for the ceiling with fingers outstretched. Come down off the toes, bring the arms down slowly (don't let them just drop to your side), and bring them up to the hips or waist, whichever is more comfortable. Keeping your hands on your midsection, fingers in front and thumbs pointing back, bend at the waist in a deep bow and bob slightly up and down. Now begin moving the upper body around in a circle, still bobbing slightly as you move around. As you begin moving around to the right, feel the muscles in the left side of your waist stretch. Make yourself aware of this feeling as it moves across your stomach and to the right. As you do this, keep your feet flat on the floor and don't let your head droop. Keep your neck aligned with your back at all times. You may find this exercise easier to do without the bobbing motion, especially when bending backward. But every chance you get, without disturbing the basic posture, glance in the mirror. You may not like what you see at first, but overcome your distaste by thinking about how your body will look as this movement whittles away sagging tummy flesh and takes inches off your waistline. This exercise also strengthens back and stomach muscles, which offsets another problem of depression: poor posture. The depressive's shoulders often droop with a defeated air and the back is slumped. This adds to whatever other problems may exist by constricting the whole upper body, causing more shallow respiration and often creating back pain or discomfort. In fact, in many cases the depressive's complaints of shortness of breath or of lower back pain can be eliminated just by doing exercises to strengthen the back and shoulder muscles. A depressive's bad posture often comes from the simple problem of just not having sufficient energy to hold the back straight because the muscles there are weak and out of shape.

The person who begins using his or her body after a long, sedentary period may notice some side effects initially. There may be a tingling of the skin which sometimes creates an itchy feeling, especially if the exercise has an impact effect, such as jogging or jumping rope. The skin may even turn red. This is normal. There may also be a slight dizziness or ringing in the ears after exercise is started or immediately after finishing. This too is normal, although any symptoms of dizziness or ear-ringing should be reported to your physician.

One good effect for those only slightly depressed but overweight is the appetite may disappear for several hours after exercising. However, this could be a problem for the person with a more serious case of depression who has already lost any appetite for food. Exercise should not be undertaken in a person whose body is severely undernourished. In fact, it might be a good idea to incorporate food into the exercise ritual: two hours before beginning, a light, high-protein snack should be eaten. Keep it light, because you don't want the stomach to be digesting when you begin exercising. Then another snack can be eaten one hour after the exercise ends.

Another factor which will help your regimen (or the one you are helping a friend to use) is regularity. Whenever possible, the exercise program should be scheduled for the same time every day or evening. As for that scheduled time, give some thought to which hour is best for you. Some people find it easier to work out when they first get up; others have a better feeling about exercising in the evening. For many depressives, the morning isn't that good an idea, because in endogenous depression the worst effects are in the morning. The sad feelings and lack of energy may lift a little as the day goes on, and late in the afternoon the depressive may feel an intense desire to go to sleep. In that case, the best time for exercising is around noon, since many people with depression go through a period of drowsiness in the mid-morning, between ten and eleven, and again around three in the afternoon.

There's also a rule of thumb which anyone with depression should keep repeating: *it takes energy to make energy.* As you spend energy exercising, you will find your energy level increasing. This can be regarded as a gift which comes as a reward for sticking to it.

There will be several stages that can be expected as a regular program of exercise is established. I have already mentioned the initial enthusiasm which will fade to a reluctance to begin. After that usually comes a feeling of hostility toward the exercise itself, an attitude of "*I don't want to be doing this and don't see why I should, even though I know what the reasons are.*" After this comes a sort of resigned acceptance that this is now a regular routine, a stage which can last for a long time. There's no enthusiasm for the daily workout, but reluctance is no longer a problem. By this time, the benefits are becoming too obvious to ignore. Many people at this point become like missionaries, raving about how good their exercise has made them feel and trying to convince others to do the same thing. (Remember that ever since exercise became a national craze, with health clubs and other commercial ventures springing up to meet the demand, nearly everyone has undertaken a program of exercise already, and if they have given it up for reasons of their own, they really don't want to hear about how good it's making you feel.)

Perhaps the most important thing to keep in mind is the goal of exercise as an anti-depressant. Many people have taken up some exercise ritual because it's so overwhelmingly faddish, and many exercisers do it for purely physical reasons. They want to lose weight, they want to tone up a sagging body, they want to stretch their endurance or extend their strength. Exercise for depression is done for one reason: to move as much of the body as possible so that a workout produces *emotional* rather than physical effects. In other words, it is *movement* which produces the desired effects, and the type of movement, as long as it is fairly strenuous, doesn't matter. You can, of course, choose the type of movement (jogging, swimming, playing golf) that will give you the specific physical effects which seem most desirable, but those physical effects should be thought of only as a by-product rather than a goal. Because of this, the depressive's state of mind will be different from the attitudes of those who use exercise for physical reasons. In using exercise to combat depression, there should be no interest in competition, either with one's self or with others. Being aware of lap times or scores can be a devastating obstacle. Remember, depression produces serious convictions of inferiority. A competitive attitude can cause someone with depression to give up because he or she may feel that it's impossible to ever be as good as anyone else or because there will be a certainty that this exercise session was worse than yesterday's because of a feeling of daily deterioration. The feeling of becoming worse each day is a common one in depression, and even if this feeling can be disproved by stopwatches, scores, and logic, it must always be remembered the proof can't overturn a depressive's basic conviction of worthlessness. Because of this lack of self-esteem, it's a very bad idea to associate a beneficial treatment with any part of the ego. Competition seriously concerns ego and self-esteem, so a noncompetitive attitude is necessary. This is one of the reasons dancing and stretching exercises are among the best: it's almost impossible to use that form of movement with any kind of competitive attitude.

Timing the Workout

Time is a big problem for most people with depression. In some cases, adding an expected time responsibility like an exercise schedule may be too much of a mental effort. Even a minor case of the illness may have so exhausted energy that performing a minimum of daily tasks takes all day. It's helpful if there's a support system—family or friends who will take over some of the chores to allow for exercise "therapy." It should be regarded as therapy. Everyone involved, including the person with depression, should think of the exercise period as important —just as important (and sometimes even more so) as a weekly visit to a therapist.

The length of time for each exercise period should vary with the individual, of course, but it should be a minimum of a half hour spent each session. While this is most efficient when done all at once, it can be split up into segments if a daily schedule leaves no other choice. A busy schedule is often the excuse offered for being unable to exercise with any regularity, but that difficulty can always be overcome in one way or another. Gail Morris is a perfect example.

Gail's depression was most likely caused by her situation, which created a long-term, unrelieved stress period. She was in her mid-thirties when she decided to divorce her husband, even though she had no way of earning enough money to survive by herself at the time. While her husband had earned a bare living during their marriage, he was irresponsible at the best of times and extremely bitter after the divorce. Gail had given no thought to the problems of raising her 7-year-old daughter should her ex-husband stop supporting her. Shortly after the divorce, the man moved to another state and all child-support money stopped.

Gail was left with the necessity of getting a job, and with very few skills she was unable to command the salary that would allow her to pay for child care.

Knowing that the only way to make a decent life for herself and her daughter was to get some vocational training, Gail enrolled in night school. But the problems of arranging for babysitters, the guilt of frequently leaving her little daughter alone, and the sheer load of motherhood, job, and school began to wear her down. Gail found herself breaking into tears without warning and without any real reason, beginning to experience anxiety attacks and bowel problems, and waking up at the slightest noise in the morning—a car going by, the dog coming in the bedroom—even though her schedule kept her from getting enough sleep in the first place.

Gail had a close friend who noticed the changes in her personality, and offered to keep Christy, Gail's daughter, for a few weeks to give Gail a vacation. During that time, Gail began running late at night after getting home from school. Someone had told her that it would relieve tension, and she found that it worked.

After Christy came back home, it became impossible to keep up the running ritual because the extra energy needed to care for her daughter just didn't leave her with enough energy to run for half an hour every night. Gail decided to try lifting weights, since it was something she could do in the house. But because of Christy's demands for attention, there never seemed to be a regularly free half hour. However, there were *always* a few minutes here and there, and Gail decided to use them for exercise. She worked out ten minutes each morning, another ten when she came home from work, and another ten just before going to sleep. When school started for Christy, Gail began leaving a little earlier so she could park the car farther away from work and walk a few extra blocks to and from the car.

"In about six weeks of working out, I had an exercise schedule based on blocks of minutes," she told me. "I had worked it up to about an hour and ten minutes a day of physical activity. Strangely enough, instead of being more tired, I found myself far more energetic, and I wasn't snapping at Christy so much. In fact, I seemed to be getting along with everyone a whole lot better. The crying stopped, and I began being able to sleep soundly in the morning."

Over the next few months, Gail found she had the energy to look for a better job, and, even more important, she had the *mental* energy to look for the kind of job which would make the best and most financially rewarding use of the vocational education she had already received. The increase in emotional energy, which exercise seems to provide, allowed her to improve her situation more than any other factor. Although it took about two months before she fully recovered from the drain of her depression, she found that she was able to keep the full effects of her exercise schedule with a minimum of forty minutes every other day.

You or a depressed person you're trying to help may not see any free time, even blocks of minutes. But there are always spare moments that can be used to exercise the body. If measuring exercise in terms of *time* seems to be a problem, try measuring in units, or numbers of times an exercise is performed, instead. Set a goal of twenty push-ups a day, thirty kneebends, or whatever else seems desirable to give all the muscles of the body a full workout when the movements are put together. Then decide which times of the day a few of each of these exercises can be done—immediately upon rising, just before a shower, after coming home from work, just before bed, and so on. Keep track of how many are done so that the goal is met. If you're helping someone else through depression, you may find it easier (and healthier for you) to do the exercises *with* them. Constant encouragement will make it a routine part of daily life, and once a routine is established, there will be a greater tendency to stick to it and not give up. There are only two things to keep in the front of your mind at all times. The first is to avoid any concept of physical "improvement." Determine the variety and specific sets of exercise at the beginning, and don't change the routine. This is not, and should never be considered, a competition against the self. While it may be necessary for someone who has spent a long while being sedentary to work up to a good exercise routine, the competition-with-self becomes a self-defeating pressure which will do even more damage to the depressive's already vulnerable self-esteem.

The second important thing is to set a reasonable goal. Many people begin regular exercising with a kind of mental endurance contest, setting far too high a goal for themselves. Be careful not to get caught in the *I should* trap, as in *I should be able to run a mile a day*. There are no *should's* when exercise is used for the relief of depression. Even if you or the person you're helping latches onto exercise as the miracle which will end the emotional pain, don't get carried away by the amount of time or sets which are scheduled every day. Remember that there will be a lot of initial enthusiasm at first, but that this will fade very shortly. If the goal set was too high, the reluctance which can be expected will be even harder to fight, and the failure to overcome that reluctance may increase the symptoms of depression which the exercise was supposed to relieve in the first place.

Diet

There are so many fad diets and fad theories that even a nutritionist may have a hard time choosing something useful. In actual fact, we know surprisingly little about the medicinal qualities of food. Food is not thought of as medicinal. We are constantly reading bulletins by the medical profession which announce with surprise that some old wives' tale has been found to be factual. A balanced diet is considered good for nutritional reasons and specialized diets, such as a bland or salt-free diet, are used for specific conditions, but rarely is one specific food suggested by a doctor to help with a specific medical condition. Only in the last few years have doctors begun to tell patients on antibiotics to eat yogurt to prevent constipation. But we have yet to reach the point where a doctor will tell a patient to eat a lot of organ meats rather than take tranquilizers for stress.

Most nutritional ideas originate in popular culture or from recognized nutritionists rather than from the medical profession. Herbal doctors were advising patients to eat asparagus for kidney infections long before medical science aknowledged its benefit, even though in some parts of the world asparagus is known by the name "kidney broom." The use of vitamin E as a healing agent was touted by health food stores for decades before it achieved medical respectability, and even now there are doctors who will quibble about the medicinal effects of various vitamins.

It's unfortunate that food and medicine are considered two totally separate things, with food perhaps being thought of at best as an assistance to medicine—the "nurse" to the healing "doctoring" of pills. It's true that pills are a much more concentrated form of medicine and in cases where a quick cure is necessary they are far better than any diet or specific food used alone, but the beneficial qualities of nutrients in the form of edibles should not be disregarded.

One of the unfortunate aspects of food fads is that no scientific method is used to judge their validity. Therefore, people with very little nutritional or medicinal knowledge can eat what they believe to be an excellent diet while ending up with serious nutritional deficiencies. We all know the person with shelves and shelves of vitamin pills, all organic and carefully orchestrated to provide full complements of necessary nutrients. But the person who devotes such care (and such a large part of his or her bank account) to this vitamin collection may not be aware of the conditions needed by the body to metabolize these vitamins, and may take enormous amounts, for example, of the B and C vitamins, only to pass most of them out of the body in urine. We have already discussed water soluble and fat soluble vitamins, along with deficiency symptoms, in a previous chapter, so there's no need to go into more detail about vitamins. But in that chapter, I refer to the fact that vitamins are not medicine, but nutrients. The problem is that people rarely think of their entire diet as a form of medicine, and one of the best preventative medicines for depression and stress. We know that some foods are harmful to the body, and when we think of those, we usually think of the ones which are known or suspected carcinogens. But there is little or no research on anything other than the physical effects of food. If a food additive can cause cancer, can it also affect the emotions? Some preliminary research tends to show that it can.

In 1976, just as the controversy about the coloring agent Red number 2 was reaching its peak, a Los Angeles health food store embarked on a number of experiments with food additives. The store agreed to provide food to a commune if the members of the commune would agree to act as guinea pigs in a nutritional experiment. Seventeen members of the commune were given diets specifically designed by the store's owners to test the emotional factors which might be connected to food additives. Among the additives tested was Red number 2, which was already being considered for removal from the FDA's GRAS (Generally Recognized as Safe) list. The research was done in as scientific a method as possible, yet it could not provide the clear results that a strict laboratory test would have, since a number of the people being tested also used drugs which would alter the test findings. Yet one fact was made clear despite the confusion introduced by possible drug use. There was a definite connection between feelings of depression and ingestion of Red number 2. Shortly afterward, a doctor made headlines with his research which showed a connection between hyperactive children and this additive, used to a great degree in candies. The coloring was ordered removed from food products, but unfortunately, no further research was done on whether this coloring agent *did* affect the mind.

The lack of research into the mental effects of foods and additives is most unfortunate. Even worse is the lack of medical interest in experiments of this sort. We are already familiar with the most obvious mental effects of certain food substances: sugar will give you a brief period of mental alertness, coffee and tea will keep you from sleeping, a diet of nothing but brown rice will cause a type of calm bordering on lethargy after a period of months. Yet for the most part, we think of food's effects only in the physical area. Bread will make you fat if eaten to excess, but what effect does it have on mood? Chocolate has been discovered to have an alkaloid which produces a type of euphoria. Does that have anything to do with the fact that many depressives begin to crave chocolate?

We don't know the answers to these kinds of questions yet because we have not seriously begun to examine the possible damage to the mind from food additives, pollution, or toxic wastes. However, with the little research I have been able to discover—and with the help of a large number of people who have allowed me to experiment on them—I have come up with a few findings which can be used both to help prevent and to ease the symptoms of depression. I must tell you in advance that I have little or no *medical* proof that these facts are valid, but I have been able to prove their effectiveness thoroughly enough so that three doctors who examined the research now use it in treating depressed patients.

The Freshness Factor

Two years ago a lifelong dream of mine came true when I finally bought a home of my own. I had gone to several real estate agents, telling each one that I didn't care as much about the kind of house I bought as about having a half acre of level land. When the agent brought me to the house I finally bought, she went inside. I went out to the back yard. By the time I looked around, examined the soil, and checked its fertility by the size of the weeds, I had made up my mind. After I told her I would buy it, she said in amazement, "But you haven't seen the whole house yet! How can you decide to buy it?"

She didn't understand that while a house can be changed to suit an owner's needs, it's much harder to change a piece of land. And by then I had already discovered something that made a large back yard essential: a garden is perhaps the best anti-depressant available. It's not because of the exercise in making the garden (although, of course, that's a wonderful benefit), or the self-esteem involved in being able to grow some of your own food (although that is important too). But freshness in food provides something which has not yet been isolated, though its benefits are as great as regular exercise.

In the future, I am sure there will be discoveries which show that eating food which is not fresh is as bad as eating highly preserved or refined items. Everyone knows how much better a vine-picked tomato tastes than one several days old. The taste of fresh-picked corn cannot compare to the kind you get from a store, whether "fresh," canned, or frozen.

What you are tasting when you enjoy the pleasure of something from the garden is the full complement of vitamins. While meat eaters get most of their dietary B complex from meat, a diet of meat alone would produce serious nutritional deficiencies. We get the bulk of our natural (as opposed to tablet) vitamins C, A, K (the fertility vitamin), and minerals from vegetables. While minerals are fairly stable in foods, vitamins are not. A vegetable begins "dying" from the moment it's picked. The biggest sign of this "death" is a loss of vitamins. This is why the older a vegetable is, the less tasty it will be. Fruits, which are enclosed by a peel that gives some protective value, will stay fresh longer than most vegetables (avacados and bananas are two examples of fruits which can be kept for a long time in an unripened state), yet the vitamin content of any fruit or vegetable, no matter how well it stores, will deteriorate according to the length of time it is kept.

In spite of the vast body of nutritional knowledge, there are still many food factors we know nothing about. Some years ago, a test showed seventeen newly discovered factors in human breast milk. Obviously these were not essential to life, since millions of babies have thrived on diets of cow's milk and prepared formula, but how essential are they to the *quality* of life? In the same way, there are countless undiscovered factors in fruits and vegetables which begin to disappear as soon as they are no longer being fed by roots or branches.

Our taste buds have more sense than we give them credit for. They can actually *taste* vitamin C, for example. That tart sweetness of a fresh tomato, the puckery taste of a lemon, that slightly acid bite of an orange—that is the taste of vitamin C. A fresh carrot has a slightly bitter taste, where one which has been around for a while will taste sweeter. The sweeter that aged taste, the less vitamin A the carrot will have.

Vitamins also disappear according to how food is stored. A food may be full of those anti-depressant vitamins B and C in its natural state, but exposure to heat and oxygen as well as light will decrease the amounts of those vitamins contained in the foods. The lack of nutrition in refined products is not due to their having been changed from their natural appearance, but instead caused by the processing, which usually involves heating.

I began my first garden in 1970. It was a large garden, and I shared the produce with several friends. Over a period of a few years, I began to notice a connection between our combined states of mental and physical health and the amount of food eaten directly from the garden. This was during the days when "health food" consisted largely of food co-ops which bought direct from the produce market in Los Angeles, which meant that whatever wasn't coming from the garden was coming from a direct line which eliminated the store as middleman. So we were all getting our produce either just picked or at least three days fresher than it would have been if bought from the store.

Aside from the more obvious effects, such as a greatly decreased number of colds and viruses among the people who were eating this way, I noticed that there was a greater ability to cope with stress and a decrease in depressions and mood swings. Although I was still in the process of doing the research for this book, I didn't feel the "freshness factor" theory was developed enough yet to include in the book as valid research. It was only after completing the manuscript that I began turning my attention to the beneficial qualities of fresh food over store-bought produce, and only because what I had by then observed was too obvious to ignore.

In 1979, I was finally able to conduct an experiment with enough of a scientific method to show accurate results. Since the house had enough land for a quarter-acre garden, I planted a selection of vegetables which would allow me to use three families consisting of fourteen people, plus my son and myself, as subjects. The man in one of the families had a history of manic-depressive illness and had spent time in an institution. He was no longer on medication, but he did have a terrible time with mood swings which he fought constantly. Needless to say, I gave that family the bulk of the fresh produce, since he was such a perfect guinea pig!

I also included four other people: a man whose garden provided him with all the produce he ate, and a family whose garden served the same purpose for them. Each participant was provided with a mood chart similar to the one in this book, which pinpointed what foods were eaten daily, where they came from, and each person's emotional state.

The reason I'm boring you with all these technical details is because most statements made concerning food or diets today are suspect, especially if the statement is made by someone without a medical degree. Yet an experiment which works is valid, regardless of whether or not the person performing it has a university seal of approval, providing, of course, that the research is done in a scientific manner. And the results of this experiment were astounding, even though I was hoping for them in the first place.

Each participant was asked to fill out the chart without being told exactly what it was I was looking for, and there were several ringers thrown in for good measure so that everyone would be led to think I was looking for physical effects rather than emotional ones. (As an aside, most of the participants over thirty—which most were—said their vision had improved.)

But as for the chart results (this part does not include the three children under 10 years of age): sixteen of the seventeen over-10 participants reported an increased sense of well-being. Thirteen said their lives felt less stressful, even though there had been no major changes in their lives, other than school starting for the children. All said they felt more energetic (which may have been subjective because they expected to feel that way from eating garden vegetables). But here is the most interesting part. The charts were each of two weeks duration, which meant that every two weeks the participants would begin filling out a new chart and give me the completed one. This was done so that daily findings would not be influenced by a previous chart line. At the beginning of the experiment, the gardens weren't providing the total amount of produce eaten because it was too early in the year. As the gardens became more productive, the amount of store-bought food decreased until it disappeared. And as the amount of fresh produce eaten increased, so did alertness, feelings of calmness, ability to cope with life, feelings of greater intelligence. And what *decreased* were feelings of sadness, irritation, fatigue, depression. Jim, the man with the mood swings, said that while he still vacillated up and down, he noticed the swings not only weren't as wide, but he could cope easily with them. He had been on the verge of going back to his medication (Lithium), but no longer felt he needed it. *All reported improvement in their memories!*

I did not include the three children under 10 because I felt their parents may have influenced their answers by the way the questions on the chart could have been asked. Yet each parent made a point of telling me that his or her children seemed less whiny, and came down with far fewer colds. As an additional factor, only two of the families knew each other, so the possibility of comparison between participants was practically eliminated.

There's another element to the freshness factor. When meat has aged for a while, it passes the point where the aging adds flavor and tenderness, and it begins to taste and smell of putrification. When you taste meat which has gone bad, it's the effects of the bacteria and the toxins which you are tasting. There are many people who believe that there are toxins in aged meat which are connected to the aging process in people who eat that meat, as well as to various illnesses in the gastro-intestinal region. However, the freshness of meat isn't considered important unless the meat has actually gone bad.

It's quite possible that vegetables and fruits which have been picked a long time before being eaten may not only have lost much of their nutritional benefits, but may actually have begun to produce certain subtle toxins that have a corresponding subtle effect on the human organism. The stages a vegetable goes through during its passage from freshness to loss of nutrients to actual putrification may involve changes which can act directly on the metabolism or in conjunction with other factors, and which may cause actual changes in the central nervous system. Just as scientists have no real knowledge of what causes a sense of well-being when someone exercises regularly, there is no real knowledge of what makes a person feel so much better emotionally when a large amount of his food is fresh-picked produce.

If you live in an area where you must depend entirely upon a market for all your produce, you have very little chance of testing the benefits of fresh vegetables. The stuff which is sold at the produce section can be kept fresh-looking with waxes and sealants as well as constant mistings of water. You have no idea how long it's been sitting there to be fingered by other shoppers. Likewise, you have no way of knowing if frozen vegetables have been kept at a temperature constant enough to insure their maximum nutrient value; and with both frozen and canned food, you have no way of knowing what conditions the vegetables were kept in while they were being washed, trimmed, and prepared for packaging.

Your best bet in getting the freshest possible food is to find out if there is a wholesale produce market in your city, though this may have the drawback of selling in large amounts you can't possibly use. If you have no space to plant any kind of food for yourself, you might join one of the gardening programs that most cities have begun, where city- or county-owned land is made available in small plots to gardeners for a small sum. If none of these are feasible, the best remaining choice is canned vegetables, providing you also drink the juice. These have had the least chance of being affected by the environment once they have been packaged. If you buy fresh stuff at the produce counter, you can use the following guides to selecting the freshest possible produce: leafy vegetables such as lettuce or cabbage should have a fresh-looking cut on the stem. If there are spaces where you can see that leaves were trimmed from the outside, it usually means that old, withered leaves were removed to give the item a fresher appearance. When selecting carrots, turnips, and most other root vegetables, buy them without tops, because the root will continue to provide nutrients to the tops after being picked, which decreases the nutrients in the root itself. A darkened area where the top leaves grew indicates age, especially with carrots. Spinach is a very good food for depressives, and when buying it, look for roots that are fresh and moist looking, with smaller roots coming off the main one that still appear plump. The test for most vegetables is crispness. If something breaks with a snap when you bend it, it's a lot fresher than something which is limp and "gives" quite a bit before breaking. Gloss is another freshness indicator, especially where strawberries, eggplant, tomatoes, and citrus fruit are concerned. By all means, avoid any type of fruit or vegetables which is soft, discolored, or has a soft dark spot, especially if there is any indication of mold around the spot. Molds and fungi send long "roots" deep into the area before they become obvious in the form of white or gray fuzziness, and just cutting out the bad part may not be sufficient. Molds and fungi have a proven effect on the mind and nervous system. (LSD is derived from a fungus on rye grain which is known to have caused temporary insanity among the population in parts of Europe where people ate bread baked with rye containing this fungus. The hallucinogenic mushrooms, of which over a dozen species are known, contain some of the strongest mind-altering substances available.) Molds and fungi appear almost solely during the process of decay, and have a hard time gaining a foothold in fresh, healthy food.

The Happy Pill

You probably know the kind of nutrients you want in a depression-prevention diet. You want high-protein foods with as much vitamin C and B as possible. But the most important thing the proteins and vitamins do is to give you the essential amino acids. These are specific nutrients used by the brain and the nervous system, and they affect such things as alertness, sleep cycles, and electrical impulses used in the brain. You can see how involved they are in the symptoms of depression just by the things that they do, either in their direct form or in a different form after being metabolized.

The amino acids are more easily affected by factors such as drugs, alcohol, or personal habits than are vitamins. They're also a lot more picky. If you eat a meal in which any one of these essential amino acids is missing, you won't be able to assimilate *any* of the other amino acids in that meal! But there is one of these nutrients which can be called the star nutrient for anyone with depression or high stress levels. It's called tryptophane, and it can make an amazing difference in your mood.

A recent issue of the *Journal of the American Medical Association* acknowledged that tryptophane not only makes anti-depressant drugs work more efficiently, but that in some cases, it could be used alone and would *clear up the depressive illness with no other medication.* Tryptophane is an essential amino acid, and it has long been used by the medical profession as a cure for mild insomnia, early morning awakening, and light sleep. Yet it does far more than that.

To explain it in a very simple way, tryptophane is metabolized into seratonin, the hormone that regulates sleep cycles. The excess eventually reverts back into a form of the B vitamin which can be used directly by the brain. Tryptophane is actually formed by the central nervous system from the B vitamins. Since one very frequent cause of endogenous depression is an inability to metabolize vitamin B efficiently, tryptophane can bypass that problem by changing into those necessary nutrients once it has already been metabolized. There's also some evidence that tryptophane replaces those nutrients that are used up by stress, and helps diminish the toxic effects of stress.

But the biggest use of tryptophane is for those people who suffer from minor depressions which aren't serious enough to require a doctor or medication to suppress. It works not only for minor depression, but for minor cases of manic depression as well.

Unfortunately, it's one of the most expensive food supplements you can buy. A small bottle with about a month's supply—that's taking two a day—will cost ten dollars or more. But when you compare that to the cost of anti-depressants or therapy, it's really quite cheap. And if it cures a minor depression which may have kept you, or a loved one, from being all you are capable of being, then the value far outweighs the price.

If you or someone you know has ever been bothered even slightly by the symptoms of depression, you should make sure that there's always a bottle of tryptophane within reach. It's especially good for that dull, fatigued feeling that comes after too little sleep. As with all food supplements, it should be taken only with food, and the best times to take it are during breakfast and just before going to sleep, with a glass of milk. You should take it if you notice that you are more easily annoyed than usual. You should use it to increase your mental alertness when your mind seems tired and slow. While tryptophane is becoming more well known, its benefits are not yet common knowledge. Yet if it's taken just as feelings of depression begin, it can often end them right there and then.

If you're using it to suppress the symptoms of manic depression, it should be taken with both niacinamide (a special type of niacin available from health food stores) and vitamin B_6.

One thing to remember: the body seems to adapt to tryptophane if it's taken daily. That's why I would suggest that it only be used when needed, either because of the way you feel or because of something in your diet which you know may have affected the amount of vitamin B in your body. Since the body doesn't store this vitamin, you should always be aware of what factors destroy the amount you *do* have. These are: lack of sleep, alcoholic beverages, oils which have become rancid—that includes almost any snack from a vending machine or any fried fast food—and too much coffee.

Don't figure that if one tryptophane tablet makes you feel good, three will make you feel even better. Since this nutrient has many of the same properties as the B vitamins, it also will pass out of the body if too much has been taken. But once you start using it, you will be amazed at two things: that a simple nondrug food supplement can make such a difference, and that the news about what tryptophane can do to relieve depression hasn't received more publicity.

The Acid Test
People who are interested in nutrition are so busy with vitamins and minerals that they often overlook other areas which deserve equal attention. One of these areas is something you will be hearing a lot more about in the future—the acid/alkaline balance in the body.

You probably know someone who enjoys a salad dressing so vinegary that you find it inedible. You may have even heard someone say that he likes food so sour that a swig of vinegar right from the bottle tastes good.

Sourness, the quality which gives bite to vinegar, lemons, and certain kinds of cultured dairy products, is caused by organic (meaning natural to food) acids. It's opposite, alkalinity, is a type of salt, usually a metallic or mineral salt. Both acid and alkaline substances have a lot of properties in common. They are both caustic in concentrated form, and they both can burn or irritate, even though their content in foods is naturally balanced enough not to be at all harmful. Our bodies also need a balanced amount of both. But like vitamins, each individual requires an individual balance. And this balance is an essential factor in the prevention of depression or the lessening of its effects.

Many people have discovered the benefits of changing their

body's acid/alkaline balance for themselves, though it's usually done through cravings rather than intentional awareness. Many women develop a craving for salads just before their periods. It's not the fresh greens they need, but the acid in the salad dressing. The doctors who are doing the major research on changing acid requirements in the body are only beginning to put their conclusions into publishable form, so it will be some time before the full explanation will reach popular culture or be presented in a fashion which makes it acceptable by the medical world, but you can still put these proven discoveries to use.

I mentioned before that we don't give our taste buds enough credit. That statement also applies to food cravings. Our bodies have a very good instinct about what foods give us the specific nutrients we need to operate in the best of health. But the body can't say, "Hey, I need some potassium." Instead, you may suddenly get a craving for a chocolate bar or a banana. These cravings are subtle and easily ignored, but the more attention you give to them, the better the body is trained to let you know what nutrients are necessary. You can judge which food cravings are based on greed by using a knowledge of nutrition to substitute. During my depression, I developed a very heavy chocolate craving, and ate one of those large Swiss bars every day. In later years I noticed that I was a cyclic "chocoholic." There were times when a chocolate bar was nothing very desirable and other times when I would make a special trip to get one because I wanted it so much. By accident, I discovered that eating a banana would take away the chocolate craving, which my waistline could no longer afford to satisfy. I realized that the nutrient both had in common was potassium, which is an alkaline substance. Many depressives begin to crave chocolate especially during the recovery period, and most recently a euphoriant alkaloid has been discovered in chocolate which is now being investigated for possible use in treating minor depressions. It was at this point that I began paying more attention to food cravings. You can experiment on yourself to find out what your body requires by seeing if food cravings are actually nutrient cravings. Anytime you feel hungry, think about what food you would most like to eat. Write down as many types of food as you can that would taste delicious to you at that moment. Then check to see if all these foods can be grouped according to what they contain. You may see that at one period you desire starchy foods, that potatoes and breads, cakes and puddings would be the most satisfying things you could eat. You may go through a period of craving vitamin C, and your mouth may water at fresh cherries and other fruits, at salads and lightly steamed vegetables. Or you may need acid and get a longing for pickles or lemon-flavored food.

We all know the jokes about pregnant women craving pickles. The sudden acid requirement is strongest in women going through hormonal changes associated with the reproductive process. Many women have found that pre-menstrual tension can be lessened by increasing the acid content of the diet a few days before onset of the period.

To train your body to tell you what you need, you have to substitute good foods containing the same nutrient as the bad food you may crave at first. It's easier to think in terms of cream-filled cakes rather than a fresh vegetable, because we usually like the taste of sugar more than more nutritious food. It will take you at least a year to get to know your body well enough to translate "name brand" cravings into nutrients, so that when you think an almond cookie would be the most yummy thing in the world, you're really craving the B factor found in the almonds. But learning about your body in this way gives you the best anti-depressant weapon you have. We are only beginning to be aware of how individual a thing nutrition is. The announcement that women on the birth control pill need at least three times as much of the B and C vitamins as other people should not have come as the surprise it did. The finding that people who smoke deplete their vitamin C supply should have been common knowledge a long time ago. It's only in the past decade that we have become aware of how much external factors affect the way our bodies use and are *able* to use even the best of diets, and it's only now that there is acceptance of the fact that minimum daily requirements should not be depended upon to provide the best individual nutrition.

Since the best way to fight depression is to act fast, it's important to pay attention to factors most associated with the changing nutrient needs of a person coming down with depression, especially where an acid requirement is involved. Try to keep a jar of pickles or capers in your refrigerator so you can satisfy even the slightest craving for acid, and check any mood changes you notice at this time. See if there's a connection between increased stress or lowered energy and a desire for pickly-tasting food, or if there's an increased amount of energy and a feeling of being more able to cope with the stress after this desire has been satisfied. Remember, the most scientific research is still done for an average, and any nutritional statement made must be qualified by the term, "for the mass of people." No one but you can figure out your own personal dietary needs. The only way you can learn about your body in a methodical and efficient way is to write down what you observe. This will also allow you to keep track of any cycles that may be involved. Women are aware of one major cycle they have because of menstruation, but there are less obvious cycles in both men and women which, if they are undesirable, can be minimized through proper diet. You may notice that at certain times you feel more creative or that at other times you have a great feeling of satisfaction in life, even though there have been no changes in your life. These can also frequently be cycles, and if you can keep track of subtle mood cycles and what foods are eaten or desired during those times, you may be able to train your mind to work in top condition just the way health-conscious people now train their bodies. It's unfortunate that there has been common acceptance of the fact that there are many things you can do to increase your body's efficiency, while the separation between mind and body has retarded any great amount of research on what kind of training can be used to make the mind work better and decrease the negative qualities such as depression.

Natural Stimulants

Long before chemical medicine reached such prominence, during the time when people depended on herbs instead of over-the-counter preparations for headaches, stomach aches, and indigestion, certain remedies were accepted that have since fallen out of favor. One of these was the use of red pepper as a stimulant in cases of fatigue, lack of energy, and depression. Even today, books on herb medicine will describe cayenne pepper as a specific for depression. While most doctors will scoff at the idea, a few drops of hot sauce can make an obvious change in a depressed mood. But in using this old remedy, you must keep several things in mind. First, if you have any disorder of the gastro-intestinal system, including diverticulitis or ulcers, or if you have an easily irritated colon, pepper may prove to be harmful rather than beneficial. Keep observing how you feel after eating anything hot.

Cayenne is suggested by herbalists as having the greatest concentration of stimulating alkaloids, but many people just don't like to have their tongues burned. The "burn" is actually an irritation of the mucous membranes, and herbal doctors advise taking cayenne by capsule. Many herbal stores sell it this way, or you can buy empty gelatin capsules and fill them yourself. But because of the irritant factor, you should keep a written record of not only your mood changes, but any gastric distress or any trouble when having a bowel movement. If you suffer any physical discomfort, even if there are positive mental benefits, don't use cayenne as an anti-depressant.

The most important part of fighting depression is preventing it from getting out of hand, and you can exercise a great control over your central nervous system with diet and exercise. But remember that faddism is the opposite of common sense. Don't believe anything anyone else says until you have proven it on your own body. Some minor depressions can be relieved in some people by a diet high in organ meats. But there are actually some cases where eating liver has made the symptoms worse. We still don't take the idea for granted that nutrition is an individual subject, yet thousands of people who are subject to depression have learned to control it by learning what their own bodies need. The rise in food faddism and the interest in self-prescribed preventative medicine has come about only as a result of the lag in medical attention being paid to such things. Doctors are healers rather than preventors, which means they work with existing conditions rather than try to keep them from happening in the first place. This attitude is swiftly changing, but there's still a great knowledge gap. Until all the research is in on various diets, you have to use your own investigative powers. If regular exercise provides that extra little bit of psychic energy which allows you to make full use of all your potential, if eating a certain category of foods makes you feel good or if it relieves the symptoms of depression and gives you better coping ability when under stress, then you can take control of perhaps one of the most important areas of your life—the ability to use your mind to make your life whatever you want it to be.